Discontinuity in Learning

In this groundbreaking book, Andrea R. English challenges common assumptions by arguing that discontinuous experiences, such as uncertainty and struggle, are essential to the learning process. To make this argument, Dr. English draws from the works of two seminal thinkers in philosophy of education – nineteenth-century German philosopher J. F. Herbart and American pragmatist John Dewey. Dr. English's analysis considers Herbart's influence on Dewey, inverting the accepted interpretation of Dewey's thought as a dramatic break from modern European understandings of education. Three key concepts – transformational learning, tact in teaching, and perfectibility – emerge from this analysis to revitalize our understanding of education as a transformational process. Dr. English's comparative approach interweaves European and Anglo-American traditions of educational thought with a contemporary scholarly perspective, contributing to a work that is both intellectually rewarding and applicable to a classroom setting. The result is a book that is essential reading for philosophers and scholars of education, as well as for educators.

Andrea R. English is Assistant Professor of Philosophy of Education at Mount Saint Vincent University in Canada. Dr. English, an American scholar, previously taught at Humboldt University Berlin, Germany, from which she received her doctorate in 2005. Her work on theories of teaching and learning has appeared internationally in scholarly journals and essay collections.

Discontinuity in Learning

Dewey, Herbart, and Education
as Transformation

ANDREA R. ENGLISH

Mount Saint Vincent University

CAMBRIDGE
UNIVERSITY PRESS

KH

CAMBRIDGE UNIVERSITY PRESS
Cambridge, New York, Melbourne, Madrid, Cape Town,
Singapore, São Paulo, Delhi, Mexico City

Cambridge University Press
32 Avenue of the Americas, New York, NY 10013-2473, USA

www.cambridge.org
Information on this title: www.cambridge.org/9781107025219

First published 2013

Printed in the United States of America

A catalog record for this publication is available from the British Library.

Library of Congress Cataloging in Publication Data
English, Andrea R., 1975–
Discontinuity in Learning : Dewey, Herbart and Education as transformation / Andrea R.
English, Mount Saint Vincent University.
pages   cm
Includes bibliographical references.
ISBN 978-1-107-02521-9
1. Education – Philosophy.   2. Learning, Psychology of.   3. Dewey, John, 1859–1952.
4. Herbart, Johann Friedrich, 1776–1841.   I. Title.
LB14.7.E565   2013
370.1–dc23
2012031864

ISBN 978-1-107-02521-9 Hardback

10/6/14

to my Dad

Contents

Acknowledgments

During my initial research on Herbart and Dewey, I was moved by their thoughts, in particular, on human beings and how we learn. The ideas throughout this book have developed over more than ten years through publications, conference presentations, teaching, and international collaborative work with colleagues in philosophy of education. I would like to acknowledge the funding support I received for this project from Humboldt University Berlin, Germany, and Mount Saint Vincent University, Canada.

I am grateful to Cosima Fanselow and Karl-Franz Göstemeyer at Humboldt University Berlin, for facilitating my recent guest lectureship there, and to Cosima for her gracious help with my archival research. And thanks to my students in Germany and Canada, who have inspired me with their insightful comments and questions.

I also thank the societies that have given me the opportunity to present my work, including the John Dewey Society, the International Herbart Society, the Philosophy of Education Society, the Philosophy of Education Society of Great Britain, the Canadian Philosophy of Education Society, the American Educational Research Association, and the American Educational Studies Association.

I am grateful to have been invited to present my work, at various stages of its development, at the *Katholieke Universiteit* in Leuven, Belgium (where I presented a version of Chapter 6); the *Institute of Education* in London, England (where I presented part of Chapter 7); and *Cardinal Stefan Wyszyński University* in Warsaw, Poland (where I presented parts of Chapters 2 and 3). Many thanks to the hosts at these institutions, Stephan Ramaekers, Paul Standish, and Dariusz Stępkowski, respectively, and to all the audience participants for their insightful comments on my work.

I have had a great amount of support from colleagues who believed in this project and gave me encouragement throughout the process. I would like to express my gratitude to my colleagues, with whom I have worked collaboratively on articles, conference panels, and edited volumes: Gert Biesta, Rainer Bolle, Nicholas Burbules, Stefaan Cuypers, David Denyer, Michelle Forrest, Mordechai Gordon, Sophie Haroutunian-Gordon, Megan Laverty, Christopher Martin, Elizabeth Meadows, Konstantin Mitgutsch, and Barbara Stengel.

I am also very grateful for the encouragement, insightful comments, and constructive criticism of my work through feedback and conversations with colleagues over the years. Many have helped me in countless ways to develop and complete this project, including Nez Elik, Michael Katz, Deborah Kerdeman, Robbie McClintock, and Iain Thomson. William Hare, Walter Okshevsky, and Naoko Saito gave valuable comments on chapters in this book. Special thanks to Paul Standish for continued support and critical feedback as I have developed this project. I am also grateful to Leonard Waks for introducing me to a research group working on the topic of listening, for our many conversations on listening, and for valuable feedback on parts of this book.

I want to express my immense appreciation to Meinert Meyer, who has given valuable feedback and showed great enthusiasm about this project since the very beginning. This list would not be complete without my sincere gratitude to Dietrich Benner for welcoming me into a community of thinkers in Berlin, for introducing me to Herbart's work, and for the encouragement, guidance, and continued support of my work throughout the years – *herzlichen Dank*.

At Cambridge University Press, I thank the editors, in particular Adina Berk, Eve Mayer, and Simina Calin. Also, thanks to the anonymous reviewers for their helpful comments on my manuscript.

Finally, I thank my husband, Adam.

~~~

The following is a list of my published works that have been incorporated, in reworked and expanded form, into sections of this book:

Sections of Chapters 1, 6, 7, and 8: "Negativity, Experience and Transformation: Educational Possibilities at the Margins of Experience – Insights from the German Tradition of Philosophy of Education." In *Education and the Kyoto School of Philosophy: Pedagogy for Human Transformation*, edited by Paul Standish and Naoko Saito, 203–20. Dordrecht: Springer Publishers, 2012 © Springer Science+Business Media Dordrecht 2012.
Sections of Chapters 1 and 2: "Critical Listening and the Dialogic Aspect of Moral Education: J. F. Herbart's Concept of the Teacher as Moral

Guide." *Educational Theory*, 61, no. 2 (Special Issue "Philosophies of Listening," edited by Sophie Haroutunian-Gordon and Megan Laverty), 2011: 171–89.

Sections of the Epilogue: "Should Teachers Think? Autonomy, Accountability and Philosophy of Education." *Teacher: Newsmagazine of the BC Teachers' Federation*, 23, no. 5, March 2011: 5.

Sections of Chapter 7: "Listening as a Teacher: Educative Listening, Interruptions and Reflective Practice." *Paideusis: International Journal of Philosophy of Education* (Special Issue "Open-Mindedness and the Virtues in Education" honoring William Hare, edited by Michelle E. Forrest), 18, no. 1, 2009b: 69–79.

Sections of Chapters 1 and 6: "Transformation and Education: The Voice of the Learner in Peters' Concept of Teaching." *Journal of Philosophy of Education*, 43, Issue Supplement s1 (Special Issue "Reading R. S. Peters Today: Analysis, Ethics and the Aims of Education, edited by Stefaan Cuypers and Christopher Martin), 2009a: 75–95.

Sections of Chapters 3 and 4: "Wo *doing* aufhört und *learning* anfängt: John Dewey über Lernen und die Negativität in Erfahrung und Denken." In *Dem Lernen auf der Spur*, edited by Konstantin Mitgutsch, Elizabeth Sattler, Kristin Westphal, and Ines M. Breinbauer, 145–58. Stuttgart: Klett-Cotta, 2008.

Sections of Chapters 2, 3, and 4: "Die Experimentelle Struktur menschliches Lehrens und Lernens: Versuche über die Rolle negativer Erfahrung in den Lehr-Lerntheorien von Herbart und Dewey." In *Johann Friedrich Herbart: 200 Jahre Allgemeine Pädagogik. Wirkungsgeschichtliche Impulse*, edited by Rainer Bolle and Gabriele Weigand, 97–112. Berlin: Waxmann, 2007a.

Sections of Chapter 4: "Nietzsche, Deception and Education: A Response to Katz's Nietzschean Puzzle." In *Philosophy of Education 2006*, edited by Daniel Vokey, 401–03. Urbana, IL: Philosophy of Education Society, 2007b.

Sections of Chapter 4: "Interrupted Experiences: Reflection, Listening and *Negativity* in the Practice of Teaching." *Learning Inquiry*, 1 (Special Issue "Listening and Reflecting," edited by Leonard J. Waks), no. 2, 2007c: 133–42.

Sections of Part One and Chapter 8: *Bildung – Negativität – Moralität: Systematisch-vergleichende Analysen zu Herbarts und Deweys Konzepten der Erziehung*. Dissertation, Berlin: Humboldt University Berlin Library Archives, 2005c.

Sections of Chapter 3: "Negativität der Erfahrung, Pragmatismus und die
   Grundstruktur des Lernens – Erziehungswissenschaftliche Reflexion
   zur Bedeutung des Pragmatismus von Peirce, James und Mead für
   Deweys Theorie der reflective experience." *Zeitschrift für Pädagogik*, 49
   (Special Issue "Erziehung, Bildung, Negativität" edited by Dietrich
   Benner), 2005b: 49–61.
Sections of Chapters 3 and 4: "*Negativity* and the *New* in John Dewey's
   Theory of Learning and Democracy: Toward a Renewed Look at
   Learning Cultures." *Zeitschrift für Erziehungswissenschaft*, 8, no. 1, 2005a:
   28–37.

Abbreviations

Note on the Translation

I have modified the standard translation of Herbart's texts in various ways. It is important to note that I am making a significant change to the standard translation of Herbart's term *Zucht*, which in the standard translation is translated as "discipline," but which I translate as "moral guidance." Also, Herbart's term *Vielseitigkeit*, which relates to his theory of instruction, is translated in the standard translation as "manysidedness"; however, I have determined that a better-suited translation is "multifacetedness." In cases where I have modified the standard translation of a text passage, I note this with the words "translation modified." As for all of the untranslated German texts of Herbart and other authors, I have translated these texts myself, and note this as "translation mine."

Note on Usage

Throughout this book, with reference to the use of generic singular nouns and pronouns, my usage should be understood as inclusive of all human beings. When it does not hinder reading, I use "or" (e.g., "he or she"). In all other cases (e.g., when referring in the singular to teachers, learners, individuals, etc.), I vary between using generic male and female nouns and pronouns.

Prologue: Why *Herbart* and Dewey?

Questions concerning the structure of learning date back at least as far as Western Antiquity. From Plato through to the modern era, philosophers have recognized and investigated the aporetic and paradoxical aspects of human experience and learning. Certain authors in this tradition have highlighted the fact that learning necessarily involves discontinuous moments. This runs contrary to the more common understanding of learning as a smooth, continuous transition from ignorance to knowledge. Discontinuous moments in learning can be described as points at which the learner is confused, perplexed, filled with doubt, or engaged in a struggle with new and unfamiliar objects or ideas.

Two modern philosophers have placed particular significance on the discontinuous moments in learning processes, namely, the well-known American pragmatist John Dewey, and one of his predecessors, the lesser-known nineteenth-century German philosopher, Johann F. Herbart.[1] It is generally widely recognized in Dewey scholarship that – by his own account – learning is a process that begins with the learner's experience of

---

[1] J. F. Herbart (1776–1841) was a philosophy student of German philosopher Johann Gottlieb Fichte at the University of Jena, and later worked as professor of philosophy at Göttingen University and the University of Königsberg, where he took the former post of Immanuel Kant. Herbart made it his central aim to investigate educational questions; he can be considered one of the foundational thinkers in modern pedagogy. Herbart's followers created the educational movement known as Herbartianism, a movement that was influential in the United States and Europe. In the United States, the Herbartians formed the National Herbart Society around 1895, a society in which John Dewey was an active member (but he was not considered a Herbartian); see Harold B. Dunkel, *Herbart and Education* (New York: Random House, 1969). Although Dewey (1859–1952) is better known than Herbart, it is worth mentioning that he studied at Johns Hopkins University with George S. Morris and gained prominence during his time on the faculty at the University of Chicago, where he initiated the Laboratory School. He later moved to the philosophy department at Columbia University, New York, where he remained until his retirement. On these and other aspects of Dewey's biography and intellectual life, see Robert B. Westbrook, *John Dewey and American Democracy* (Ithaca, NY: Cornell University Press, 1991).

"doubt," "difficulty," or "frustration," and leads to reflective thinking. Far less considered is how this central tenet of Dewey's thought connects his work to the Continental tradition of *philosophy of education* (in German, *Allgemeine Pädagogik*), in particular to the work of Herbart. For the most part, the American reception of Dewey has focused on understanding him as a dramatic break from modern European understandings of education that had taken hold in late nineteenth-century America, including, and perhaps especially, that of Herbart.[2] At least part of the reason for this reception may be owing to the fact that Dewey himself – although acknowledging Herbart as an influence – criticized the Herbartian movement in his 1916 canonical work *Democracy and Education*. To this day, those aspects of Deweyan philosophy that demonstrate significant continuity with the Continental tradition of education philosophy have gone almost entirely unrecognized. This marks a significant gap in the research.

Discontinuity in Learning: Dewey, Herbart, and Education as Transformation addresses this gap. In this book, I argue that both Herbart and Dewey provide answers to the question concerning the structure of learning. Their works on education demonstrate the central educational meaning of *discontinuity* in learning and, in turn, in teaching processes. Through detailed analysis of these authors' works, this book seeks to enrich our understanding of discontinuity in education with the aim of productively reorienting how we approach education.

This book is situated in an international discourse on education currently taking place in both the English- and German-speaking worlds. In these contexts, philosophers have examined and established the importance of understanding learning as a complex process – one that entails what I have termed "discontinuous moments." In the English-speaking world, these moments are discussed in a variety of ways, without necessarily using the concept "discontinuity." For example, philosophers have discussed aspects of learning such as doubt, fear, discomfort, difficulty, disorientation, and

---

[2] Recently, scholars have taken an increased interest in the well-known nineteenth-century German philosopher (and contemporary of Herbart) G. W. F. Hegel's influence on Dewey's thought in a way that begins to contribute to understanding Dewey in the context of Continental philosophy. See, for example, James A. Good, *A Search for Unity in Diversity: The 'Permanent Hegelian Deposit' in the Philosophy of John Dewey* (New York: Lexington Books, 2005). For an examination of the emerging scholarship on Hegel and Dewey, see James Garrison, "The 'Permanent Deposit' of Hegelian Thought in Dewey's Theory of Inquiry," *Educational Theory*, 56, no. 1, 2006: 1–37). See also David I. Waddington, "Uncovering Hegelian Connections: A New Look at Dewey's Early Educational Ideas," *Education and Culture*, 26, no. 1, 2010: 67–81. Despite this important scholarship, extended study into J. F. Herbart as a foundational influence on Dewey's educational thought remains largely unexamined.

ignorance as central aspects of educational processes.[3] Although each of these ideas demarcates different phenomena, they all describe aspects of learning that are conceptually connected to the idea of discontinuity, as I will demonstrate.

Within the present-day German-speaking philosophical discourse on education, the idea of discontinuity is more prevalently discussed than it is in English. German educational philosophers have drawn on the tradition of *philosophy of experience*, as developed in particular by Husserl, Heidegger, Gadamer, and Merleau-Ponty, to analyze processes of learning and teaching. Within this discourse, concepts have been developed that provide a way of talking about discontinuities in learning and teaching using the idea of the "negativity of experience" (*Negativität der Erfahrung*) and also "negative experience" (*negative Erfahrung*).[4] In this context, the term "negative" has a different sense from what it does in colloquial English, in that it is not meant pejoratively. The negativity of experience arises in our encounters with difference and otherness, that is, in encounters that are the basis for learning, since learning necessarily involves confronting something that is as yet unfamiliar and new.

Why do we need the term "negativity" in English-speaking discourse?

To use the terms "negative" and "negativity" to describe experience likely brings a bad taste to the English-speaker's palate. In everyday language, these terms commonly describe something bad, such as an undesirable experience. Although these and related terms have to some extent been incorporated into English-language philosophical discourse, the terms were given meaning primarily with reference to the German philosophical tradition, such as Hegel's "the negation of negation" (*Negation der Negation*) or Heidegger's "the nothing noths" (*das Nichts nichtet*). These usages in English-language contexts have maintained a distinctly foreign quality to their tone.

Yet, the terminology of the *negative*, especially the concept of *negativity of experience*, has proven to be significant for discussions of teaching and learning. The concept of negativity provides the philosophical basis to

---

[3] Each of these concepts and the authors dealing with these phenomena will be referenced in various ways throughout the book, for example, Nicholas Burbules's work on doubt, Gert Biesta's work on difficulty, Deborah Kerdeman's work on disorientation, and relevant work by others.

[4] This German discourse will be taken up throughout the book, referring to the works of authors such as Günther Buck, Fritz Oser, Käte Meyer-Drawe, Dietrich Benner, and others who have discussed notions of negativity of experience in relation to teaching and learning.

examine and describe phenomena at the margins of experience in ways that can get lost or be easily overlooked without this terminology. Using this terminology, we can discuss the connection between different kinds of learning experiences (such as doubt or fear) in ways that are not possible within the limits of the current English-speaking discourse in philosophy of education.

Thus, the term "negative" is used here as a way of philosophically demarcating the moment when a person experiences a limit to his or her present ability or knowledge. These are moments in experience when our ideas or ways of acting become untenable, and thus are often coupled with doubt, discomfort, or frustration. They make us aware that experience and learning are not merely positive and continuous, but also negative and discontinuous. By examining connections between negativity and learning, we can open up the possibility of grasping meaningful differences between learning as mere *correction of error* and learning as *transformation of self and world*.

The aforementioned English- and German-language discourses in educational philosophy (although operating largely without reference to one another) serve to resist the overwhelmingly common conception of learning as merely a series of positive steps toward the acquisition of knowledge. Unfortunately, current trends in educational *policy* tend to frame learning as merely the continuous step-by-step achievement of predefined outcomes. On such models, the student's difficulties, frustrations, or doubts are considered signs of a *halt* in the learning process and are associated with the learner's failure. Accordingly, the student's difficulties with a particular subject matter in school are viewed by teachers and administrators as undesirable and problematic. In this way, the concept of learning has become dramatically simplified and reified.

These current trends have serious implications for teaching. Teaching is increasingly construed as transmitting predetermined outcomes to students and then using standardized testing to verify that students have achieved these outcomes. In practice, teachers are pressured to eliminate any signs of student failure from the classroom, at the risk of losing employment or resources. The result is that students' difficulties are not perceived as meaningful for their learning processes. The danger is that teachers may entirely overlook the educative value of difficulty and doubt, that is, of forms of discontinuity and negativity in experience and learning.

On this basis, a pressing need exists for a sustained examination of the educative value of discontinuities in learning. Indeed, it is a significant point of this book to argue that experiences such as difficulty, perplexity, doubt, suffering, and struggle are constitutive of learning processes. These experiences should not be avoided by teachers; rather, they should be cultivated in educational ways. To make this perhaps counterintuitive argument, this book brings together a rich line of educational thought across philosophical traditions represented in the works of Dewey and Herbart, two seminal thinkers in philosophy of education. The book also connects these traditions of thought to the contemporary discourses on teaching and learning mentioned earlier.

Furthermore, the book brings the important educational concept of the negative aspect of experience into an English-speaking context. It demonstrates that this concept is necessary for philosophical inquiry into the limits of human experience, knowledge, and understanding in a way that harkens back to those paradoxical aspects of experience and learning discussed since the Socratic tradition. More specifically, this book addresses questions concerning *where learning begins* and *how the learner experiences the world and learns to interact with other human beings.* A basic premise of this book is that, without answering these questions, we cannot begin to educate another person.

In addressing these central questions of learning, this book develops connections to other important educational concepts including critical thinking, moral judgment, teaching as a reflective practice, and recognition of the other. In this book, I also illustrate implications for teaching practice by demonstrating how a learner's experiences of frustration, confusion, and resistance can *support*, rather than *hinder*, the learner's ability to learn. Furthermore, I show how a teacher's experience of teaching is also discontinuous – the teacher's experience can be interrupted such that he or she falls into difficulty and doubt. Yet, as I underscore throughout this book, such experiences of interruption in both learners' and teachers' experiences are vital for cultivating educative learning environments. Ultimately, this book aims to demonstrate how understanding the role of discontinuity – and the related concept of *negativity of experience* – in education can deepen our understanding of education as a transformational process.

Therefore, in this book, I aim to:

Provide a sustained study of the educative meaning of discontinuity in teaching and learning processes.

Provide a conceptual apparatus for philosophers and educators to further analyze and critique educational theories and practices that ignore the educative meaning of discontinuity. The concepts developed in this book

are essential for reinvigorating the meaning of learning as a transformational process.

*Bring together Continental and Anglo-American approaches to philosoph-
ical questions about the nature of education.* By investigating this topic
across philosophical traditions, this book goes against common conceptions of Dewey as a dramatic break in the tradition of philosophy of
education. Instead, it demonstrates that Dewey's thinking was influenced by and aligned with thinkers in the Continental tradition of
philosophy of education, particularly Herbart. In doing so, I offer a
new reading of Dewey.

Provide an in-depth treatment of Herbart's educational works. It is the only
such treatment available in the English language in more than forty
years.[5]

By highlighting discontinuity as a central aspect of educational thought, this
book tells an untold story of the connections between Herbart and Dewey in a
way that does not conflate the myriad distinctions between these thinkers, but
rather illustrates how they each have something important to say about
education as a transformational process. An underlying concern here is
thus to highlight the meaning of the negativity of experience as a constitutive
aspect of teaching and learning that has been under-investigated and risks
being eliminated from educational discourse. By providing philosophers and
educators within the international community a way of discussing this aspect
of learning and teaching, this book seeks to further cross-cultural dialogue
about education in the twenty-first century.

The book is divided into two parts. In Part One, I offer a historical and
philosophical examination of the idea of discontinuity in education by examining the central educational works of Herbart and Dewey. In Chapter 1, I
provide some philosophical background to Herbart's thinking about the
human being as a learner, which forms the basis of my analysis of his theory
of education (in Chapter 2). I highlight how Herbart's concept of education
and its connection to morality was influenced by his more widely known
contemporary, Immanuel Kant. Furthermore, I examine his concept of "perfectibility" (*Bildsamkeit*) as the underlying anthropological notion framing
his thinking about education. This idea connects his work to well-known

---

[5] Prior to this book, Harold Dunkel's work provides the most recent sustained look at Herbart's
educational works in English: Harold B. Dunkel, *Herbart and Education* (New York: Random
House, 1969) and Harold B. Dunkel, *Herbart and Herbartianism: An Educational Ghost Story*
(University of Chicago Press, 1970).

educational philosophers Jean-Jacques Rousseau and Wilhelm von Humboldt.

In Chapter 2, I address Herbart's two-part theory of education by examining his notions of the teacher's task as both supporting the learner's expansion of horizons through "educative instruction" and providing "moral guidance," respectively. By examining each of these interrelated ideas of teaching, I discuss the significance Herbart placed on discontinuity in the learner's process of learning. I reveal that, whereas Herbart viewed *cognitive* learning as primarily a continuous process, he viewed *moral* learning as a discontinuous process. I provide a criticism of his conception of continuity in cognitive learning, in order to locate and define the significance of discontinuity. The central concept I develop in connection with Herbart's view of moral learning is that of "inner struggle" (*innerer Kampf*). With this concept, I highlight a form of discontinuity constitutive of learning processes and begin to illuminate the educative meaning of negativity of experience. I emphasize how Herbart's account helps us understand the teacher's task as one of cultivating the learner's inner struggle in order to support the learner's path toward becoming a moral person who recognizes the other. In closing, I turn to examine Herbart's concept of "pedagogical tact" (*pädagogischer Takt*) in teaching to illustrate how experiences of discontinuity are educative not only for the learner, but also for the teacher.

In Chapters 3 and 4, I analyze the role of discontinuity in Dewey's theories of learning and teaching. Chapter 3 introduces the concept of discontinuity as a learning-theoretical concept by addressing how it relates to key ideas in the tradition of pragmatism. I demonstrate that the idea of discontinuity in experience can be found in key works of Dewey's fellow American pragmatists, namely, Charles S. Peirce, William James, and George Herbert Mead. I examine Dewey's concept of learning and develop what I call "learning in-between." I argue that we can understand learning as a process in which spaces and gaps are opened up in experience through *interruptions*. These spaces can be viewed as openings for experimentation with new ideas and new modes of action. My examination of the discontinuity of experience and learning highlights the central role of negative experiences such as doubt, difficulty, and frustration in Dewey's concept of reflective learning processes.

In Chapter 4, I analyze Dewey's concept of teaching and argue for an understanding of teaching as "teaching in-between." I argue that, for Dewey, reflective teaching provokes learners to dwell in the realm *between* right and wrong answers. Further, I discuss how this realm for learning can and should be created in classrooms. In the context of my discussion of teaching, I also take up the idea of teaching as a reflective practice, drawing on Donald Schön, who builds on Dewey's work, and who has become widely known in teacher education for his theory of reflective practice. I extend Schön's concept to demonstrate that teaching is a unique form of reflective practice, distinct from other professional practices, in order to develop the idea of teaching in-between as *interrupting experiences* of learners. To close this chapter, I examine how discontinuous learning and teaching processes relate to Dewey's ideas of teaching as a moral task and to his notion of democratic education.

Chapter 5 forms the conclusion to Part One. Here, I examine Herbart and Dewey comparatively and discuss both Herbart's influence on Dewey, as well as the ways in which Dewey's concept of education surpassed that of Herbart. Additionally, I address broader implications of these philosophers' ideas for our present-day understanding of morality and democracy.

In Part Two, I take up three particular concepts, namely, *learning in-between*, *pedagogical tact*, and *perfectibility*, which emerge from my discussion in Part One. Part Two is divided into three chapters (Chapters 6–8), with each of the concepts forming one chapter. I contend that these concepts are particularly important for understanding the educational relation between teacher and learner and its connection to the cultivation of transformational learning processes. I further develop these and examine them in ways that connect classical and contemporary thinkers from both the Continental and the Anglo-American traditions of philosophy of education. Thereby, I seek not only to draw out the concepts of teaching and learning developed in Part One with Herbart and Dewey, but also to show interrelations in the current discourse on education, in particular interrelations between notions of discontinuity in teaching and learning developed in the traditions of pragmatism, phenomenology, hermeneutics, and existentialism.

Specifically, in Chapter 6, I further develop the concept of learning in-between as a space of learning opened up by interruptions in experience, in which we explore new possibilities for thinking and acting in the world. Here, I tie the idea of learning in-between to the German notion of *Umlernen*, which describes learning as a complex transformative experience.

Chapter 7 further develops the concept of pedagogical tact. I inquire into the unexpected that pervades the practice of teaching and that arises from the discontinuity in both the teacher's and learner's experiences. In this context, I further develop the notion of teaching in-between and describe teaching as involving learning to productively turn toward the blinds spots of teaching practice. Ideas of risk, improvisation, and listening in teaching are the focus of this chapter. I conclude Chapter 7 with a model of "Reflective

Teacher-Learner Engagement," which illustrates how the concepts developed throughout the book are interconnected in a teacher's reflective practice.

Chapter 8 discusses the need to highlight the concept of perfectibility in contemporary educational discourse. I demonstrate that this concept connects to educational concerns that reach beyond language barriers and cultural contexts to broader questions of education and humanity.

Part Two concludes by considering what it might mean to preserve the "in-between" in education. There, I define the corporeal-existential, theoretical-experimental, and pragmatic-moral dimensions of negativity of experience in learning, with a look ahead as to how we can continue to articulate the meaning of these aspects of human experience in educational theory and practice.

In the epilogue, I consider the implications my argument has for beginning to rediscover the meaning of philosophy for the education of teachers.

A note to readers: This book is written for theorists and practitioners, philosophers as well as educators in all fields. Some readers may prefer to begin with Part Two, which is primarily concerned with contemporary educational theory and practice. Most of the concepts dealt with in Part Two have been developed throughout Part One, and relevant internal chapter references have been included to help guide readers.

PART ONE

EDUCATION, DISCONTINUITY, AND TRANSFORMATION

Chapter 1

The Moral Dimension of Education

Johann Friedrich Herbart, one of the founders of modern educational theory, is, for the most part, no longer discussed in Anglo-American educational philosophy, and this is at least in part due to John Dewey's critique of aspects of Herbart's work. The neglect of Herbart's work in contemporary educational discourse has, unfortunately, led to a loss of insight into the fruitful aspects of his theory of education. In his central educational work, *The Science of Education*,[1] from 1806, Herbart develops a theory of education that illuminates important distinctions between socialization and education. These distinctions provide a framework for understanding the basis of the educational relationship between teacher and learner as one that entails and cultivates certain forms of discontinuity in learning.

Much of Herbart's thinking about how education differs from mere socialization hinges on the idea that education aims at autonomy, or self-determination, of the learner. In our current postmodern world, the idea of autonomy, as formulated by Enlightenment thinkers, has been criticized as too individualistic, a vision of a rational human being devoid of emotion and lacking a connection to the social world. However, for Herbart, the idea of self-determination (*Selbstbestimmung*) is connected to the ability to critique not only oneself, one's own thoughts and actions, but also the values and norms that govern society at large. Part of my aim in examining Herbart's standpoint is to demonstrate that self-determination is interconnected with

---

[1] Johann Friedrich Herbart, "Allgemeine Pädagogik aus dem Zweck der Erziehung abgeleitet (1806)," in *Joh. Friedr. Herbart's Sämtliche Werke in Chronologischer Reihenfolge*, Vol. 2, edited by Karl Kehrbach, pp. 1–139 (Langensalza: Hermann Beyer und Söhne, 1887), cited here using both the German and the English translation, "The Science of Education," in *The Science of Education, its General Principles Deduced from its Aim, and The Aesthetic Revelation of the World*, translated by Henry M. Felkin and Emmie Felkin, pp. 94–268 (Boston: D. C. Heath & Co., 1902). In the following, the German text will be cited as *AP* and the English version as *SE*.

an openness to the other, such that education toward autonomy has to be at the same time conceived of as education toward openness to the other. On this account, self-determination – that is, thinking critically for oneself and not blindly following the authority of others – entails a relation to and understanding of the other; the self-determined individual is one whose judgments take honest account of other human beings and the world around them.

In aiming toward the self-determination of individuals, education, as Herbart views it, takes on moral meaning: its "whole purpose is morality."[2] The underlying idea of Herbart's claim that morality is not simply the "highest" purpose but the "whole" purpose of education is that *all* education has an effect on the learner's ability to think and act according to his or her own judgments; the actions of educators and others in a child's life either *help* or *hinder* this ability. The central question for philosophers and educators then becomes, which forms of education help and which hinder the learner?

Of course, the answer to this question is never straightforward; it entails a complex understanding of what educating another person involves. This means reflecting not only on the possibilities but also on the limits of what can and should be involved in educating and teaching another person. Herbart began to answer this question by distinguishing his own concept of education from two other problematic notions of education. He opposed, on the one hand, forms of education that he termed "education without instruction" (*Erziehung ohne Unterricht*), or, more appropriately translated, "discipline without instruction," because when using such models the teacher seeks to "educate" learners by pure disciplinary measures (*SE* 85–86/*AP* 11). These modes of interaction hinder the learner's self-determination because they force the learner to conform to the teacher's will; they demand blind obedience. On the other hand, Herbart also opposed forms of education that seek merely to transmit knowledge through instruction in subject matter that learners are expected to take in and then regurgitate. On such a concept of education, or, more precisely, "instruction without education" (*Unterricht ohne Erziehung*), learners are viewed as passive recipients of knowledge who

---

[2] Johann Friedrich Herbart, "Über die *ästhetische Darstellung der Welt, als das Hauptgeschäft der Erziehung* (1802–1804)," In *Joh. Friedr. Herbart's Sämtliche Werke in Chronologischer Reihenfolge*, edited by Karl Kehrbach, Vol. 1, pp. 259–74, 259 (Langensalza: Hermann Beyer und Söhne, 1887), cited here using the English translation, "On the Aesthetic Revelation of the World (1804)," in *The Science of Education, its General Principles Deduced from its Aim, and The Aesthetic Revelation of the World*, translated by Henry M. Felkin and Emmie Felkin, pp. 57–77, 57 (Boston: D.C. Heath & Co., 1902), translation modified. In the following, cited as *ARW*.

do not learn to relate this knowledge to their self-understanding and practical judgment.

In each of these concepts we can see that the learner's self-critical judgment is not developed; for Herbart, they fail to fulfill the necessary precondition of self-determination. In the context of the present discussion of discontinuity in learning, we can say that such concepts fail to address a certain kind of discontinuity found in those learning processes which are directed toward critical thinking – an idea I will continue to unfold throughout the book. The former "disciplinary model" forces the will of the teacher on the learner, and the latter "transmission model" forces learners to accept knowledge without providing the basis on which this knowledge can be critically examined, questioned, and related to choices for action. Countering these positions, Herbart developed the idea of "education *through* instruction" (*Erziehung durch Unterricht*). Education through instruction, or *educative instruction*, is one essential part of Herbart's twofold definition of education proper, which includes educative instruction and moral guidance. By examining Herbart's concept of education, we can see that although it entails certain forms of continuity, it also identifies significant forms of discontinuity indispensable to learners' experiences of learning how to make choices for action. Specifically, his concept entails a notion of the learner's *inner struggle* as an educative aspect of moral learning processes. Herbart's idea of inner struggle provides a central thread to both this chapter and the next.

It is important to note that, from a historical standpoint, Herbart's thinking represents a strong break with traditional concepts of education. Herbart's idea of the educator takes into account that modern educators must reckon with the fact that they have to educate someone for an unknown future; the future of the learner can only be decided *by* the learner. In part, Herbart is addressing the historical changes of his time and the opposing notions of education of the *ancien régime*, which assume that the next generation's future is decided by the previous generation. In other words, such notions assume that each individual learner's future is determined by the past, by tradition and socialization.

From a philosophical standpoint, Herbart's thinking also represents an understanding of the human being as essentially capable of independent thinking and capable of learning to decide to act toward the Good. In this chapter, my aim is to introduce readers to the concepts underlying Herbart's theory of education. My analysis focuses on understanding Herbart's concept of the human being as one who is capable of morality. In the first section, I analyze the paradox of education, which we can call the paradox of "autonomy through heteronomy," or, in German, "*Selbstbestimmung durch*

Fremdbestimmung" (self-determination through determination-by-another). I discuss how this paradox represents Herbart's starting point and a presupposition of his contemplation of both the possibilities and limits of educating individuals who are capable of morality. In the second section I inquire further into Herbart's understanding of the human being by examining his concept of "perfectibility" (*Bildsamkeit*) as an important limit for educators to recognize, a limit that lies in the fact that we cannot know what each individual is capable of learning. With this concept, Herbart provides the anthropological grounding of education in the idea of the human being as a learning being.

1 THE MORAL INDIVIDUAL AND THE EDUCATIONAL PARADOX

In his influential early essay "On the Aesthetic Revelation of the World as the Chief Work of Education," Herbart defines his notion of the moral individual most concretely when he writes, "the moral man commands himself" (*ARW* 62). Herbart sees this idea represented in Kant's Categorical Imperative and seeks to highlight the intersubjective relationship between self and other formulated therein, namely that the Categorical Imperative expresses a judgment of oneself in light of one's recognition of the other. This comes forth most clearly in Kant's second formulation: "Act in such a way that you treat humanity whether in your own person or in the person of any other always at the same time as an end and never merely as a means to an end."[3]

In Herbart's view, the categorical imperative is central to understanding morality. However, the concept of the moral person as one who is capable of judging her own will according to principles of universalizability and humanity sets up a dilemma for educators that Herbart believed Kant did not adequately address. This dilemma lies in the fact that the learner's ability to judge *for herself* what is good and right needs to be cultivated through education. Furthermore, to cultivate each learner's ability for self-determined judgment, educators must *influence* the learner's choices *without* choosing for her and without manipulating her.[4] Herbart's concern underscores the paradox of education that lies in the fact that education toward autonomy is

---

[3] Immanuel Kant, *Fundamental Principles of the Metaphysics of Morals* (1785), translated by T. K. Abbott, p. 58 (New York: Prometheus Books, 1988), translation modified.

[4] For Herbart's further discussion of Kant, see *SE*, and *ARW*. For a discussion of the limits of Herbart's view of Kant, see Dietrich Benner and Wolfdietrich Schmied–Kowarzik, *Herbarts Praktische Philosophie und Pädagogik. Möglichkeit und Grenzen einer Erziehungsphänomenologie* (Herbart's Practical Philosophy and Pedagogy: Possibilities and Limits of a Phenomenology of Education)

achieved through heteronomy, or, put another way, an individual's ability to mediate thought and action with reason and judgment is made possible by intergenerational and intersubjective educational relationships.

To address this concern, Herbart argues that educators must understand how individuals make choices. He makes the point that it is not transcendental freedom, but concrete "freedom of choice" that educators need to understand, for that is the only type of freedom on which they can have an influence (*ARW* 61). Herbart takes a phenomenological approach to analyzing how human beings make choices. Specifically, he inquires into what is involved in one's choice of the Good. His underlying question is: What happens in the moment in which an individual chooses *not* to follow his inclinations or self-interested desires, and instead chooses to act in recognition of and respect for the other? (*ARW* 62–64). In Herbart's account, in moments of moral crisis, the individual experiences a break with oneself, becomes distanced from oneself, and begins to observe and judge oneself. Accordingly, we can understand the self as divided into two selves, that is, both as a *subject* judging and an *object* being judged. Herbart refers to these two sides of ourselves as parts of our character, one *subjective* and one *objective* (*SE* 200–01/*AP* 90–91).

Although Herbart's terminology may seem outdated, the distinction between subjective and objective selves is helpful for understanding his view of moral decision-making processes. The "objective character" comprises all the choices one has made thus far in one's life. This side of oneself is objective because it is already formed through choices that, to a large extent, have become habits and routines. The "subjective character" refers to the reflective self, who judges the objective self, potentially critiques past choices, and creates new rules for future conduct (*SE* 200–01/*AP* 90–91).These two sides of ourselves come forth as divided when we are faced with new and unfamiliar situations. If we choose to follow routine, then our past is dictating our choices, such that we are guided by our objective side. If we make a conscious decision to break a habit by deciding to act differently than in the past, then we are following insights of our subjective side.

(Ratingen: A. Henn, 1967). For an examination of Kant's ideas pertaining to moral education and the role of dialogue in teacher-learner interaction that aims to evaluate whether a learner understands the Categorical Imperative, see Walter Okshevsky, "Kant's Catechism for Moral Education: From Particularity Through Universality to Morality," *Philosophy of Education 2000*, edited by Lynda Stone, pp. 94–102 (Urbana, IL: Philosophy of Education Society, 2001). Martin offers a valuable discussion of Kant's notion of education in connection to morality; see Christopher Martin, "Education Without Moral Worth? Kantian Moral Theory and the Obligation to Educate Others," *Journal of Philosophy of Education*, 4, no. 3, 2011: 475–92.

The break one experiences with oneself in moral dilemmas is significant for Herbart because it marks a certain kind of self-self relation; it marks the moment in which one is *at odds* with oneself and finds oneself in the midst of an inner conflict or "inner struggle" (*innerer Kampf*), as I will refer to it throughout this book (*SE* 200–01/*AP* 90–91). To understand Herbart's concept of the moral individual, it is necessary to take a closer look at this concept of inner struggle. When we experience inner struggle, it is because our past decisions come into conflict with the demands of the present situation – thus, our objective side comes into conflict with our subjective side. Inner struggle marks the point at which we can make changes in the way we act in the world. The moment of inner struggle, Herbart notes, is an existential moment that we experience so forcefully that it can threaten "mental" and "bodily health" (*SE* 204/ AP 93). These moments of inner struggle are not necessarily moral; they can be part of all sorts of decision-making processes in an otherwise inwardly harmonious person. Our inner struggle becomes part of moral decision making when it marks the point at which we have the choice to move away from egoistic actions and move toward actions that respect others. These are the moments in which we ask ourselves, "What should I do?"

To draw out the moral implications of the struggle, Herbart underscores the dialogic aspect of this self-self relation implicit in Kant's notion of moral judgment. Herbart argues that when an individual is faced with a moral crisis, for example, whether to lie or to tell the truth in a given situation, we can imagine that the "voice of the moral imperative" comes forth in the individual and distinguishes the "worthy and good" on one side and the "common and bad" on the other (*ARW* 63). This voice arises within the space of self-observation – that is, it arises as part of the subjective side of our character – when we find ourselves in a struggle as to whether to follow self-interested desires and inclinations or to take a new path that respects the other.

Herbart emphasizes that this voice of the moral imperative has nothing necessarily in common with the self it judges. This commanding voice that we hear inside ourselves has a moral aspect, insofar as it is *self-critical* and is informed by ethical ideas. In other words, it is *heard* as a "censor" (*Censur*) – a negative judgment – by the person who is inclined to follow self-serving interests and desires.[5] A person must *learn* to hear this voice, that is, she must learn to hear her own inner censor and follow her own command into action.

---

[5] *ARW* 63; see also *SE* 204–9/*AP* 92–7, translation modified. In the standard English translation of *The Science of Education*, the German term "*Censur*," which Herbart uses, is translated at times as inner "monitor" (for example, *SE* 204). I translate this term consistently as "censor."

An individual's choice to listen to the voice of the moral imperative and act *against* self-interest and *toward* the other is an act of "inner freedom" (*Innere Freiheit*) that Herbart views as an essential aspect of all human beings and, significantly, one over which educators have influence. The idea of "inner freedom" delimits the moral relation of oneself to oneself, specifically the relation of a person's will to the critical judgment she casts upon her own will.[6] This idea highlights the human capacity for self-reflection that separates human beings from other animals, that is, our ability to make ourselves *inwardly free* from our *inclinations* by restraining ourselves from action, turning inward onto ourselves, thinking critically and judging our inclinations with approval or disapproval. Accordingly, the moral person is able to act against self-centered inclinations and make inner freedom "practical" by acting on one's judgment of the Good. For Herbart, the concept of "inner freedom," together with the concepts of "completeness" or "coming to fullness" (*Vollkommenheit*), "benevolence" (*Wohlwollen*), "right" (*Recht*), and "justice" (*Billigkeit*), form the moral ideas that are central for education that I examine in depth in the next chapter.[7]

---

[6] See in particular pages 33–36 in Johann Friedrich Herbart, *Allgemeine Praktische Philosophie* (1808), in *Joh. Friedr. Herbart's Sämtliche Werke*, edited by Karl Kehrbach, Vol. 2 (Langensalza: Hermann Beyer and Söhne, 1887), cited in the following as *APP*; see also *SE* 210/*AP* 97–98.

[7] In his theory of education, Herbart states that three central moral ideas are important for guiding the educational processes of learners. He names *Inner Freedom*, as well as *Goodness* (*Güte*, which combines the ideas of benevolence and completeness) and *Rectitude* (*Rechtlichkeit*, which combines the ideas of right and justice.) Herbart combines these moral ideas for educators, which he differentiates in his ethics, on the grounds that learners first learn these concepts in situations in which these ideas are not so easily differentiated; learners then at a later point learn to distinguish conceptually what they had experienced as connected. In Chapter 2, I discuss each of these ideas separately in more detail. Here, it is important to note that I am not keeping with the standard translation (both Felkin and Felkin's translation and Dunkel's translation) of Herbart's idea of *Vollkommenheit*, which, in the standard translations, has been translated as *Perfection*, but I am translating as *Completeness*. This idea is not meant to imply that there is a specific endpoint to be achieved. Rather, it is more aptly translated as I have noted (and as Felkin and Felkin note in their translation) as the idea of "coming to fullness"; see Herbart, *Letters and Lectures on Education*, translated by Henry M. Felkin and Emmie Felkin, p. 107 (London: Swan Sonnenschein and Co. Ltd., 1898), and Harold B. Dunkel, *Herbart and Education*, pp. 32–33 (New York: Random House, 1969). Also, I translate the last idea *Billigkeit*, "justice," slightly differently than in the standard translations. Felkin and Felkin translate *Billigkeit* as equity/retribution (see Johann Friedrich Herbart, *Letters and Lectures on Education*, p. 107), whereas Dunkel translates this idea as requital/recompense (see Dunkel, *Herbart and Education*, pp. 32–33). In an earlier essay, I translated Herbart's moral idea of *Billigkeit* as "equity," but find "justice" to be more accurate. See Andrea English, "Critical Listening and the Dialogic Aspect of Moral Education: J. F. Herbart's Concept of the Teacher as Moral Guide," *Educational Theory*, 61, no. 2 (Special Issue "Philosophical Perspectives on Listening," edited by Sophie Haroutunian-Gordon and Megan Laverty), 2011: 171–89.

Herbart's concept of the struggle in moral decision-making processes points to the meaning of discontinuity in moral learning as an experience of a break with oneself. This form of discontinuity is significant for understanding the idea of education toward self-determination: the struggle marks the point at which there is an *opening* in an individual's experience, a *space* in which she has the *choice* to break with her past choices and act differently in the future. Only on account of this discontinuity in learning does one's choice to think and do otherwise arise; for Herbart, it is a precondition for learning in the realm of morality that educators can and must support.

Implicit in Herbart's analysis of the moral individual is the idea that to be moral, one must listen to oneself in a particular way – namely, one must listen to the commands of one's own *inner censor* in the context of moral dilemmas. This draws on the moral sense of the notion of listening-to-oneself reminiscent of the *daemon* that comes to Socrates as a voice telling him what not to do.[8] In these moments, we can say that we begin to listen *inwardly* and begin an inner dialogue of the sort that phenomenologist Bernhard Waldenfels describes when he states that in inner dialogue, "the speaker breaks away from his past and commands himself to act differently in the future."[9] Taken in this way, the idea of a person *listening to an inner voice as an inner censor* connects to the idea of human beings as self-questioning and learning beings who can question their own motives and call into doubt their plans for action. The idea of the human being as one capable of learning is captured in the notion of perfectibility (*Bildsamkeit*), which I examine next.

[8] Plato, "Apology", in *Plato Complete Works*, translated by G. M. A. Grube, edited by John M. Cooper and D. S. Hutchinson pp. 17–36. (Cambridge, MA: Hatckett Publishing Company, 1997). On this idea, see also in particular chapter 9, "Solitude, Silence, Listening," in Nigel Blake, Paul Smeyers, Richard Smith, and Paul Standish, *Education in an Age of Nihilism* (London: Routledge, 2000); see also Dietrich Benner, "Kritik und Negativität. Ein Versuch zur Pluralisierung von Kritik in Erziehung, Pädagogik und Erziehungswissenschaft" [Critique and Negativity: Towards the Pluralisation of Critique in Educational Practice, Theory and Research], *Zeitschrift für Pädagogik*, 46, 2003: 96–110; and, for an expanded English-language version of that article, see Dietrich Benner and Andrea English, "Critique and Negativity: Toward the Pluralisation of Critique in Educational Practice, Theory and Research," *Journal of Philosophy of Education*, 38, no. 3, 2004: 409–28; see also the response to this article in Rosa Nidia Buenfil Burgos, "Negativity: A Disturbing Constitutive Matter in Education," *Journal of Philosophy of Education*, 38, no. 3, 2004: 429–40.

[9] Bernhard Waldenfels, "Sich-sprechen Hören. Zur Aufzeichnung der phänomenologischen Stimme" (Hearing Oneself Speak. Sketch of a Phenomenology of the Voice), in *Deutsch-Französiche Gedankengänge*, p. 96 (Frankfurt am Main: Suhrkamp, 1995), translation mine.

2 THE LEARNING BEING: PERFECTIBILITY WITHOUT
PERFECTION (*BILDSAMKEIT*)

The concept of *Bildsamkeit*, which can be translated as educability, plasticity, or perfectibility, addresses the very possibility of one person learning from another. *Bildsamkeit* describes an aspect of the human condition that educators have to presuppose, namely, that the individual is both capable of being formed through her interaction with the world *and* of forming herself within that interaction. Herbart put forth the idea of *Bildsamkeit* as an indispensable educational concept when he proclaimed in his 1835 *Outlines of Educational Doctrine* that the "educability [*Bildsamkeit*] of the individual" is the "founding principle of education."[10] The idea may seem tautological because the concept holds that, in order to educate, we have to assume education is possible.[11] Herbart's point, however, is to underscore that without making explicit the assumption that educators can have an influence on another person, there is no basis for theoretical discussion about the limits or possibilities of pedagogical interaction. Thus, without such a concept, neither a science (*Wissenschaft*) of education nor practice of education would be possible.[12] Herbart's statement underscores the idea that pedagogical interaction is grounded in the human capacity for learning through encounters with difference and otherness. In defining Herbart's concept of *educability* more closely, we can look at two other concepts that inform it, namely Jean-Jacques Rousseau's notion of *perfectibilité* and Wilhelm von Humboldt's notion of *Bildung*.

Rousseau's concept of *perfectibilité* expresses the idea that the human being is capable of learning in all areas of life.[13] In *Discourse on the Origin and Foundations of Inequality Among Men* (1755), Rousseau highlights the term *perfectibility* as a way of making a distinction between the human being and

---

[10] Johann Friedrich Herbart, "Umriss pädagogischer Vorlesung" (1835 and 1841), in *Joh. Friedr. Herbart's Sämtliche Werke in Chronologischer Reihenfolge*, edited by Karl Kehrbach, Vol. 10, pp. 65–206 (Langensalza: Hermann Beyer und Söhne, 1902), cited here using the English translation, Herbart, *Outlines of Educational Doctrine*, translated by Alexis F. Lange, p. 1 (New York: MacMillan Company, 1913), translation modified. In the Felkin and Felkin translation, rather than "educability," the term *Bildsamkeit* is translated as "the capacity for cultivation"; see Herbart, *Letters and Lectures on Education*, p. 102.

[11] On this point, see Otto Friedrich Bollnow, *Existenzphilosophie und Pädagogik* (Existentialism and Pedagogy), p. 16 (Stuttgart: Kohlhammer, 1965).

[12] Benner and Schmied-Kowarzik, *Herbarts Praktische Philosophie*, p. 95–97.

[13] Jean-Jacques Rousseau, *Emile or On Education* (1764), translated and edited by Allan Bloom, p. 61 (New York: Basic Books, 1979).

other animals.[14] This distinction lies in the fact that human beings, unlike other animals, have the potential *not* to follow their instincts, but to move past these with reason and understanding.[15] Thus, we can say that Rousseau's concept locates the basis for human self-transformation and learning, which lies in the human capacity to go against inclinations, to break with oneself and, in doing so, to change direction of thought and action.

Herbart's notion of *Bildsamkeit* emphasizes this human ability to break with oneself and go against self-interested inclinations as the basis for the human capacity to become *moral*.[16] This break with oneself, which we can call a form of *self-alienation*, relates to how we learn through encounters with things in the world that are unfamiliar, unexpected, and strange. This type of interaction with otherness as a basis for learning about the world and about oneself is expressed in the idea of *Bildung*, which is most often translated as *education* or *formation*. Both terms, *Bildung* and *Bildsamkeit*, stem from the root word *bild*, which means *form*, and the term *bildsam* can be connected to the Latin *formabilis* or *docilis*, meaning formable or teachable, respectively. Herbart's use of the term *Bildsamkeit* reflects these meanings. The concept captures the individual's capacity *to form* and *to be formed* and thereby connects to the notion of *Bildung*.[17]

The notion of *Bildung* brings forth a concept of education as a transformational process. This idea has, in particular, been a theme in the modern German tradition of educational philosophy, yet, as philosopher of education Jörg Ruhloff points out, the category "*Bildung*" goes back as far as the Greek Sophist and Socratic traditions as a way of delimiting problems of the legitimacy of our basic human dispositions.[18] He explains, "Bildung, as a category," thematizes and calls into question the self-evidence of "our

---

[14] Jean-Jacques Rousseau, *Discourse on the Origin of Inequality* (1755), edited by Patrick Coleman, translated by Franklin Philip (Oxford: Oxford University Press, 1999).

[15] Ibid., pp. 33–34.

[16] Herbart, *Outlines of Educational Doctrine*; see also Herbart, *ARW*.

[17] See also similarities in Gadamer's reading of Hegel's concept of *Bildung* in Hans-Georg Gadamer, *Truth and Method*, Second revised edition, translation revised by Joel Weinsheimer and Donald G. Marshall (New York: Continuum 2000). See also the introduction to the idea of Bildung in an English-language volume on the concept, Lars Løvlie and Paul Standish, "Introduction: Bildung and the Idea of Liberal Education," *Journal of Philosophy of Education*, **36**, no. 3, August 2002: 317–40. For a critical treatment of Heidegger's relation to education (*Bildung*), see Iain Thomson, *Heidegger on Ontotheology: Technology and the Politics of Education* (New York: Cambridge University Press, 2005).

[18] Jörg Ruhloff, "Bildung – nur ein Paradigma im pädagogischen Denken?" [Bildung – only a paradigm in educational thought?] in *Skepsis und Widerstreit: Neue Beiträge zur skeptisch-transzendentalkritischen Pädagogik*, edited by Wolfgang Fischer and Jörg Ruhloff, p. 176 (Sankt Augustin: Academia Verlag, 1993), translation mine.

perceptions, interpretations, feelings, needs and wishes, our ways of communicating, acting and interacting as well as our intergenerational forms of socialisation, upbringing, and instruction."[19]

In modern educational theory, questions of how human beings move beyond primary modes of perception and understanding are addressed in Humboldt's fragment "Theory of *Bildung*" (1793). Therein, Humboldt draws out the understanding of education as *Bildung* by explicating that, in order to learn and grow, the human being relies on a world being something *other* than himself, that is, "*NichtMensch.*"[20] In encounters with the world, the human being meets difference and learns through the process of active *and* receptive interplay with that world.[21] Humboldt illustrates that inner growth and change is dependent upon encounters with the otherness of the world as follows: "Just as mere abilities can be developed only in interaction with objects, and just as thoughts can be sustained only in reference to substance, so man needs a world outside himself."[22] Our encounters with the world are transformative in that they are mediated by "self-alienation," that is, alienation from our taken-for-granted and habitual self-understandings. This alienation arises out of recognition of the limits of such understandings; by gaining new perspective and new understanding, we find the "warmth" of a "return" to ourselves.[23] *Bildung* refers to the active and receptive self-other relation implicit in educational processes. Thus, the "interplay" Humboldt speaks of cannot be captured in an understanding of the mind as an "autopoietic system" interacting with itself; rather, it involves the human being's confrontation with an external world that potentially resists his attempts to change and transform it.[24]

---

[19] Ibid., translation mine.

[20] Wilhelm von Humboldt, "Theorie der Bildung des Menschen," in *Wilhelm von Humboldt, Werke in Fünf Bände.* edited by Andreas Flitner and Klaus Giel., Vol. 1: Schriften zur Anthropologie und Geschichte, p. 235 (Darmstadt: Wissenschaftliche Buchgesellschaft, 1969); see also the English translation, Wilhelm von Humboldt, "Theory of Bildung," in *Teaching as a Reflective Practice: The German Didaktik Tradition*, translated by Gillian Horton-Krüger, edited by Ian Westbury, Stephan Hopmann, and Kurt Riquarts (Mahwah NJ: Lawrence Erlbaum Associates, 2001).

[21] Humboldt, "Theorie der Bildung des Menschen," p. 235–36; see also Wilhelm von Humboldt, "Über den Geist der Menschheit," in *Wilhelm von Humboldt, Werke in Fünf Bände*, edited by Andreas Flitner and Klaus Giel, Vol. 1: Schriften zur Anthropologie und Geschichte, pp. 506–18 (Darmstadt: Wissenschaftliche Buchgesellschaft, 1969).

[22] Humboldt, "Theorie der Bildung des Menschen," p. 235, translation mine.

[23] Compare Humboldt, "Theorie der Bildung des Menschen," p. 237.

[24] Compare Käte Meyer-Drawe, "Die Herausforderung durch die Dinge: Das Andere im Lernprozess" (The Challenge by the Object: The Other in the Learning Process), *Zeitschrift für Pädagogik*, 46, 1999: 329–36, translation mine. See also Dietrich Benner's discussion of learning from the other, Dietrich Benner, "Der Andere und Das Andere als Problem und Aufgabe in der Erziehung und Bildung" (The Other as Human, The Other as Object: A Problem and Task in

Herbart's term *Bildsamkeit* (*perfectibility* or *educability*) expresses the process of change through *Bildung*, of which all human beings are capable, without making claims about a blank starting point or a predetermined final destination to this process. It differs fundamentally from concepts of the human being as deficient from the start or as a being that follows a path to completion. On the latter point, Herbart agrees with Rousseau's statement that, "we do not know what our nature permits us to be."[25] For Herbart, we can say *Bildsamkeit* expresses an understanding of human beings as "changeable beings," both in relation to their organic nature and in relation to their will, but the change each person is capable of is "*indeterminate*," a qualification that reveals Herbart's concept of perfectibility is ateleological.

However, this capacity for change and formation through the teacher-learner relation and through encounters with the world, though indeterminate, is not limitless, and should not be seen as such to the educator. Herbart defined two limits to the individual's capacity for change that are equally limits for the educator: the circumstances of the situation and the "individuality" (*Individualität*) or uniqueness of the human being, expressed in one's capacity to make choices based in one's own unique history.[26] The notion of *Bildsamkeit* thus expresses the idea of the human being as a *learning being*, a fact that all forms of education must address: "The object (*Gegenstand*) upon which all education (*Erziehung*) must orient itself is without a doubt none other than man himself, namely, man as a changeable being, as a being, who can transition from one state to another, and at the same time maintain something of himself in the new situation."[27]

Teaching and Education), in *Bildungstheorie und Bildungsforschung* (Paderborn: Ferdinand Schoningh, 2008). I draw out certain connections between the idea of *Bildung* and the work of R. S. Peters; see Andrea English, "Transformation and Education: The Voice of the Learner in Peters' Concept of Teaching," *Journal of Philosophy of Education*, 43 (Special Issue "Reading R. S. Peters Today: Analysis, Ethics and the Aims of Education," edited by Stefaan Cuypers and Christopher Martin), no. S1, 2009: 75–95.

[25] Rousseau, *Emile*, p. 62. See also *SE*; on this point in Herbart, see Günther Buck, *Herbarts Grundlegung der Pädagogik*. (Heidelberg: Carl Winter, 1985). Herbart criticizes doctrines of fatalism and transcendental freedom on account of the fact that they cannot be consistent with the idea of *Bildsamkeit*. For Herbart, those doctrines do not allow for an understanding of the historicity of the individual and therefore do not allow for discussions of how education influences the individual's choices. See Herbart, *Outlines of Educational Doctrine*, p. 2.

[26] Herbart, *Outlines of Educational Doctrine*, p. 4; see also Benner and Schmied-Kowarzik, *Herbarts praktische Philosophie*; and Dietrich Benner, *Allgemeine Pädagogik* (Weinheim: Juventa, 2001).

[27] Johann Friedrich Herbart, "Zwei Vorlesungen über Pädagogik (1802)," in *Joh. Friedr. Herbart's Sämtliche Werke in Chronologischer Reihenfolge*, edited by Karl Kehrbach, Vol. 1, p. 131 (Langensalza: Hermann Beyer and Söhne, 1887), and the English translation, Herbart, "Introductory Lecture to Students in Pedagogy," in *Herbart's ABC of Sense-Perception and Minor Pedagogical Works*, edited and translated by William J. Eckoff, pp. 13–28, pp. 27–28 (New York: D. Appleton, 1896), translation modified.

The recognition of the human being as a learning being is indispensable for understanding the limits and possibilities of educative interactions between teachers and learners. Specifically, from Herbart's understanding of perfectibility as the founding principle of education, we can draw out two significant consequences for the teacher that will be important in the next chapter, where I examine Herbart's concept of the teacher's task in relation to cognitive and moral learning. First, it means that the teacher must recognize her ability to have an influence on the learner and, therefore, take responsibility to make conscious choices about how she will influence the learner. In this sense, *Bildsamkeit* has a prescriptive quality for the teacher.[28] Second, the human as a learning being expresses the idea that neither the educator nor society at large can determine an individual's future. *Bildsamkeit* is an ateleological notion that says it is up to each learner to decide for herself in particular cases, and in life on the whole, what to think and do. Thus, as philosophers of education Dietrich Benner and Friedhelm Brüggen emphasize, *Bildsamkeit* is "that unknown something" ("*das unbekannte etwas*") of human nature.[29] In this sense, to describe the human being as *bildsam* (i.e., *perfectible* or *capable of learning* – the latter of which is the most apt translation) reminds us that, in principle, there always remains something unknown and unknowable, and, in Herbart's sense "indeterminate" (*unbestimmt*) about human nature.

---

[28] Compare Benner and Schmied-Kowarzik, *Herbarts praktische Philosophie*.

[29] Dietrich Benner and Friedhelm Brüggen, "Bildsamkeit und Bildung" (Perfectibility and Bildung) in *Historisches Wörterbuch der Pädagogik*, edited by Dietrich Benner and Jürgen Oelkers, pp. 174–225, p. 195 (Weinheim: Beltz, 2004).

Chapter 2

The Problem of Continuity, the Need for Struggle, the Role of Tact

Herbart sought a form of education that supports learners to come into a moral relation with themselves by presenting them with options and providing them the means, through instruction, to broaden their circle of thought. Education thereby creates situations in which the Categorical Imperative has meaning for learners, such that they want to judge and *act* according to it. In concrete educational situations, the learner's inner struggle poses a problem for both teacher and learner, and the interpersonal relation formed between them is at stake. Whereas the learner may seek to avoid inner conflict and follow habit, the teacher has the difficult task of cultivating inner conflict in the learner by bringing in different viewpoints and ideas that contradict the learner's viewpoints. Only in this way can learners begin to experience the power of *inner freedom* that occurs when they see that they can distance themselves from their initial inclinations and choose not to follow them. For Herbart, this type of moral experience is not possible without a form of instruction that provides a strong basis in varied and pluralist views of the world, views that support learners' ability to expand their horizons of thought beyond their immediate community in a way that reveals to them a multitude of choices. This stance forms the basis of Herbart's argument that instruction and moral education must reciprocally support one another.

Herbart's account of moral decision making, as I delineated in the last chapter, problematizes the idea that education amounts to initiating others blindly into an existing ethical order, or into a new ethical order anticipated by the educators themselves. Furthermore, he rejects child-centered notions of education that leave all judgments in the learner's hands, without guidance. Instead, for Herbart, there are two opposing ideas at the heart of education: first, that educators have a responsibility not to leave it up to chance whether learners choose self-interested action or action that recognizes the other, and, second, that educators must allow learners to decide for themselves how to act, be it self-interestedly or morally. The central question is then: What form of education would allow teachers to guide learners into moral self-relations without making learners dependent upon the judgments of others?

Herbart's answer is twofold. He argues that education involves both "educative instruction" (*erziehender Unterricht*) and "moral guidance" (*Zucht*).[1] Accordingly, educative instruction is grounded in cultivating cognitive learning processes, which support the learners' expansion of knowledge and experience beyond the immediacy of their observed world so that they come to see the plurality of choices they *could* make in the world. Moral guidance is grounded in dialogue that supports moral learning processes, which develop the learners' critical thinking about the choices they *should* make in the world (*SE* 109/ *AP* 28). Herbart envisions each of these realms of education as entailing separate tasks for the teacher.[2]

Each of Herbart's concepts of learning (one addressing cognitive growth, the other moral growth) connects to his understanding of the perfectibility of the human being and how it is to be cultivated by educators. The notion of perfectibility (discussed in Chapter 1) begins to tell us something about the structure of learning. It hints at the fact that learning involves a break with ourselves that occurs in the context of our interaction with the otherness of the world; a break that makes moral action possible. However, to recognize that the human being *can* change and learn does not yet answer the question of how learning takes place. To answer the question of how we learn, we have

---

[1] As I mentioned in the "Note on the Translation," I am diverging from the standard translation of the term *Zucht*. Herbart refers to forms of pedagogical action that prevent a child from physically harming himself or others as *Regierung*, which is rendered in the standard translation as "government," but on my view is more appropriately translated in this context as "discipline." However, although I am not dealing with the idea of *Regierung* in this text, it is important to note that Herbart differentiates discipline (*Regierung*) from moral education, and did not see it as part of education proper. That is, discipline focuses on the results of learners' actions, with the aim of preventing learners from immediately harming themselves or others; moral education focuses on understanding the thought behind learners' actions, a task we can refer to as moral guidance (*Zucht*). Herbart sees discipline as an indispensable precondition for formative education; however, he notes that it is not part of true education because it only works negatively to prevent harm, and thus should not have an intentional formative influence. Herbart refers to the teacher's task in the development of moral character as *Zucht*. The term *Zucht* comes from the German verb *ziehen*, meaning "to pull forth." This idea of educational practice as *Zucht* describes a form of educating that has a formative effect on learners' development of moral character, which is why I contend that the concept is better addressed in English as "moral guidance."

[2] In German, Herbart uses both the terms "Erzieher" (guide or someone responsible for upbringing) and "Lehrer" (teacher), with the latter most often referring to one who is mediating content of the world to the learner (e.g., through instruction in subject matter in or out of school context). I will use the word "teacher" when referring to either the task of "educative instruction" or the task of "moral guidance."

to examine the role of the "new" in our experience. How is it that we take in something new, different, and unfamiliar in a way that enters our thought and becomes part of our consideration for action?

Herbart provides two separate answers to the question of how we learn, one for cognitive learning and one for moral learning (in later chapters, we will see how Dewey developed a unified theory of learning). For Herbart, cognitive learning proceeds primarily by the continuous step-by-step acquisition of the new, whereas moral learning proceeds through discontinuous experiences of self-questioning and inner struggle in confrontation with the new. To understand this distinction, we might say that, for Herbart, the new encounters us and in turn challenges us in the process of learning in different ways. In cognitive learning, it encounters us as question of knowledge or what to think, whereas, in moral learning, it encounters us as a question of what to do; it is up to each individual to connect thought and action in making particular choices.

In this chapter, I consider each of Herbart's concepts of the structure of learning in turn, in order to demonstrate how they each reveal something distinct about how to understand learning as a discontinuous process. Although, as I have already suggested, Herbart does not make discontinuity integral to his theory of cognitive learning, his analysis of cognitive learning proves important for understanding the limits of theories of learning (such as his own) that only theorize continuity. Such theories, as I explicate, hide the ruptures in our experience of the new embedded in processes of learning, and therefore fail to address the educative potential of discontinuity.

In the first section, I discuss certain salient features of Herbart's notion of cognitive learning in order to problematize the notion of continuity underlying his theory of learning and of teaching in this realm. In this way, I begin the chapter with a critique of Herbart's understanding of the *process* of cognitive learning, while demonstrating the fruitfulness of his understanding of the *aim* of cognitive learning. My discussion in the first section then provides a point of contrast for my discussion on Herbart's view of moral learning as a discontinuous process guided by the teacher, which I take up in the second section. Throughout the chapter, I consider the teacher's role in guiding the learning process of the learner. I close the chapter with an analysis of Herbart's notion of tact in teaching, which helps us to begin to discover the *teacher's* experience of discontinuity.

1   LEARNING TO SEE DIFFERENCE WITHOUT DISRUPTION

The very idea of perfectibility entails for Herbart that an individual is capable of expanding her mind outside the realm of the familiar and everyday and beyond the contingencies of birth. But, what happens between our encounter with something new and different and our understanding of that object or idea? For Herbart, the path of cognitive learning is a path on which the learner learns about different, as yet unfamiliar objects and ideas with the aim of learning to distinguish between different types of knowledge (*Erkenntnis*) and different concepts of social participation (*Teilnahme*) in the world. For Herbart, the ability to make such distinctions is indispensable to the learner's moral growth and *Bildung*. However, his account of the learner's path toward the new in the realm of cognitive learning, as I will demonstrate, does not theorize the *experience* of the new for the learner; rather, learning is conceived of primarily as a path without the disruption of discontinuity.

Herbart conceived of cognitive learning processes as leading individuals to become "multifaceted," and, in doing so, he was at once connecting cognitive learning processes to what he deemed the larger project of education: education is a path away from the egoism of "one-sidedness." Herbart's notion of developing a person toward "multifacetedness," although perhaps uncommon-sounding in English, connects to German classical notions of *Bildung* as "general education" developing all aspects of the human being, as philosopher of education Wolfgang Klafki explains.[3] In this sense, *Bildung* is grounded in the idea that the "*multidimensional*" relations a human being can potentially make to "natural and historical reality" must connect back to the "*unity* of the responsible person."[4]

Before delving further into what Herbart conceived of as the path of learning that leads to multifacetedness, it is helpful to understand the basis for his conceptual distinction between "one-sidedness" (*Einseitigkeit*) and "multifacetedness" (*Vielseitigkeit*). The one-sided individual and the multi-faceted individual each relate differently to the new in experience. The one-sided individual can only understand familiar and trusted things in her surroundings, such that she either cannot perceive unfamiliar objects, simply ignores difference, or, perhaps more problematic, distorts everything else to the point of "falsifying" it entirely through a "habitual frame of mind" (*SE* 124/ *AP* 38); such an individual only sees "the old in the new" (*SE* 127/*AP* 40; see also *AP* 48). This type of person is unable to take in the new *as* new – that is, as something she has not previously encountered either at all or in this partic-ular way – and so it does not cause her pause to consider the difference

---

[3] Wolfgang Klafki, *Neue Studien zur Bildungstheorie und Didaktik. Zeitgemässe Allgemeinbildung und kritisch-konstruktive Didaktik*, 6th ed., p. 30 (Beltz: Weinheim, 2007).

[4] Ibid., emphasis mine. Klafki also demonstrates therein that "multifacetedness" is still today an important aim for education and schooling in pluralistic societies.

between *known* and *unknown, old* and *new*. Thus, the one-sided individual is stuck in her habits of thought and routine interactions to the point that these color, or even distort, her new experiences.

So, in Herbart's terms, we can say that a one-sided individual has a mind that has not been awakened to the many ways we can see and be in the world. Contrastingly, a person who has "many facets" describes someone who is moved by the new, such that she becomes *"interested"* in the new objects and ideas that she encounters. Herbart uses the term "interest" in a way that distinguishes an interest from a fixed habit. With the term "interest," Herbart is denoting a state of mind in which a person is "inwardly active," yet does not necessarily move forward toward action (or, put another way, does not necessarily become outwardly active), but rather "clings to the contemplated present" (*SE* 129/*AP* 42).[5]

Herbart is capturing the meaning of interest as *inter-esse* (i.e., "to be or lie between"). For Herbart, this is a state of being between "observation and attainment" when we notice something new, such that our mind is captivated by it, and we want to understand both the object and our relation to the object (*SE* 129/*AP* 42).[6] Herbart's concept of "a person of multifaceted interest" thus describes a person who does not take immediate action on the things that interest her, but rather views these as objects of learning that open up the possibility for change and new choices.[7]

Herbart's juxtaposition of the one-sided person and the multifaceted person is important for understanding his theory of cognitive learning for two central reasons. First, he is pointing out the human tendency to remain one-sided, curb any desire to learn from the new, and remain satisfied with the stability and comfort of the familiar – a claim based in his anthropological assumption that we will later see is also shared by Dewey. On this view, insofar as human beings do not wander through new learning processes, they tend toward one-sidedness, seeking routine rather than new experiences.

---

[5] A connection can be made here to Leonard Waks's idea of inwardly listening, in which he seeks to describe a state of listening related to inner contemplation; Leonard J. Waks, "Two Types of Interpersonal Listening," *Teachers College Record*, 112, no. 11, 2010: 2743–62.

[6] On this point, see also Dietrich Benner, *Johann Friedrich Herbart: Systematische Pädagogik [Johann Friedrich Herbart: Systematic Pedagogy]*, Vol. 2, Interpretationen, p. 67 (Weinheim: Deutsche Studien Verlag, 1997).

[7] Herbart also cautioned that the aim of education is not to create what he called "all-faceted" individuals (*SE* 122/*AP* 37, translation modified). To have such an aim would imply that educators (or society at large) knew what the educated person should look like, that is, it would imply that we knew the end of education. By rejecting the idea that instruction should aim to create "all-faceted" individuals, Herbart remains consistent with his ateleological notion of perfectibility that I discussed in Chapter 1.

Second, with this juxtaposition, Herbart is grounding the need for teachers to cultivate each learner's ability to expand her horizons of thought through cognitive learning processes that are supported by *educative instruction*. Educative instruction seeks to extend the learner's immediate everyday forms of experiencing and interacting with others in the world through mediated aesthetic experiences. These aim to develop multifaceted individuals, those who freely choose to continue to expand their own minds and thereby continue to learn. Without the aesthetic experiences that provide fodder for our understanding of the "many facets" of the world (even those that we cannot immediately see), we are confined to only learning about a world that is within our vision – the world of everyday experiences.

Herbart is making educators aware of a significant point: the world we find before us, however it may be, determines to a large extent whether we are able to extend our thoughts in multifaceted directions or remain narrow and one-sided in our vision of what is possible. He warns educators that, although all children "observe" the objects and people within their surroundings and "– at least in thought – imitate, taste and choose," there remains a danger that the learner will be "seized" by what excites him, such that he begins to "calculate" (*ARW* 68, translation modified). With this warning, Herbart underscores how an individual becomes one-sided: the one-sided individual is held by his subjective desires and calculates what needs to be done in order to satisfy those desires; he is "lost to true morality" because his relationships to the world and others turn to means-ends relationships (*ARW* 68, translation modified).

Cognitive learning processes, guided by the teacher through instruction, aim to help the learner expand his or her mind from potential one-sidedness toward an understanding of multifaceted ways of seeing and being in the world. Through cognitive learning processes, as Herbart viewed them, learners move from their starting point in everyday experiences to develop an interest in distinguishing among empirical, aesthetic, and scientific forms of knowing, and among social, political, and religious forms of communicating with and participating in the world.[8] However, in Herbart's conception of the learner's path toward making such distinctions between old and new, familiar

---

[8] These distinctions relate to Herbart's material concept of multifacetedness. He understands the learning process as expanding the learner's everyday knowledge toward empirical, scientific, and aesthetic knowledge, and the learner's everyday mode of interaction with others toward social, political, and religious participation in the world (*SE* 132-35/*AP* 44-45). I will not be developing the concrete subject matter of instruction here further as my focus is on the process of learning. However, later in this chapter, I give a few examples that help illuminate the relation between the process of learning and the material of learning on Herbart's model.

and unfamiliar, he fails to take systematic account of the gaps and breaks – the discontinuity and negativity of experience – that learners experience when encountering something new. Rather, he constructed the path of cognitive learning according to the principles of a theory of association in which the learner steadily and continuously associates the old with the next closely related new object.

On his account, the process begins with the learner "immersing" (*Vertiefung*) herself into the object by first "noticing" (*Merken*) an object "clearly" (*Klarheit*) (*SE* 123–33/*AP* 38–43). Herbart illuminates his meaning of these terms by poetically stating that seeing something clearly means grasping it mentally as if "with clean hands" and not allowing "confused markings" to be "scratched" upon the mind (*SE* 124/*AP* 38). The process continues with a following stage of "associating" (*Assoziation*) that clear object with other known and familiar objects (*SE* 123–33/*AP* 38–43). In the stage of association, the learner brings together things that have been noticed clearly, and while certain "expectations" (*Erwarten*) of how the new object is (although new) still related to other known objects inform her understanding, Herbart emphasizes that it must be ensured that "contradictory" objects, or aspects of these objects, are not connected in the learner's mind (*SE* 124–25/*AP* 38–39). The stages of immersion are followed by two stages of "reflection" (*Besinnung*) in which the learner "orders" (*System*) the new object into a system of other known and related objects.[9] The process concludes with a

---

[9] Herbart makes clear that it is not part of the teacher's task in instruction to lead learners to take particular actions in the world because, in his view, actions form habits and thus can limit the learner's future choices. If habits are formed as a result of instruction, the teacher would be predetermining and narrowing the learner's choices, rather than expanding these and leaving final decisions to act for the learner to determine. For that reason, for Herbart, the learner's answer to questions of "what to do" cannot stem directly from instruction, but must be negotiated in the learner's struggle with himself, as I discussed in Chapter 1 and return to later in this chapter. Herbart conceived of the realm of instruction as an "action free-zone" and viewed these stages of building the child's interest as connected to the age of the child, such that the small child "notices," the young boy develops "expectations," the youth "demands" (*Fordern*), so that "the man can act (*Handeln*)" (*SE* 147/*AP* 54, translation modified). The stages of reflection set up the learner for understanding his or her desire or demand of certain things and certain forms of participating in the world that can be the basis of his or her choices for reflective action. However, Herbart notes in passing that a young learner's inner activity in the context of instruction may lead by chance to *outward* activity and that the teacher should not hinder this. He writes that a child may have certain expectations and "experiment" with "having a go" and testing out an idea that may lead the child to an unexpected "strange" result that can be instructive because it promotes imagination (*SE* 131/*AP* 43, translation modified). Herbart's comments suggest that failed expectations and failed trials that lead to "strange" results are unavoidable in learning processes. The fact that Herbart notices that such discontinuity in experience can have an instructive side is significant for the current reading. However, he relegates this experience to young children who have not yet learned patience of mind and does not consider further any constitutive role that such

stage Herbart termed "method" (*Methode*), in which the learner considers the learning process she has gone through in a way that promotes her understanding of the process of learning (or *learning to learn*), so that new questions for the learner can arise (*SE* 123–28/*AP* 38–41).[10]

Herbart's theory of cognitive learning only accounts for the positive and continuous stages of learning, not the negative and discontinuous moments of our encounters with the new. So, we can say that what is hidden and not accounted for in this theory is the experience of *interruption*. The new interrupts us by its newness and otherness, so that we have to take the time to figure out whether or not, and how, it might modify or contradict our existing knowledge and understanding. The negativity of this experience of the new reveals itself when learners begin to distinguish one object, or aspect of an object, from another and notice *what constitutes* this particular object or idea and *what does not*. Although, for Herbart, the learners' ability to use thought and judgment to make such distinctions is constitutive of their learning processes, his theory of association does not answer the question of wherein the negativity lies on our path toward making distinctions between old and new. In other words, he does not answer the questions: What happens when the learner is still *coming* to know something clearly, but is still unclear? What happens in thought, when the learner is still awestruck by the new and is unable to associate the new and strange with things she already knows and trusts? What about those moments when the learner has noticed contradictions in thought, but has not yet found a method for inquiring into those contradictions and learning anew? Although Herbart gives us an important sense of learning as a process, not simply a product, Herbart's theory of the positive stages of learning overlooks how learning processes entail *an experience of difference*, an experience wrought with perplexity and confusion on the way toward clarity; doubt and resistance on the way toward understanding the new and strange.

Teaching for Continuity or Not Minding the Gaps in Learning

Models of learning that address continuity at the expense of discontinuity imply concepts of teaching that view teaching as oriented on maintaining

experimental forms of experience could have for cognitive learning processes. Considerations of that sort, as they appear in Dewey's work, will be discussed in the following chapters.

[10] Herbart scholar Stephanie Hellekamps calls this stage "a thinking-over of the newly acquired content of the world and its connection to one's mind"; see Stephanie Hellekamps, *Erziehender Unterricht und Didaktik* (Educative Instruction and Didactics), p. 80 (Weinheim: Deutscher Studien Verlag, 1991), translation mine. For American readers, this process of stages is perhaps the most familiar part of Herbart's work.

continuity in the learner's experience of learning. Such concepts of teaching ensure that the learner arrives at the positive stages of learning, but overlook the negative moments in learning and, in turn, overlook the educative potential of these moments. We can see this issue arising in Herbart's theory of teaching through "educative instruction." Although, on Herbart's model, the teacher must place importance on introducing learners to the multi-faceted new, the teacher leads learners to distinctions in thought in a way that provides for their experience of continuity between old and new, but not for their experience of the discontinuity associated with the experience of the otherness of the new. To understand the inadequacies of what I will call a *continuity theory of learning*, I will briefly illustrate the problems of Herbart's model of the teacher's task in instruction, after which I will address where we might find a hint in Herbart's discussion of the potential significance of discontinuity in cognitive learning.

Herbart gives a sense of his vision of the teacher's task in instruction in his short explanation of how history should be taught. He explained that children should be made aware of the continuity between the ancient world and their own present world. He states: "Starting at an early age, the souls of (the learners) should be rooted in the world of the past from which there is a *continuous* progression through to the present."[11] Although he acknowledged that the differences between the old and new world will be noticed by learners – learners "will come across foreign elements, such as oriental or old Germanic things" – he emphasized that these foreign elements "are not suited to be used as aids for a continuously progressing education."[12] Herbart's example demonstrates that, in his vision of teaching, the teacher is meant to maintain the learner's steady progression from historical knowledge of the past to that of the present by focusing on things that are connected with what the learner already knows. Such focus is to be maintained to the point of not allowing the learner to be disturbed by the unexpected moments entailed by the unfamiliar historical objects and ideas, or, in Herbart's terms, "foreign elements," with which the learner cannot associate. In other words, on Herbart's view, what the learner notices *unclearly*, what does not make immediate sense, or cannot be immediately associated with existing

---

[11] Johann Friedrich Herbart, "Kurze Anleitung für Erzieher, die Odyssee mit Knaben zu Lesen," in *Joh. Friedr. Herbart's Sämtliche Werke in Chronologischer Reihenfolge*, edited by K. Kehrbach, Vol. 3, pp. 3–6, 5 (Langensalza: Hermann Beyer und Söhne, 1888), emphasis in original, translation mine.

[12] Herbart, "Kurze Anleitung für Erzieher," 5, translation mine.

knowledge, is not of central importance and should not form a significant part of instruction in history; correspondingly, it should not form a significant aspect of the learner's learning process.

By acknowledging that there are certain things that learners will unavoidably notice and that will be too strange or different for them to take in, Herbart was to some extent recognizing the fact that learners may be thrown off course by what they read or come into contact with in any given lesson. However, there are two problematic assumptions underlying Herbart's view of the teacher's task in instruction: first, the assumption that the teacher can predetermine what the learner will or will not expect in the material, and, second, the assumption that the teacher should keep the lesson within the realm of the expected. The result of such assumptions is a model of teaching according to which the teacher only looks for the positive features of the learner's existing knowledge and experience. In other words, in ensuring that the *new* is always connected to what the learner *knows* and the *foreign* is always connected to what the learner is *familiar* with, the teacher only allows connected ideas to regulate the learner's learning process.

In consequence, while the teacher focuses on the positive features of the child's previous knowledge and experience – those that identify how the learner's knowledge and experience *connect* to the subject matter being taught – the teacher overlooks the negative features – those that identify how the learner's knowledge and experience *do not connect* to what is being taught. The latter identify what knowledge or ability the learner is missing, what difficulties or problems she is having, what she does not know, what may prevent her from associating prior experiences with the new, what causes awe and puzzlement, what is strange to her, and what she may resist taking in.

Thus, the underlying problem with such a teaching model is that, in searching for the positivities of learning, the teacher ignores or skips over the learners' negative experiences that occur within their interaction with the new – the unclarity or confusion that occurs *between* first seeing an object and then seeing it clearly in its relations to other things. In skipping over the learner's negative experiences with the unexpected for the sake of arriving at the positive stages of learning, Herbart's theory of cognitive learning processes (and the theory of teaching that promotes these processes) potentially skips over the possibility for the learner to learn from his or her negative experiences. So, although we can say that Herbart would acknowledge that arriving at positive distinctions in knowledge and understanding involves knowing what something is not – that is, that positive knowledge entails what philosopher Fritz Oser calls "negative knowledge"[13] – he does not systematically theorize the fact that the process of arriving at both positive and negative knowledge entails an experience of the negative and discontinuous moments in learning, moments of getting it wrong, of getting lost, and of being unclear about how to move on.

It is important to note that in envisioning the teacher's task in instruction as promoting the learner's smooth transition from old to new, Herbart was aiming to address the teacher's need to find a balance between over- and underchallenging the learner. He believed that introducing learners to things that are too disconnected from their existing knowledge and experience runs the risk that they will retract into the comfort of one-sidedness and the narrow field of the everyday. What Herbart was after was developing an understanding of instruction that promoted each learner's ability to gain *distance* on the everyday.

Herbart scholar Stephanie Hellekamps illuminates this idea of "distancing" underlying Herbart's theory of educative instruction in a way that sheds light on the constitutive role of negative experience in learning. She explains that when we make an object of the everyday into an object of instruction (as Herbart's model asks us to do), we take "a step toward distancing ourselves from the everyday."[14] Instruction increases this distance on the everyday, she adds, when, in a lesson, new elements are added to the whole, elements that cannot be found in ordinary experience. These new elements can only be grasped by (our) change of perspective . . . So, our perspective on colloquial language changes once grammar lessons ask us to grasp the inner structure of the language. The learner learns something new, for example, when instruction awakens in him an initial grasp of the fact that *his* social reality is not the only one that exists, but rather that other cultures also exist and have existed prior to his own.[15]

---

[13] Fritz Oser has written much on negative knowledge. See Fritz Oser, "Negatives Wissen und Moral" (Negative Knowledge and Morality), *Zeitschrift für Pädagogik*, **49**, 2005: 171–81; see also the discussion on this concept for instruction in today's schools in Fritz Oser, Tina Hascher, and Maria Spychiger, "Lernen aus Fehlern. Zur Psychologie des 'negativen' Wissens" ["Learning from Mistakes. On the Psychology of 'Negative' Knowledge"], in *Fehlerwelten-Vom Fehlermachen und Lernen aus Fehlern*, edited by Wolfgang Althof, pp. 11–41 (Opladen: Leske and Budrich, 1999), and Henning Schluss, "Negativität im Unterricht" ["Negativity in instruction"], *Zeitschrift für Pädagogik*, **49** (Special Issue *"Erziehung-Bildung-Negativität"* ["Education-Bildung-Negativity"], edited by Dietrich Benner, 2005): 182–96; see also Martin Gartmeier, Johannes Bauer, Hans Gruber, and Helmut Heid, "Negative Knowledge: Understanding Professional Learning and Expertise," *Vocations and Learning: Studies in Vocational and Professional Education*, **1**, July 2008: 87–103.

[14] Hellekamps, *Erziehender Unterricht*, p. 84, translation mine.

[15] Ibid., translation mine, emphasis mine.

Hellekamps's remarks highlight an important premise of Herbart's theory namely, that to understand the *different* and *unfamiliar*, we need distance on the familiar, the known, the comfortable and secure, and that, in gaining distance from the world, we gain distance on ourselves – *we change perspective*.[16] However, on its own, Herbart's premise does not provide an explanation of the negativity of this experience of gaining distance on the known that comes forth in our encounters with the unknown. The *experience of difference* entailed in the process of distancing from one's world and oneself, the break with oneself entailed by our change of perspective on the known, does not become explicitly integrated into Herbart's theory of the structure of cognitive learning; in turn, it is not assimilated into his notion of the teacher's task in instruction.

The Potential of Discontinuity: First Traces

We experience *difference* when, in trying to grasp the new and gain distance on the familiar, the new resists our attempts to understand it. Learners experience difference, for example, when, in grammar lessons, they learn of correct forms of grammar that *modify* or *negate* how they speak in everyday life, or, when in history and literature lessons, they learn about ways of life that do not make sense to them. The discontinuous and negative moments that arise in the experience of learning are revealed to us when we find out that we do not know what we thought we knew, when we experience confusion or doubt – when we are interrupted by the world in a way that creates openings for grasping newness and difference. These moments have educative potential because they can force us to call our previously acquired knowledge into question and open ourselves up to the new; in these moments, we can say we become disillusioned.[17] This experience of disillusionment is

---

[16] A relation here can be made to Ludwig Huber's contemporary argument that schooling today can and should promote learners' changes of perspective (*Perspektivenwechsel*) and that this is done through interdisciplinary education; see Ludwig Huber, "Stichwort Fachliches Lernen. Das Fachprinzip in der Kritik." *Zeitschrift für Erziehungswissenschaft*, 3, 2001: 307–31. Also, this seems to me to relate to Ramaekers's ideas about the possibilities of seeing multicultural education as an invitation to return to oneself, to rethink oneself through confrontation with the new, so that we can learn from the new. His remarks demonstrate the significance of multicultural education as a certain away of promoting distance from oneself or one's own cultural heritage and thus moves beyond the simple duality of multicultural education as preserving or giving up one's cultural identity. See Stefan Ramaekers, "Multicultural education: embeddedness, voice and change," *Ethics and Education*, 5, no. 1, 2010: 55–66.

[17] The notion of disillusionment (*Enttäuschung*) has been brought into the contemporary German education philosophical discourse specifically in its connection to the idea of *Umlernen* (transformative learning). See, for example, Käte Meyer-Drawe, "Lernen als Umlernen – Zur

hinted at in the notion of *distancing* – a phenomenon of separating oneself from the certainty of acquired knowledge and ability – needed to make the necessary distinctions Herbart deemed indispensable for the type of learning that leads individuals toward a multifaceted interest in the world. Although in his central educational work, *The Science of Education*, Herbart did not fully theorize the educative potential of moments of discontinuity as essential in cognitive learning, he was nonetheless aware that discontinuity can have significant educative meaning. In a particular passage of an earlier work,[18] he indicates the significance of *disillusionment* in a way that illuminates the educational meaning of discontinuity in cognitive learning, which I argue is relevant to all learning processes.

Herbart speaks of the role of disillusionment in learning when he notes the care the teacher must take to question the learner, so that the learner finds the errors in his or her thinking.The aim of teacher-learner interaction in these instances is to lay bare the learner's self-deception:

All self-deception, that makes one think that something which is not understood is understood, or that something which is not familiar is familiar, has to come to light [in the process of instruction]. The weakness of [the learner's] thought must become apparent to him. But not just weakness, – also strength, also his perfectibility has to be revealed to [the learner] through instruction . . . What was once incomprehensible, what appeared unreachable, what made his mind come to a halt: that must become completely clear to him, such that it can be executed with ease.[19]

Negativität des Lernprozesses" (Learning as Transformative Learning – On the Negativity of the Learning Process), in *Lernen und seine Horizonte. Phänomenologische Konzeptionen Menschlichen Lernens – Didaktische Konsequenzen*, edited by Käte Meyer-Drawe and Winfried Lippitz, pp. 19–45 (Frankfurt: Scriptor, 1984), and Konstantin Mitgutsch, "Lernen durch Erfahren: Über Bruchlinien im Vollzug des Lernens" [Learning through Experience: Fault Lines in the Process of Learning] in *Dem Lernen Auf Der Spur*, edited by Konstantin Mitgutsch, Elizabeth Sattler, Kristin Westphal, and Ines M. Breinbauer, pp. 263–77 (Stuttgart: Klett-Cotta, 2008). I discuss these ideas further in Chapter 6.

[18] Johann Friedrich Herbart, "The ABC of Sense-Perception (1802 and 1804)," in *Herbart's ABC of Sense-Perception and Minor Pedagogical Works*, edited and translated by William J. Eckoff, p. 146 (New York: D. Appleton, 1896) and *Minor Pedagogical Works*, translated by. William J. Eckoff, p. 146 (New York: D. Appleton, 1896); see also the original in German:, Johann Friedrich Herbart, "Pestalozzi's Idee eines ABC der Anschauung (1802 and 1804)," in *Joh. Friedr. Herbart's Sämtliche Werke in Chronologischer Reihenfolge*, edited by Karl Kehrbach, volume Vol. 1, p. 164 (Langensalza: Hermann Beyer & Söhne, 1887). In this case, Herbart was speaking of mathematics instruction, but he viewed mathematics as central to the general development of the learner's thinking processes.

[19] Herbart, "The ABC of Sense Perception," p. 146, translation modified. Herbart notes that the difficulty of finding where the learner is unclear is a difficulty teachers will have primarily early on in the instructional process, before the teacher has learned how to get the student to follow the steady flow of cognitive learning processes. Herbart seems to suggest that these moments of

This passage reveals not only that the unknown and untrue can be hidden in what we know and hold true, but also that an essential part of the learning process is uncovering these moments. Only through a process of confronting and questioning given knowledge and ability can the learner locate where the limitations of his knowledge and ability lie. Herbart's remark underscores that discontinuity in experience – the break with one's prior ways of thinking – is at the same time an *opening*, and, as an opening, it has educative potential. In other words, the limit marks a "weakness" in the learner's thinking up to that point; however, this limit at the same time marks an opening for learning, a new possibility to demonstrate "strength." It is not despite the negative experience of seeing how one's thinking was misguided, but rather by means of this experience that the learner learns. *The learner learns from negative experience.* As philosopher of education Lutz Koch points out, such experiences are vital for growth and *Bildung*: the "negative moments" of learning "allow us to see what Hegel called the experience of consciousness."[20] The experience of consciousness occurs in the moment one is interrupted and begins to break with taken-for-granted knowledge and ability; one become conscious of oneself, and the possibility for self-transformation opens up. Herbart's remarks give us insight into the fact that this consciousness of oneself that occurs in the moment of disillusionment makes room for the consciousness of one's own perfectibility, that is, in moments of disillusionment, one becomes open to seeing one's potential to learn.

Thus, in this brief passage, Herbart leaves us a trace of the meaning of learning from negative experience. He reveals the educative side of disillusionment in a twofold fashion: when we are disillusioned, we become aware of our own fallibility,[21] and we also can become aware of our own perfectibility. Although it is true that we enter every experience with some foreknowledge and prior experience, there is something about learning that makes us confront what we know, such that it can break down. Whereas ignorance of the new and the path of self-deception allows us to operate within a false framework and to continue engaging in the world with one-sidedness and egoism, the experience of disillusionment reframes our thinking on account of our

discontinuity in the learner's thinking are necessary to address, but separately rather than as part of the essential process of learning.

[20] Lutz Koch, "Eine pädagogische Apologie des Negativen" ("A pedagogical Apologia of the negative"), *Zeitschrift für Pädagogik*, 49 (Special Issue "Erziehung – Bildung – Negativität," edited Dietrich Benner), 2005: 101; see also, Lutz Koch, *Bildung und Negativität. Grundzüge einer negativen Bildungstheorie* (Education and Negativity: Grounding Features of a Negative Theory of Education) (Weinheim: Deutscher Studien Verlag, 1995).

[21] See Günther Buck, *Herbarts Grundlegung der Pädagogik*, p. 83–84 (Heidelberg: C. Winter, 1985).

encounters with the new. Once the learner has traversed through the difficulty of becoming disillusioned, he has a choice to change his way of thinking, reveal to himself his strength, and, in doing so, reveal to himself that he is capable of learning, that is, he is capable of taking in the new in a way that transforms him. In Herbart's remarks, we can see that, in his ideas of instruction and cognitive learning, Herbart reserves a place for the educational importance of the Socratic *elenchus* in two ways: he deemed it vital for the learner to examine the untruths within her truths, and he deemed it vital for the teacher to question the learner in a way that leads the learner to begin to question herself. Dialogue in teaching and its connection to discontinuity in learning becomes an integral part of Herbart's theory of moral learning, which I take up in the next section.

2   THE STRUGGLE OF LEARNING, TEACHER AS MORAL GUIDE

Educational processes that lead to critical thought, judgment, and action are more than mere cognitive processes; they include the existential and interpersonal difficulties wrapped up with making decisions against self-interested inclinations. As I discussed in Chapter 1, Herbart captures this idea using the concept of *inner struggle*. In his explanation of the development of moral character, Herbart explains that even the slightest, smallest, or weakest conflict between subjective and objective character can have an educational effect, as long as the struggle is endured and not simply ignored (as one's force of habit may recommend). The problem for Herbart, one that he seeks to address with his concept of the teacher as moral guide, is that the inner struggle (encountered by all human beings in their experiences) could be simply ignored rather than endured and incorporated into a learning process.

New experiences that become coupled with moral questions of *what to do* ask us to confront our own inner struggle rather than run from it. Inner struggle is constitutive of moral learning processes on Herbart's account, but it does not necessarily lead to learning unless we inquire into it. Such inquiry demands of a person that she confront the otherness of herself. Such self-confrontation and self-inquiry cannot be left to chance for Herbart, so he develops the notion of the teacher as a moral guide, one who guides the learner through this process of self-inquiry. This process of moral learning leads to what Herbart terms *moral strength of character*. Inner struggle is a form of negative experience characterized by the self-alienation that we experience within ourselves. Here, I develop the connection between inner struggle and learning further than in the previous chapter by focusing my analysis on the role of the teacher in moral learning processes. I demonstrate that Herbart's account of teaching as moral guidance clarifies the essential role of the teacher in moral education: for inner struggle to become educative for the learner (and not just suffered through or ignored), the learner needs a teacher who can guide the learning process through the difficulty of inner struggle.

A Distinction: Herbart on Rousseau's Notion of Teacher as Guide

In the context of his discussion of moral education, Herbart points to a central dilemma in educational practice, one that still has relevance for teaching practice today. Herbart notes that the teacher can only bear witness to the child's choice – good or bad – *after* the child has acted on it. For the teacher, the child's morality is an event in the world, a "happening" (*Ereignis*) (*ARW* 61). The dilemma thus lies in the fact that, to influence the formation of the learner's moral character and development, teachers cannot wait for the learner to have acted; rather, they must be able to influence the learner *before* the learner has made concrete choices in the world. Even a child's *good* choices may not, in fact, be moral if they are the result of imitation and not self-reflective judgment. Herbart explicated that the only way around this dilemma is to conceive of the teacher's task as a form of moral guidance that aims to understand and to influence the thought process *behind* the learner's choices. On this view, moral guidance entails a form of dialogue with the learner. Through dialogue, the teacher questions the learner in a manner that leads the learner to question herself, that is, to question her own assumptions and motives for action. In this way, dialogue with the learner involves *interrupting* the learner's taken-for-granted modes of thinking and acting, such that she engages in an inner struggle with regard to her own motives. So, in Herbart's concepts of moral guidance, we can identify a form of educating that seeks to cultivate discontinuity as an indispensable part of moral learning processes.

To understand this concept of the teacher as moral guide and how it relates to Herbart's concept of moral learning, it is helpful to look at how he differentiates his idea of the teacher from that of Jean-Jacques Rousseau, whose model we may also associate with the educator as a guide in the cultivation of the moral individual. Although Herbart shares with Rousseau a concern for every individual's growth and freedom, and, like Rousseau, sees education as a means of cultivating that freedom, he differs from Rousseau in his approach to education. On more than one occasion in his work, Herbart specifically criticizes Rousseau's vision of the educator as Emile's "companion at every step."[22] Although Herbart's critique seems relatively harmless at first, in fact, he was getting at a significant problem at the heart of Rousseau's conception, namely, that the close companionship between the educator and Emile does not allow Emile the freedom for exploration of the kind that children may actually engage in on their own.[23] Furthermore, the educator does not have the freedom to gain the type of *distance* from the learner necessary for critical judgment of the learner's thoughts and actions.[24] So, although Herbart acknowledges that Rousseau believed in both the theoretical and real possibility of education that leads an individual to freedom from blind adherence to authority, he contends that Rousseau's method would actually achieve the opposite end: the teacher on Rousseau's model is like a "slave chained to the boy" in a way that hinders the freedom of both teacher and learner.[25] Ultimately, Herbart deems Rousseau's method of educating "the natural man" not only difficult for the teacher, but also for the learner, because the

[22] Johann Friedrich Herbart, "Introductory Lecture to Students in Pedagogy (1802)," in *Herbart's ABC of Sense-Perception, and Minor Pedagogical Works*, edited and translated by William J. Eckoff, pp. 13–28, 23 (New York: D. Appleton, 1896); see also *SE* 79/*AP* 5, translation modified.

[23] Certainly, Herbart would not say that the child's freedom was entirely limited. The freedom Rousseau imagined for the learner is shown in his idea that, in early childhood, the child should not be allowed to develop fixed habits: "the only habit the child should contract is none"; Jean-Jacques Rousseau, *Emile or On Education*, edited and translated by Allan Bloom, p. 63 (New York: Basic Books, 1979). This point is important for Herbart also, who agreed with Rousseau that the child should not be habituated at an early age to think or act in certain ways because, he maintained, this limits the child's interests in later life.

[24] To extend Herbart's critique, we can add that many of Rousseau's examples are based in contrived and, to a certain extent, manipulative situations aimed at getting Emile to have the "right" learning experience. See, for example, how Emile is taught not to be afraid of masks and other scary objects. For a discussion of Rousseau's conception of fear, see Andrea English and Barbara Stengel, "Exploring Fear: Rousseau, Dewey and Freire on Fear and Learning," *Educational Theory*, 60, no. 5, 2010: 521–42.

[25] Herbart, "Introductory Lecture to Students in Pedagogy," p. 23, translation modified. In a later essay, Herbart added that although Rousseau's image of the educator is too centered on the education of *one* child, teachers who are more concerned with having *many* students around them than with *educating* these students miss the finer nuance of the educational relation. Herbart's views are part of his larger critique of schools. He believed schools, in their very early development, were straining the educative relationships that can be formed between teachers and learners and warned that if teachers are not given the proper time and opportunity to form these relationships, they will in turn lose the desire to cultivate such relationships; see Johann Friedrich Herbart, Über Erziehung unter öffentlicher Mitwirkung *(1810) (On Education with Public Cooperation), in Joh. Friedr. Herbart's Sämtliche Werke in Chronologischer Reihenfolge*, edited by Karl Kehrbach. Vol. 3, 73–82. Langensalza: Hermann Beyer und Söhne, 1888. Such a remark bears on the school situation of today. For a critical and imaginative look at the problem of the contemporary conflation between education and schooling and how we must address this as a society today, see Robbie McClintock, *Enough: A Pedagogical Speculation* (New York: The Reflective Commons, 2012).

learner does not gain the type of varied experiences necessary for learning how to be free in the sense of being able to live "in the middle of heterogeneous society" (*SE* 79/ *AP* 6).

Herbart's contrasting idea of the teacher in the realm of moral learning is stated in his "Introductory Lecture to Students in Pedagogy." In this lecture, Herbart encapsulates what he means by moral guidance (*Zucht*): the educator must be "a wise guide from afar, who by profoundly penetrating words and firm action" knows "when to protect the learner" and "when to leave him to his own devices."[26] Accordingly, in opposition to Rousseau's model of a companion at every step, Herbart believed that the teacher requires a certain amount of distance from the learner to critically observe and judge the learner's choices. On Herbart's account, it is only through educative distance that the teacher can understand how the child is influenced by the immediately observed world (with all of its limits) and thereby recognize where the child's thoughts about and interactions with the world need expansion or modification. The teacher as moral guide is always seeking to find to what extent the learner is considering *others* in her thoughts and choices. Teachers may ask themselves, "To what extent does this learner see the consequences of his or her actions?"; "Is the learner able to suspend action and contemplate his or her choices, or, is the learner acting capriciously and instinctually?"; "Is the learner imitating what others do or say, or searching to find and understand ideas of the Good?"

Dialogue in Moral Guidance

Educational practice that simply *tells* the learner what to do or what is good and right cannot answer these difficult ethical and pedagogical questions. As Herbart emphasized, no amount of unidirectional speeches or admonitions can help teachers understand learners – and without understanding the learner as an individual, teachers are not able to judge how to guide each learner to become aware of and to open to the *other* in a moral sense. Through moral guidance, the teacher has the task of helping the learner attend to her own moral learning process by problematizing past experiences, understanding the limits of her own knowledge and ability, and making new decisions for action on that basis. By thematizing the "struggle" of making the choice between old and new experiences and ideas as a basis for his discussion of moral education, Herbart makes clear that a human being is something more than a mindless automaton: human beings have the freedom to act differently

---

[26] Herbart, "Introductory Lecture to Students in Pedagogy," p. 23, translation modified.

than they have in the past, given a new situation. To act according to this freedom is not to ignore the struggle one faces or simply to wish it would come to an end. Rather, as Herbart maintains, to act according to freedom is to choose to confront the conflict and explicitly question wherein it lies.

In his theory of moral guidance, Herbart developed four forms of dialogic interaction that aim to cultivate moral learning by cultivating the learner's ability to expand thought in such a way that the learner begins to question herself and thereby enter into a moral self-relation. These forms of interaction can be described as moral guidance that (1) *"gives pause"* (*halten* or *anhalten*) to the learner, so she does not act capriciously and so she remembers her past choices, good and bad, and remains consistent with past decisions insofar as these were representative of recognition of others; (2) helps the learner *"determine"* (*bestimmen*) present choices compatible with a "warmth for the good"; (3) requires that the learner *"create rules"* (*regeln*) for future action on the basis of such choices; and (4) *"supports"* (*unterstützen*) the learner's inner struggle (*innere Kampf*) by supporting her act of self-restraint – that is, of opposing her initial self-serving interest and following through with actions that are based in a new understanding of the good or right thing to do.[27] Through this interaction, the teacher seeks to understand how the learner is judging herself. The teacher then has the responsibility of supporting the learner in regulating her self-understanding and self-judgment on the basis of the aesthetic relations set forth in the moral ideas of "inner freedom," "completeness" "benevolence," "right," and "justice."

On the Moral Ideas

A brief consideration of the aforementioned moral ideas is important at this point, not only because these ideas reveal how Herbart connected his ethics to his educational theory, but also because they tell us something more about the basis of the ethical relation between teacher and learner that Herbart was attempting to articulate in his notion of moral guidance. Each of the five basic moral ideas represent basic aesthetic judgments that are meant to orient one's view of the relations of one's will to itself, to other wills, and to objects in the world. Herbart saw these as an expansion on the idea of a Good Will expressed in Kant's different formulations of the Categorical Imperative.[28]

---

[27] On these ideas, see *SE* 242–50/*AP* 118–126. (translation modified).

[28] The following discussion of these five moral ideas is based on Herbart's delineation of these in his *APP*; specifically compare pp. 355–75. On the connection to the Categorical Imperative, see Dietrich Benner, "Negative Moralisierung und experimentelle Ethik als zeitgemässe Formen der

These relations of the will are made possible in the moment of self-alienation (discussed in Chapter 1), when we find ourselves faced with a decision for action. I will address each of the five ideas, beginning with a reiteration of the concept of inner freedom that I explained in Chapter 1, since this idea provides the basis for Herbart's development of the other moral ideas.

Inner Freedom

As mentioned in Chapter 1, *inner freedom* (*innere Freiheit*) represents the idea that the human being can make a judgment on his or her own will, so this idea is therefore implicit in all the other moral ideas. Inner freedom demands that one not place precedence on one's own self-interested will, but rather make judgments on this self-interested will and only act according to those judgments.

Completeness

The second idea, *completeness* or *"coming to fullness"* (*Vollkommenheit*), comes into play when an individual's will is pulled by different "strivings" (*Strebungen*), each of differing strength, one weak and one strong. The judgment here is not a judgment about the content of the will (i.e., the object the will is striving toward), but rather a judgment about whether to follow the stronger or weaker striving. The idea of completeness says that one ought not to follow a stronger striving simply because it is stronger. Herbart's broader point in this idea is that a stronger striving or desire may be motivationally stronger merely because of contingencies of what one has experienced and become familiar with through socialization thus far in one's life, but not because that desire has been subject to critical judgment. Thus, with the idea of completeness, Herbart is saying that morality cannot be based in the arbitrary circumstances influencing one's individual history: morality must be grounded in forms of education that provide learners with various ways of seeing the world, so that decisions to act are based in the learner's reflective judgment. On this account, the idea of completeness demands that one imagine something other than one's own stronger or weaker idea of what to do.[29] This entails that the individual continue to expand her own horizons of thought toward multifacetedness until she can see beyond the two original

Moralerziehung" ["Negative Moralisation and Experimental Ethics as Contemporary for Moral Education"], in *Bildungstheorie und Bildungsforschung*, p. 161 (Paderborn: Ferdinand Schöningh, 2008), and Benner, *Johann Friedrich Herbart*. In his ethics (*APP*), Herbart also extends these five individual moral ideas to five social moral ideas.

[29] A connection can be made here to William James's "Talks to Teachers." Although James is not discussing Herbart's moral ideas (he does mention Herbart in the text, but also is known to have distanced himself from Herbart's psychology), he makes an interesting point that relates to

strivings.[30] An ethics that propounds that we should always follow a stronger desire for its own sake (i.e., "might makes right") is thereby rendered unethical.

Benevolence

Each of Herbart's moral ideas is based in an understanding of the human being as a historical being; a being who is influenced, but not entirely determined, by her own history – a history that may recommend a certain desire be followed – but who can reflect upon her own history, judge and act differently than she had in the past, and continue to learn. Whereas the first two moral ideas are concerned with the individual's self-self relation, the third moral idea, *benevolence* (*Wohlwollen*), considers what the relation between self (or one's own will) and an imagined other (or the will of another person with whom one imagines to be interacting, yet with whom one has not concretely interacted) looks like when moral action becomes concretely possible. The idea of benevolence commands goodwill toward the imagined other, so that, in every judgment of action, one considers the will of an imagined other and not simply one's own will.

Right

In the fourth idea, the idea of *right* (*Recht*), Herbart considers the relation between an individual's will as it comes into relations with concrete other wills in the world. Right regulates the relations between persons when two people strive toward the same object in the world such that a conflict between them arises. The idea of right regulates the relation of one will to the other and demands that an agreement be made between the interacting wills. As Herbart scholar Harold Dunkel points out, for Herbart, each one of the moral ideas considered "individually was wholly inadequate as a standard for morality; each must be conditioned and modified by the others. Otherwise

---

Herbart's notion of completeness when he says, "So you see that volition, in the narrower sense, takes place only when there are a number of conflicting systems of ideas, and depends on our having a complex field of consciousness. A strong and urgent motor idea in the focus may be neutralized and made inoperative by the presence of the very faintest contradictory idea in the margin." William James, "Talks to Teachers (1899)" in *The Works of William James: Electronic Edition*, edited by Frederick H. Burkhardt, Fredson Bowers, and Ignas K. Skrupskelis, Vol. 12: "Talks to Teachers on Psychology," pp. 13–115, 105 (Charlottesville, VA: InteLex Corporation 2008). Herbart's idea of completeness demands that we allow such contradictory ideas to arise as part of our decision-making process; however, further exploration of connections to James here would lead us too far afield.

[30] This idea connects to what Herbart sees as the task of instruction to cultivate the learners' ability to expand their horizons of thought and experience.

a one-sided morality or even immorality would result."[31] This interconnection between the moral ideas can be illustrated in the idea of *right*, as Dietrich Benner explains.[32] Benner illustrates that the idea of right entails that each person, each will, judges himself according to the other ideas, so that each person critiques his own self-interest (following a notion of *inner freedom*), expands his own idea of what is possible (following the notion of *completeness*), "takes the other person's will into consideration" (thus following the notion of *benevolence*), and, in doing so, is able to come to an agreement that mediates existing conflict and hinders future conflict between the two people, as the idea of right demands.[33]

Justice

Herbart's considerations illuminate the idea that an attempt to resolve a moral dilemma is not a simple rational act of knowing the objectively right and wrong, nor is it a utilitarian consideration of consequences. Rather, for Herbart, resolving a moral dilemma – that is, answering a question of what one *ought* to do – entails reflection on and judgment of relations, namely, the relation one stands in with oneself and the relation one stands in with others, when desiring to act in this or that particular way. There is always a chance that our estimate of the right thing to do can later be determined to be misguided or that we retreat to self-serving ways. This possibility is reflected in particular in Herbart's fifth moral idea, which demonstrates that he leaves open a space for our fallibility (and in turn our *perfectibility*) in the realm of morality. The fifth moral idea, *justice* (*Billigkeit*), reflects the notion that one may (with good or bad intention) break an agreement that one has made with another person, an act that does not recognize that person's capacity for self-determination. Justice thus demands that when an agreement has been broken, the person who broke the agreement must provide recompense to the other person who has been affected by that decision. This ability to see the error of one's ways and provide recompense underscores the idea of the human being as one who can continue to learn in the realm of morality.

The task of moral education is to develop the disposition in the learner to understand and make moral judgments reflectively, rather than normatively.[34] As philosopher and Herbart scholar Rainer Bolle emphasizes, for

---

[31] Harold Dunkel, *Herbart and Education*, p. 33 (New York: Random House, 1969).

[32] Benner, "Negative Moralisierung und experimentelle Ethik," p. 163.

[33] Compare ibid.

[34] Benner and English, "Critique and Negativity, Toward the Pluralisation of Critique in Educational Practice, Theory and Research," *Journal of Philosophy of Education*, 38, no. 3, 2004: 409–28.

Herbart, morality refers to "the ability to judge your own actions according to the moral viewpoint and to act according to that judgment."[35] To return to our discussion of moral guidance, we can say that what is being guided by the teacher is the learner's ability to make judgments upon her own will according to the relations set forth in the moral ideas. The teacher is not guiding the learner to particular actions. Moral guidance means that the teacher leaves it up to the learner to determine which concrete action in the world would fulfill the demands of the self-self and self other relations set forth in the moral ideas. Such a determination cannot be decided absolutely in advance of a concrete situation, nor can one's decision be made by anyone other than oneself. In this way, Herbart is setting a necessary limit on the teacher's task in moral education: it is not up to the teacher to decide *for* the learner what to do in any particular ethical dilemma. With this limit, moral education becomes something other than the purely reproductive and indoctrinating task of leading learners to the affirmation of societal norms or to the heteronomous imitation of accepted behaviors; it entails guiding learners through the process of self-critique and critique of social norms.[36]

Moral education on this account is dialogic. Through the process of dialogue, the teacher can and must bring learners to confront themselves and their own learning history by judging their past decisions and entering into a moral self-relation implicit in the five moral ideas. The teacher is thereby guiding learners toward understanding and problematizing the difference between good and bad – and transforming themselves on that basis. Herbart did not aim to suggest a concrete prescription for the educator's action. He did, however, give one example that helps clarify how the teacher as moral guide might interact with the learner in order to get the learner *to interrupt himself,* heed his own negative experience, engage his *inner struggle,*

---

[35] Rainer Bolle, "Herbart's Beitrag zur Theorie sittlicher Persönlichkeitsbildung – Weiterführende Impulse aus der Individual Psychologie Alfred Adlers" [Herbart's Contribution to the Theory of Educating the Moral Personality – Insights from Alfred Adlers' Individual Psychology], in *Johann Friedrich Herbart 200 Jahre Allgemeine Pädagogik,* edited by Rainer Bolle and Gabrielle Weigand, p. 53 (Münster: Waxmann, 2007), translation mine.

[36] Jörg Ramseger explains on this point that Herbart limits the role of moral guidance in education through the two other tasks of the educator: "So that moral guidance does not become determination by the teacher, that is the pure demonstration of power, Herbart contrasts it to discipline (*Regierung der Kinder*); so that moral guidance does not become moralising, Herbart grounds it in and binds it to educative instruction." Jörg Ramseger. *Was heisst "Durch Unterricht erziehen?": Erziehender Unterricht und Schulreform [What does "Education through Instruction" mean?: Educative Instruction and School Reform]* (Weinheim: Beltz, 1991), p. 72, translation mine.

and seek to understand and judge himself according to idea of "rectitude" (an idea which combines the notions of right and justice):[37]

[C]hildren associate with each other and exchange things and services at prices more or less fixed. The interference of adults, and the anticipation of this possible interference alone, makes rectitude among children uncertain and deprives it of their respect ... [W]e may lay down as a principle never to disturb what exists among children without good reasons, nor change their interactions into forced politeness. When disputes arise, we must first ascertain what has been settled and agreed upon amongst the children themselves, and we must take the side of the child who has in any way been deprived of his fair share. Then we must try to help each child to what he deserves, so far as this is possible without violent injury to justice. And finally we must point beyond all this to what is best for the common good ... and which will be the chief measure for future agreements ... The pupil [must never be allowed] to form a habit of making *his* right the determining ground of his actions; the right of others alone must be for him a strict law.[38]

In this example, the teacher engages in dialogue with the learner to help the learner understand what it means to hold oneself to an agreement, even when this is difficult and may conflict with self-serving interests. The teacher brings forth not only the agreements that were made among the children, but also further ideas that point to the "common good." This refers not to the good found according to the principle of maximized benefit, but the good that arises according to judgments made with respect to all five moral ideas. The learner is thus faced with the challenge of whether to follow his own self-interested desires or to look beyond these and ask what might it mean to recognize the other. This marks the moment in which the learner finds himself in a "inner struggle" (*innere Kampf*), one that forces the learner to question his assumptions and motives for action.[39]

---

[37] As I mentioned in a footnote in Chapter 1, Herbart believed that the ideas of right and justice, as well as the ideas of benevolence and completeness, although conceptually distinct, are learned in situations in which they are closely connected with one another, as the example that follows seeks to show. Thus, in his *Science of Education*, he combines the idea of right and justice into the idea of rectitude (*Rechtlichkeit*), and completeness and benevolence into the idea of goodness (*Güte*).

[38] *SE* 261/*AP* 134, translation modified.

[39] Although there are some similarities between Herbart's idea of dialogue and the theory of values clarification proposed by Louis Raths, Merrill Harmin, and Sidney Simon – such as the importance of presenting the learner with alternatives – there are also important differences. A detailed analysis is beyond the scope of my discussion; however, one central distinction between Herbart's theory of teacher-learner dialogue and values clarification theory is that the latter emphasizes the *process* of valuing over its *product*. The values theory proposes that the teacher is not aiming to

In the educative contexts, in which the learner is engaged in inner struggle to see beyond his own desires, the teacher must *listen* and figure out how "to show the pupil his better self" such that he learns "to feel" and *listen* to his own "inward reproach" (*SE* 235–36/*AP* 116). Through the process of moral education as Herbart envisions it, the learner "finds himself thrown under his own censorship" (*SE* 246/*AP* 123). This moment of inward self-reproach marks a definitive moment in the learner's educational process; it marks "the natural beginning of moral education, which is weak and uncertain in itself" (*SE* 246/*AP* 123). Facing a moral dilemma, the learner finds himself stuck in an experience between right and wrong, lost in unknown territory and entangled in a situation that may, in fact, have many morally right and wrong ways out. In these moments, the negativity of the learner's experience of difference is not (yet) educative. The learner needs a teacher to guide him out of this experience, until he can become his own guide. By interrupting the learner's taken-for-granted modes of being in the world, the teacher opens up the possibility for the learner to experience the *self* differently, to come into conflict with the self, *to feel uncertain* about what to do, to hear the voice of the inner censor. Ultimately, the learner must begin to feel and see himself choosing actions that recognize the other. This is what Herbart meant when he wrote that the task of moral education is to create possibilities for the child to "*find himself choosing the good and rejecting the bad*" (*ARW* 61, emphasis in original).

In this process of questioning and listening in teacher-learner interaction, the learner begins to understand the relation between self and other implicit in ideas of right and justice, and also to cultivate his or her inner censor, which aids the learner in judging actions on the basis of this new understanding. How the learner chooses to act, however, is not only dependent on the censor in the subjective character telling the learner what *not* to do, but also on whether the learner's objective character has developed what Herbart

get learners to see any particular values as important; rather, the teacher is relatively value-neutral, only helping learners "clarify" what they believe in and value at the present stage of their life, without helping them change problematic values. (Whether or not the teacher truly remains value-neutral on this model is another question for deliberation.) On this theory, see Louis E. Raths, Merrill Harmin, and Sidney Simon, *Values and Teaching: Working with Values in the Classroom* (Columbus, OH: Charles E. Merrill, 1966), especially p. 28, 47–48, and the examples on 72ff. This model seems to stop short of aiming to engage learners in critiquing their own self-serving interests and of bringing learners into conflict with themselves on that basis. In this way, values clarification may aim to help learners understand themselves, but it fails to explicitly attempt to help learners *transform* their self-understanding through self-critique according to the self-relations set forth in the moral ideas, which is the central aspect of moral guidance developed here. Thus, it seems that the negative experience of inner struggle and self-critique as an educative experience necessary for moral learning is not fully thought through in values theory.

called "a warmth for the good."[40] Accordingly, the teacher's task in moral guidance is twofold: it involves cultivating in the learner a sense of "positive morality" (in the objective side of character) by providing the learner with opportunities to experience and choose the good successfully; also, it involves cultivating in the learner a sense of "negative morality" (in the subjective side of character) by promoting the learner's ability to engage in inner struggle and self-critique and follow through on his or her self-critical judgments through acts of "self-restraint" (*SE* 206–09/*AP* 94–97). As Lutz Koch explains, "negative morality," for Herbart, "is the result of moral self-evaluation, that [Herbart] identified as the censor of one's own character."[41]

By cultivating positive *and* negative morality, the teacher is providing the ground on which the learner can engage in an experimental process of learning what it means to be moral. Moral learning processes involve finding the relation between one's own positive and negative morality and experimenting with self-critique. This experimental nature of moral learning is expressed when Herbart states, "in the beginning" the learner's attempt to judge his objective character according to the moral ideas "is only an attempt" (*SE* 221/*AP* 105, translation modified). However, he adds that, in order for the learner to begin to see himself differently – that is, to see that she is capable of thinking, judging, and acting in ways that respect the other – some of his "attempts" at moral action "must succeed" (*SE* 221/*AP* 105). Through moral learning processes, learners come to understand negative judgments of what is *wrong* and *bad*, while at the same time coming to know that positive judgments of *right* and *good* are always open to critique. With this insight, learners can become moral individuals because they not only can recognize wrong and bad, but also – through critique of established personal and social norms – they can contribute to the idea of the Good.

Herbart's concept of learning in the realm of morality is a statement about what education truly means: cultivation toward moral self-determination. Each of the five moral ideas are "guides" for the learner to come to understand what it means to orient oneself against egoism when faced with the discontinuity of inner struggle. The egoist does not find himself in the self-self and

---

[40] This relates to the task of instruction, which aims to expand learners' interests in multiple directions and present ideas of both good and bad, right and wrong, such that learners can differentiate between these and search for new meanings of the good. Herbart deemed history and literature to be particularly important subjects because they can give learners the ability to learn from the possibilities and mistakes of human beings. The "warmth for the good" connects to what Herbart calls the "aesthetic necessity," or the "ought," that compels us to act according to the moral imperative in moral dilemmas, see *ARW* 63–65; see also *SE* 207–208/*AP* 95–96.

[41] Lutz Koch, *Bildung und Negativität*, p. 52.

self-other relations represented by these ideas; rather, the egoist follows "his own right" as his guiding principle and thus destroys all the five ideas by placing himself – his own will – above others. By engaging the learner *so that* the learner engages his or her own inner struggle and learns to come into new self-relations – relations based in inner freedom, completeness benevolence, right, and justice – the teacher is at once guiding the learner away from egoism and toward moral self-determination. Thus, Herbart gives the teacher an indispensable role in moral education.

Listening and the Educational Relationship

Herbart's description of teacher-learner interaction in moral guidance suggests a particular understanding of the nature of the educational relation between teacher and learner that is notably still relevant today: an educational relation involves a teacher who maintains necessary guidance over learners without interfering with their freedom to decide for themselves the good and right thing to do. On this account, it is central to the teacher's task in moral guidance that the teacher *supports* each learner's inner struggle. This idea sharply counters authoritarian notions of moral education that rely on the teacher's authoritative judgment of what is right in a way that releases learners from inner conflict. It also counteracts child-centered models, in which learners can arbitrarily overlook conflicts of principles and never decide to engage in the discomfort of inner conflict about questions of the Good. Opposing these views, Herbart's theory underscores that this experience of struggle and inner conflict is a constitutive part of moral learning. Such experiences are "negative experiences" – a general term used to describe particular types of experience of arriving at one's limits – but, in the context of moral learning, they become educative forms of negative experience.[42]

---

[42] This understanding of negative experience having an educative meaning in the context of moral learning relates to Fritz Oser's thesis on "negative morality." Oser argues that our mistakes in moral learning contribute to our understanding of what it means to be moral; see Fritz Oser, "Negative Moralität und Entwicklung. Ein undurchsichtiges Verhältnis" ["Negative Morality and Development: An Opaque Relationship"], *Ethik und Sozialwissenschaft*, 9, no. 4, 1998: 597–608. Further references to negative experience in German philosophy can be found, for example, in Hans-Georg Gadamer, *Truth and Method*, Second revised edition, translation revised by Joel Weinsheimer and Donald G. Marshall, pp. 353–54. (New York: Continuum, 2000); Günther Buck, *Lernen und Erfahrung* [Learning and Experience] (Stuttgart: Kohlhammer, 1969); Dietrich Benner, "Kritik und Negativität. Ein Versuch zur Pluralisierung von Kritik in Erziehung, Pädagogik und Erziehungswissenschaft," *Zeitschrift für Pädagogik*, 46, 2003: 96–110; Dietrich Benner and Andrea English, "Critique and Negativity," pp. 409–28. I return to the discussion of negative experience and learning in the German tradition in Chapter 6.

Although Herbart did not explicitly develop a theory of listening, his theory of moral guidance radically calls into question the assumed linearity between listening and obedience to external authority with consequences for our understanding of the role of critical listening in educational relations. Using Herbart's theory of moral guidance as a basis for my examination, I identify three necessary (but not sufficient) guiding principles of listening in forms of teaching that seek to begin and maintain the educational relation. I use the term "critical" to describe the teacher's listening in order to refer to the fact that the teacher is listening for ways to understand how the learner is judging herself and is evaluating what is heard on the basis of the distinction between egoism and having regard for others. I define the educational relation as the relation between teacher and learner that supports the learner's striving toward moral self-determination and thus neither imposes the will of the teacher onto the learner nor forces the learner to blindly conform to societal norms. The three guiding principles of listening can be described as follows: (1) *listening to know where the learner is*, (2) *listening to know when to cultivate discontinuity in the learner's experience and, in turn, to support the learner's expansion of her circle of thought*, and (3) *listening to know when to end the task of moral guidance*. I examine each of these here.[43]

Of these three principles of listening, the first one is meant to orient the teacher's listening toward finding out how the learner thinks on his or her own, that is, the teacher is listening to find out where the learner is starting from in the learning process. Herbart argued that the teacher must come to understand the learner without initial prejudices because only in this way can the teacher determine where the learner can and should grow. He asserted that the teacher must listen to all of the child's "innocent wishes" without "prematurely (seeking) to correct them," for these can be connected to the child's "opinions and views" (*SE* 243/*AP* 121–22). The teacher's listening here, which I call *listening to know where the learner is*, is oriented toward the learner in order to understand how the learner thinks so as to gain an initial impression of how the learner's thoughts might influence actions.

The second principle of listening guides the teacher to know how and when to initiate the learner's self-critical and reflective thought. Following this

---

[43] These three ideas of listening were first developed in my article, "Critical Listening and the Dialogic Aspect of Moral Education: J. F. Herbart's Concept of the Teacher as Moral Guide," *Educational Theory*, 61, no. 2 (Special Issue "Philosophies of Listening," edited by Sophie Haroutunian-Gordon and Megan Laverty), 2011: 171–89. Here, I have expanded on the dimensions of listening and developed these into guiding principles of listening. In addition, I demonstrate, more so than in my earlier article, how listening connects to discontinuity in learning. In Chapter 7, I continue my discussion of listening.

principle, the teacher seeks to *listen to know when to cultivate discontinuity in the learner's experience and, in turn, to support the learner's expansion of thought.* Listening here is not neutrally listening to the learner's views, nor is it listening with the aim of affirmatively leading the learner to take on the views of the teacher. Rather, listening involves finding ways to problematize the learner's self-understanding, insofar as it is informed by egoism and self-interest rather than by respect for and recognition of the other. On this account, listening in teaching is an essential component of dialogue with the learner. The aim of dialogue in this context is to understand whether the learner is acting too quickly on self-interested ideas without careful consideration of the situation at hand. In this way, the teacher uses questions that seek to mediate between the learner's thought and action in order to cultivate the learner's process of coming into *conflict* with herself, and the teacher listens to see if this inner conflict or *inner struggle* is taking place. We can say that the teacher thereby seeks to cultivate *discontinuity* within the learner's experiences by interrupting the learner's experience, so that the learner begins to stand outside the self, gain distance on initial intentions, become self-reflective, and form critical judgments about those intentions.

To understand this sense of listening, we can turn to Herbart's example of how a teacher as moral guide would respond differently to two different learners, each of whom is caught in a lie (*SE* 240/*AP* 119). He explained that if a teacher hears a child telling a "self-interested lie" for the *first* time, then the teacher must correct the learner harshly, so that the learner recognizes the gravity and consequences of his act and wants to correct *himself*, so as not to risk losing the respect he had previously won. However, if the teacher begins to recognize that a child has become a "deliberate liar," the teacher must approach the situation differently. As Herbart notes, if the teacher were to use harsh corrective words to the child who has already made a habit of lying, the child would only become "more deceitful and insidious" (*SE* 240/*AP* 119). This child knows the teacher disapproves, but his habits show that he is not concerned with this disapproval. Herbart argues that the only way to deal with such a situation is not by isolated reprimands, but by supporting the learner's process of expanding his "circle of thought" so that he can discover and value the meaning of respect and choose other options for action.[44]

In both of these cases, the teacher is looking at and listening to the whole individual as a historical being. Although both students are telling a lie, the teacher is *hearing* the lie differently. This difference in what the teacher is

---

[44] On this point, see in particular pages *SE* 213–215/*AP* 100–101 and Herbart's concept of multi-faceted educative instruction, discussed earlier in this chapter.

hearing leads to a different understanding of how to *interrupt* the learner's experience. In the first case, the teacher is interrupting the learner's experience by pointing out to the learner how this *first* lie does not fit into the series of good choices (telling the truth) he has made thus far. The learner's self-reflection and self-questioning is promoted here so that the learner learns not to change good choices (formed in objective character) just because a self-interested opportunity has arisen. In the second case, with the child who has become a deliberate liar, the teacher is also determining how to interrupt the child's experience (a concept of teaching I develop further in Chapters 4 and 7). The child here, however, only sees one way: *his way* of doing things, that is, lying, rather than telling the truth. So, to interrupt this learner's experience, the teacher must cultivate the learner's ability to expand his horizon of thought and experience by presenting the learner with *other* ways of being in the world, so that he begins to question his own judgments, see himself differently, and see the possibility to make different choices.

Thus, the second principle of listening delimits the idea that the teacher listens to each learner not just in one isolated moment, but as a person who is in the process of change and growth. The teacher on this model must constantly make connections between the individual learner's present and past choices, and evaluate how these relate to future possibilities for change. This type of pedagogical judgment of the whole person requires a teacher who can support the expansion of the learner's "circle of thought" in multifaceted directions, which means presenting the learner with alternative ways of seeing the world, new ideas and different knowledge or experiences that present different options for action. Listening thus informs the teacher's understanding of what subject matter to teach the learner, thus connecting the teacher's task of moral guidance with the task of instruction.

Although the first two principles identify conceptually distinct aims of listening, in practice these aims are closely connected. The teacher must understand both *where the learner is starting from* in the learning process and *where the learner still needs to grow*, and this understanding may become clear in the same moment. In both cases, the learner is being "discovered" by the teacher. As Herbart says, neither practical experience nor a priori principles alone can tell us how to educate another human being: the individual must "be discovered, not deduced" (*SE* 83/*AP* 9). Each individual learner is unique and can only be understood by the teacher *in the moment*, that is, through lived experiences and interpersonal interaction. In this way, the teacher is making the learner the "point of orientation" for all decisions (*SE* 113–14/*AP* 30, translation modified). In today's diverse classrooms, it is increasingly important for teachers to understand how to discover each learner as a unique individual, without imposing prejudices or making assumptions about learners.

Further, both of these principles of listening in teaching involve determining how to initiate learning processes that aim to help the learner understand, as Herbart states, the "disharmony" within himself. By *listening to know where the learner is starting from,* the teacher can find the good within the learner, that is, the teacher can find out where the learner is already acting with inner freedom and out of respect for the other. This good within the learner – the warmth for the good that the learner has already cultivated – provides the grounds upon which the learner can create an idea of Good as his own evaluative criteria for judging himself and is therefore an indispensable starting point for the educational relation. By understanding where the learner is starting from, the teacher can understand how to support the learner's growth by helping the learner recognize self-developed notions of good and bad. To aid the learner in this process of self-understanding, the teacher must listen to find ways to initiate discontinuity in the learner's experience: the teacher "aims to get the learner to *separate* from himself; for [the learner] must educate himself."[45] In other words, the teacher is attempting to help the learner recognize his own negative experience – the interruption in his thought or action that has now thrown him off (his own) course – and inquire into this negative experience, question himself, understand his inner struggle, and find strength to move on.

On this understanding, teaching entails seeking out moments when the cultivation of discontinuity is necessary for the learner's growth, so that changes of fixed self-interested habits become possible. This sort of teaching cultivates the learner's belief in her own perfectibility in the moral realm: the learner begins to see that she can change and that, by not doing so, she has something to lose, so that she *wants* to change. The true basis for moral inner struggle is that the Good has been recognized, felt, and cultivated as a warmth for the good; once we have had the experience of honesty and loyalty among friends, the opportunity or even desire to lie weighs more heavily on us. In other words, after one has had the *experience of the Good,* one then has something to lose, namely, one's self-respect, the basis for the respect of others.

Finally, the third guiding principle of listening in educational relations is reflected in Herbart's considerations of the end of the task of moral guidance.

---

[45] Johann Friedrich Herbart, "Aphorismen zur Pädagogik," in *Johann Friedrich Herbart's Sämmtliche Werke,* edited by G. Hartenstein, Vol. 11, Part 2, Schriften zur Pädagogik, p. 486 (Leipzig: Leopold Voss, 1851), emphasis in original.

At the point when learners demonstrate an ability to make their own informed, self-determined decisions, the teacher as moral guide has the task of *ending* moral guidance. Herbart underscores that moral guidance is self-undermining; it must seek out its own end.[46] To do this, the teacher must *listen to know when to end the task of moral guidance* because the learner has become his own guide. By listening to learners, the teacher seeks to determine if they have individually learned to endure the struggle and recalcitrance of negative experiences constitutive of moral decision-making processes and to act in recognition of the other. Herbart asserted that when the learner "can pursue his right way independently," then the teacher must drop "all claims of moral guidance [*Zucht*]" and "confine himself to sympathetic, friendly, trusting observation" (*SE* 239/*AP* 119). The teacher-learner relation changes at this point, as does the dialogue between them: all advice from teacher to learner has "the purpose of getting the learner to think about the matter for himself" (*SE* 239/*AP* 119). As the process of moral guidance ends, the learner takes on a stronger role of initiating dialogue with the teacher by *asking* for advice regarding problems and dilemmas. The change in the teacher-learner relation that results from an educational relation is a change that involves the learner's self-transformation; the learner now "possesses both praise and blame within himself, and can guide and impel himself by their means" (*SE* 248-49/*AP* 125).

This third principle illuminates the role of listening in concepts of the educational relation developed by various contemporary philosophers. Nigel Tubbs, for example, examines the task of an educator to "negate" herself[47] by cultivating the learner's doubt. Nicholas Burbules states that authority in education must be self-undermining.[48] Dietrich Benner underscores that the educational relation is based in educating to "promote the learner's self-activity," a task that entails forms of teaching and educating that seek out their own end.[49] The principles of listening developed here extend such notions of the educational relation by highlighting the less-considered, yet indispensable, role of listening in teaching (I continue my discussion of listening in Chapter 7).

---

[46] Compare Herbart *SE* 239/*AP* 128-29 and *SE* 248-49/*AP* 125.

[47] Nigel Tubbs, *Philosophy of the Teacher: Journal of Philosophy of Education* **39**, no. 2 (Special Issue) 2005, p. 318.; Tubbs draws this current of thought from the Socratic tradition, continuing through the Continental tradition of philosophy such as that of Heidegger, although he does not mention Herbart.

[48] Nicholas C. Burbules, "What Is Authority?" in *Key Questions for Educators*, edited by William Hare and John Portelli, pp. 17–21, 20–21 (San Francisco: Caddo Gap Press, 2007).

[49] Dietrich Benner, *Allgemeine Pädagogik: Eine systematisch-problemgeschichtliche Einführung in die Grundstruktur pädagogischen Denkens und Handelns*, (Philosophy of Education) p. 78–79 (Weinheim: Juventa, 2001).

On this account of the nature of the educational relation, the learner's self-transformation cannot occur *in spite of*, but only *in the context of* educational relations that support discontinuity in a learner's experience brought about by inner struggle. The end of the teacher-learner relation does not mean the end of the individual learner's inner struggle (although the nature of this struggle changes as the learner changes). Rather, the end of the teacher-learner relation means that the learner's relation to her own negative experiences, to the interruptions in her experiences of the otherness of the world, has changed: the learner no longer needs a teacher to interrupt her experiences and promote her reflective inquiry into the nature of the negativity of her experiences – into her own doubt and felt resistance of the world and others. Instead, she is able to recognize the interruption in her experiences and initiate such reflective inquiry on her own.

3 PEDAGOGICAL TACT: TEACHING AS A THEORY-GUIDED PRACTICE

Herbart's theory of moral guidance suggests that understanding and responding to the learner requires teachers who listen closely to *their own* inner self-critical voice. In all aspects of education, just as in moral guidance, teachers must recognize learners as changing, learning beings, who are capable of transforming their views of the world, asking questions, and developing an inner censor. But listening critically to someone who is in the process of changing requires teachers who can change and alter their judgments of learners in new situations. It requires a teacher who is able to observe herself, to experience the *otherness* of herself, and listen to the voice of her inner censor, stopping her in action, such that she questions her judgments of the learner. In this respect, Herbart gives us an added insight into what critical listening in teaching entails; it is self-critical and requires a teacher who orients her listening *inwardly* by *listening to her own inner censor*.

By analogy, Herbart gives an illustration of the nuanced aspects of what is meant by *listening inwardly* for the teacher:

Just as a singer practices to discover the compass and finest gradations of his voice, the teacher must, in thought, practice going up and down the scale of the encounter [with the learner . . .] so that he may banish with sharp self-criticism every dissonance, attain the necessary certainty in hitting every note, the necessary flexibility to change, and the indispensable knowledge of the limits of his organ.[50]

---

[50] *SE* 237/*AP* 117, translation modified.

To extend Herbart's analogy, we can say that the teacher as moral guide is trying to "hit the right note" with each individual learner. This is a difficult task because what may have worked for one student may not work for another, and what worked once with a child may not work later with the same child. The teacher is perpetually seeking out openings for dialogue so that his words do not fall on deaf ears, so to speak. A teacher may ask himself, "Am I telling the learner something he already knows?", "Am I using too harsh of a tone to criticize an honest mistake?", "Am I accepting the learner's explanation of his actions when I should be asking more questions?" In other words, the teacher is asking himself, "*Am I getting through to the learner?*"

The teacher, in Herbart's vision, must be guided by the moral ideas *and* by the learner. The teacher must care for how he or she is heard by the learner and seek to be heard as having concern for the learner's growth and education (*Bildung*), and not as simply having interest in correcting the learner's errors or giving isolated praise (*SE* 236/*AP* 116-17).[51] Herbart develops the notion of "pedagogical tact," placing emphasis on the fact that *learning tact* is an essential part of *learning to teach*. Learning pedagogical tact is learning to maintain openness and flexibility toward the *other as learner*. Herbart's notion of tact relates to Aristotle's concept of *phronesis*, or the art of making informed, wise decisions in the moment.[52] In his "Introductory Lecture to Students in Pedagogy," Herbart refers to pedagogical tact (*pädagogischer Takt*) as the "quick evaluation and judgment – not proceeding like routine –" of what should be done in an individual situation.[53] This pedagogical activity, or tact, develops in practice, but is guided by theory.[54] When Herbart refers to tact as *pedagogical*, he means that it is a form of practical wisdom that is unique to teachers.[55]

With his concept of pedagogical tact, Herbart opens our eyes to the inevitable difference between theory and practice, which necessarily contributes to experiences of teaching, and points to the discontinuity of these experiences. Discontinuity here has a twofold meaning: first, it refers to the

---

[51] See also *SE* 243/*AP* 120.

[52] Aristotle, *Nichomachean Ethics*, translated and edited by Roger Crisp (Cambridge: Cambridge University Press, 2000). On the concept of *phronesis*, see in particular Book 6. In this edition, translated by Crisp, the term *phronesis* is translated as "practical wisdom"; see, e.g., p. 107/1140b.

[53] Herbart, "Introductory Lecture to Students in Pedagogy," p. 20, translation modified.

[54] Ibid. p. 18–20; on this point, see also Benner, *Johann Friedrich Herbart*, p. 13.

[55] On this point, see also Müssener's remark that a concept of tact that does not include the "pedagogical aspect" or a concept of pedagogical tact that does not include the "scientific theoretical aspect" would only be fragmentary for Herbart. Gerhard Müssener, *Johann Friedrich Herbarts "Pädagogik der Mitte": Sieben Analysen zu Inhalt und Form*, p. 201 (Darmstadt: Wissenschaftliche Buchgesellschaft, 1986).

discontinuity a preservice teacher experiences between *how she was taught* and *how she learns to teach*; second, it refers to the discontinuity a teacher experiences in the everyday professional practice of teaching itself. For Herbart, pedagogical tact is the "link" (*Mittelglied*) between educational theory and educational practice; it enters in the gap that "theory leaves vacant."[56] This gap cannot be closed by theory because, of course, theory moves in the realm of the general, whereas practice always deals with individual cases. But a teacher's tact, her wise decisions in the moment, are wise because they are *attuned* to theory in a way that prevents educational practice from becoming merely an imitation of past practices. As the link between theory and practice, tact also prevents educational practice from being deduced directly from theory.

Although Herbart did not fully consider the improvisational character of teaching, his notion of pedagogical tact as a link between theory and practice provides a starting point for understanding the experience of teaching as discontinuous and necessarily improvisational. Tact develops out of innovative practice that is made possible by the openings and gaps, the discontinuous moments of teaching experiences. In these moments, teachers can begin to question their own practice, to question how they were educated, and to form new theories around the central philosophical questions of education through continuous dialogue with other educators. In closing, I would like to draw on three hints in Herbart's discussion that point to the discontinuous structure of teaching experiences and reveal how tact is a form of judgment used to productively address discontinuity in teaching practice:

- *Tact aids teachers in finding their mistakes and learning from their mistakes.* For Herbart, to create the sort of educational relation in which both teacher and learner are heard by one another, teachers must be open to things not working out as planned and have the "courage" to learn from their mistakes (*SE* 268/*AP* 139). All teachers will experience mistakes when their experiences break down and their planned interactions with learners do not work. But, as Herbart notes, learning from one's mistakes is only possible for the teacher who has prepared through theory. Judgments of tact are oriented on educational theory. Without preparation for practice provided by educational theory, the teacher can only get "stuck in a rut" because his judgments of what to do in educational contexts are based in habit and routine. The teacher who is stuck in a rut ignores the discontinuity of his own

---

[56] Herbart, "Introductory Lecture to Students in Pedagogy," p. 20.

practice. As Herbart scholar Günther Buck emphasizes, this type of teacher "skips over the negative instances" of teaching experiences and is "trapped" in the "prejudice" formed by his prior experience; he is, therefore, no longer "open to learning" because he ignores the moments that do not work and relies on routine.[57] This sort of teacher, who just follows routine, cannot see his own mistakes. As Herbart states, a teacher who has no preparation in educational theory "only experiences himself"; he has nothing to which he can compare "his way," for he has not learned to discern the meaningful moments in practice from the irrelevant ones.[58]

- *Tact gives productive meaning to anything unexpected that arises in the practice of teaching.* Tact allows the teacher to "use the invasion of fate" to her "benefit."[59] This means that by developing pedagogical tact, teachers develop a sense of how to use the experience of discontinuity in teaching. Specifically, tact means utilizing the moments of being thrown off course by unplanned and unforeseen interactions with learners, not as stopping points in teacher-learner interaction (and the teacher-supported learning process of learners), but as moments for new and previously unforeseen learning opportunities for learners.

- *Tact is also a creative act of meeting the needs of the moment.* Herbart writes: "one must trust his own ingenuity, in order to meet the needs of the moment *in* the moment."[60] The term Herbart uses for "ingenuity" (*Erfindungsgabe*) means in a more literal sense the "talent for invention." Applied to teaching situations, we can say that tact involves the creative act of meeting the learner's needs, in particular, those that cannot be determined in advance, while at the same time remaining true to the principles of educational theory.

On the basis of these insights, we can say that tact is a conscious turn toward the individual learner that cannot be entirely foreseen or preplanned.

---

[57] Buck, *Herbarts Grundlegung*, 83–84.
[58] Herbart, "Introductory Lecture to Students of Pedagogy," p. 19, translation modified.
[59] Ibid., p. 24, translation modified.
[60] Ibid., p. 22, translation modified; this type of creative inventiveness connects to a further hint at discontinuity in teaching, which is found in *The Science of Education*, where Herbart writes that instruction should not be boring and should not create passivity. For Herbart, the learner's boredom is a sign of not learning, so that, in this case, the instruction should "not aim at being continuous, but permit interruptions (*Unterbrechungen*) or itself cause them" (*SE* 153/*AP* 58). Herbart does not examine fully what this entails for the teacher, but a further connection to this idea of initiating discontinuity in learning will be made in my discussion of teaching in Dewey (Chapter 4) and in Part Two of the book.

Pedagogical tact is a form of judgment that distinguishes the novice teacher from the professional: whereas the novice teacher may *per chance* meet the needs of the learner in the moment, the professional teacher who has prepared for the practice of teaching through educational theory masters what Herbart calls "the art of educating."[61] This art must be learned: tact is not based in natural intuition or in instinct. Rather, as Dietrich Benner points out, "pedagogical tact is more than a stop-gap between theory and practice. It is the educated conscience of pedagogical responsibility."[62] To *respond* to the learner in the ethical ways entailed by educational relationships requires that the teacher *make it a habit* to orient his or her practice on theory rather than on whim or routine. The ability to respond to the learner is developed when teachers' decisions about what to do in educational contexts are grounded in their theoretical understanding of the role of both continuity and discontinuity in the structure of learning.

Although Herbart's concept of pedagogical tact is an important starting point for understanding the experience of teaching, Herbart did not go far enough because he did not place emphasis on the fact that there is a difference between the function of tact for the novice teacher and the lasting function of tact for the professional teacher. Once the novice teacher develops pedagogical tact and finds ways to be attuned to theory *within* practice, there is a danger that the teacher's tactful mediation between theory and practice itself becomes *routine*. In other words, a teacher's judgment of unexpected situations that arise in teaching practice may become so habitual that the teacher no longer truly looks at the individuality of the learner involved or at the particular circumstances of the situations of learning. That is, the teacher no longer analyzes the meaning of discontinuity within her practice. Throughout a teacher's career, a teacher must allow herself to be interrupted, to address her own negative experiences, and on that basis to reflectively reevaluate and critique her own "quick decisions" made in the moment. In doing so, a tactful teacher differentiates herself from the *rut* of a teacher who lacks all connection to theory, but also from what we might call *the rut of tact* – that is, the habits, fixed dispositions, and routines – of professional educators. The "rut of tact" rears its head when experienced teachers begin to routinize their solutions to the problems of practice and, in turn, stop critical reflection on their own practice. In such instances, the teacher has stopped defining herself in terms of the learner. The belief that, as teachers, we know "what works" can hinder us from reexamining "what works" from new perspectives and

---

[61] Herbart, "Introductory Lecture to Students in Pedagogy," p. 22.
[62] Benner, *Johann Friedrich Herbart*, p. 13

discovering what does *not* work. The tactful teacher knows when to use learned judgments of tact (tried-and-true responses to unexpected situations of practice) and when to distance herself from her own judgments and reflect on her decisions, evaluate them in light of new theories of education, and create alternative modes of practice to address the needs of the moment. In this way, in using tact (or trying to use it), teachers are continually learning what tact is; they learn if their judgment worked in the moment or if it needs to be modified the next time a similar situation arises. Good teachers learn that the raison d'etre of teaching is responding to the call of the other – the learner.[63]

With German philosopher Jakob Muth, we can say that tact becomes the *inner voice* of the teacher that not only tells the teacher what *not* to do – just as Socrates' daemon – but also tells the teacher *what to do*.[64] These positive judgments of action in teaching are based in decisions made to address the perfectibility of the learner and to extend learning processes where they may have become stuck. Thereby, a tactful teacher differentiates herself from the "rut" of a teacher who lacks all connection to theory, but also from the habits, fixed dispositions, and routines of professional educators: she has prepared for practice through planning, reflected on the possibilities of practice through philosophical research, and has learned to continually critique her own practice on the basis of such preparation.

4 CONCLUSION: A LOOK BACK AND A LOOK AHEAD

Herbart's theory of education is limited in that it confines the notion of the learner's struggle to moral learning, whereas Dewey, as I will demonstrate in the next chapter, extends the notion of struggle – as difficulty, perplexity, and doubt – to be constitutive of all realms of learning. But, importantly, Herbart's theory of education emphasizes that through dialogue, teachers can create a virtual space for learners to find themselves *between* right and wrong, in the space of inner struggle, a space in which learners become open to the other and learn to judge themselves out of recognition of the other. For Herbart, only when learners are given varied options to choose *otherwise* do they engage in struggle and become compelled to contemplate what is good and choose on that basis. Thus, Herbart's theory of education gives us insight into

---

[63] On this point, see Jakob Muth, *Pädagogischer Takt. Monographie einer aktuellen Form erzieher-ischen und didaktischen Handelns* [Pedagogical Tact: Monograph of an Actual Form of Educative and Instructive Action], pp. 72–73 (Heidelberg: Quelle und Meyer, 1967).

[64] Ibid., 61–62.

the fact that the task of the teacher entails finding ways to question and listen to the learner and point out, as Herbart says, "what the learner does not see, but must see in order to live as a human being" (*ARW* 269, translation modified). Such questioning and listening in teaching cannot simply be for the sake of passing on positive teachings, but rather must aim to problematize and *interrupt* the learner's immediate connection between listening and obeying external authority or self-originating uncritical judgments.

Moral education that is predicated on the learner's blind obedience to authority works against cultivating the learner's choice, and therefore contradicts the central criteria of Herbart's notion of moral education. Whereas such authoritarian models of moral education serve only as a means of *silencing* the learner's critical inner voice by not allowing its commands to be put into action, I maintain that Herbart's insights form a basis for extending critical-reflective models of moral education that aim to initiate the learner's transformation, by supporting the learner to transform her self-relation and relation to others. To cultivate moral understandings and experiences in democratic society, learners must be introduced to various perspectives and conflicting value systems, so that they can understand the difference between the Good, the Bad, and the gray areas. Only in this way can they actively engage in experimenting with varied understandings of the Good.

In the next chapters, we will see that Dewey explicitly contemplates the role of discontinuity and negative experiences as constitutive aspects of democratic education.

Chapter 3

Discontinuity and Educational Openings in Learning

1   PRAGMATISM, DISCONTINUITY, AND LEARNING

For Dewey, our encounters with the new and unexpected play an essential role in understanding how learning begins and how we arrive in what I refer to as an *in-between realm of learning*. By analyzing Dewey's concept of learning with a focus on the role of experiences such as doubt and difficulty, we can identify the in-between realm of learning that is opened up by discontinuity in experience. As I draw out in this chapter (and the next), the in-between realm of learning can be understood as an opening or gap in experience. This opening is an educational space in which the learner finds herself bound up in a realm that lies between an encounter with the *limits* of knowledge and ability, and the *new* knowledge or ability that is *yet to be found*. Here, the learner has recognized that her previous experiences and accrued knowledge and ability do not suffice; rather, they must be expanded on, modified, or corrected. However, in this in-between realm, the learner has not yet determined what this expansion or correction consists of. In other words, the learner is in a space in which she is not yet able to answer the questions, "What must I do or know to move on?" and "How do I navigate through the difficulties in the situation I have encountered?"

Educators might assume that the best way out of the in-between realm is for the learner to get quickly to a solution to the difficulty. In present-day mainstream educational discourse, the emphasis on outcomes and results certainly implies such urgency. This urgency to get learners out of difficult situations – or to not even allow them into such situations in the first place – coincides with a more common-sense understanding of what to do in difficult and doubt-filled situations we may encounter in everyday life. In everyday life, we either seek to avoid unexpected situations that throw us off course or, if we cannot avoid them, we seek to get back on course with little hesitation.

For Dewey, the realm of the in-between, as I will address it here, is not a space to scurry through with haste, let alone ignore or run from. Rather, it is essential for learners to reside in the in-between for the sake of their own learning process: it is in this space that learners can find possibilities for experimenting with the new and, on that basis, develop new learning experiences.

I begin this chapter by examining specific ideas relating to discontinuity in experience as developed in the pragmatist tradition of Charles Sanders Peirce, William James, and George Herbert Mead.[1] In the second section, I demonstrate how Dewey's theory of learning as a *reflective experience* productively extends notions of discontinuity in learning developed by his fellow pragmatists. I underscore the idea that Dewey, unlike Herbart, who viewed discontinuity as essential primarily in moral learning, views discontinuity in experience as indispensable in all realms of learning. In my analysis of Dewey's theory of learning, I clarify the idea that the in-between realm of learning is an opening between *our encounter with the new that interrupts us* and *our newly acquired understanding of the new in experience*. In the context of my analysis, I explain how such a view of the role of discontinuity in learning has implications for how we understand Dewey's notion of continuity. In the third section, I examine Dewey's notion of "problems" as they connect to his concept of learning. I close the chapter by developing the idea that Dewey's model of learning delimits *two* beginnings of learning that must be taken into account when educating others. This chapter leads to my discussion of Dewey's concept of teaching in Chapter 4.

2 NOTIONS OF DISCONTINUITY IN PEIRCE, JAMES, AND MEAD

Peirce: On the Irritation of Doubt

C. S. Peirce develops a concept of doubt that demarcates it as a productive moment of discontinuity in experience in a way that connects to learning. Although Peirce does not use the terms discontinuity or interruption as I do, his concept of doubt identifies a moment of rupture or break in experience that occurs when we encounter the new and unfamiliar. By analyzing Peirce's concept of doubt and how it arises in our experience, I identify the meaning of discontinuity in experience as it connects to Dewey's thought on reflective experience.

---

[1] My focus will be on those particular texts of these thinkers that deal explicitly with the notion of pragmatism. Also, although I present these thinkers in the order stated, I do not wish to imply a strict developmental order from Peirce to James to Mead, since they were in some ways influenced by each other and in some cases by Dewey.

In "The Fixation of Belief," Peirce makes a significant point related to learning when he describe situations in which a person veers off the path of routine:

[L]et a man venture into an unfamiliar field, or where his results are not continually checked by experience, and all history shows that the most masculine intellect will ofttimes lose his orientation and waste his efforts in directions which bring him no nearer to his goal, or even carry him entirely astray.[2]

Although it is not Peirce's direct intent to use this passage to demonstrate how learning takes place, his description of such moments of aporia highlights the experience of discontinuity within the learning process (setting aside his questionable use of the term "masculine"). This experience of discontinuity occurs when something did not happen as planned, so that we become lost and disoriented. These moments connect to our encounters with the new and unfamiliar and involve risk; they come about when we intentionally or unintentionally digress from routine.

Peirce's concept of "doubt" marks the moment within our experience when we have reached a limit to thought and action. When we find ourselves in such a state of aporia as the one just described, we endure what Peirce calls the "irritation of doubt."[3] Doubt, in Peirce's account, is an "uneasy and dissatisfied state, from which we struggle to free ourselves";[4] it reminds one of the "irritation of a nerve."[5] Despite this, doubt is *not* a moment in experience that we should skip over or avoid. Rather, on his account, experiences that lead to the possibility of the irritation of doubt are necessary for changing our beliefs: the irritation of doubt arises when we experience the new and unfamiliar in such a way that we begin to question our existing beliefs.

Pointedly, the concept of doubt Peirce seeks to clarify stands in opposition to the formal concept of Cartesian doubt. Unlike Cartesian doubt, "real and living" doubt, as Peirce terms it, arises from problems of practice. For Peirce, real and living doubt is a form of doubt that cannot be separated from the practical problem from which it arose.[6] To be in doubt on Peirce's account means that we lack a "habit of mind" to guide action and, in turn, are in need

---

[2] Charles Sanders Peirce, "Paper 4: The Fixation of Belief," in *The Collected Papers of Charles Sanders Peirce: Electronic Edition*, edited by Charles Hartshorne and Paul Weiss, Vol. 5: Pragmatism and Pragmaticism, § 2, 368 (Charlottesville, VA: InteLex Corporation, 1994). Cited in the following as *FOB*.

[3] Peirce, *FOB*, § 3, 374 and 375.

[4] Ibid., § 3,372.

[5] Ibid., § 3,373.

[6] For Peirce, "genuine doubt" constitutes the reason we are asking the question and thus incites the struggle of inquiry toward new belief. Compare *FOB*, § 4,376.

of new beliefs to guide action.[7] Thus, Peirce is concerned with the sort of doubt that arises from something "external," as he states, most often from "surprise."[8] This point in Peirce's thought is significant because he is making clear that doubt arises within our interaction with the world around us, not simply in the isolation of thought.

The notion of surprise in particular helps get at the meaning of interruption in experience. It draws attention to those moments when something unexpected happens and our taken-for-granted experience of the world is *interrupted*. Peirce states, "it is by surprises that experience teaches all she designs to teach us."[9] We cannot altogether escape the experience of surprise. As philosopher Israel Scheffler poignantly states in his essay on surprise, the very fact that we have something called "surprise" is a recognition of the possibility of human fallibility.[10] Doubt, for Peirce, is a state of experiencing our own fallibility; doubt is a signal that we have experienced the new and unfamiliar in a way that disorients us.

A central question underlying Peirce's argument is, in my view, a learning-theoretical question: How can we learn from the experience of doubt? Or, more broadly stated, how can we learn from the experience of discontinuity, from *interruption*? Peirce's answer places the scientific method of inquiry at the center of understandings of how to learn from doubt.

Real and living doubt for Peirce (as opposed to Cartesian doubt and feigned doubt)[11] places us in a "struggle" that takes the form of a search to seek out

---

[7] Charles Sanders Peirce, "Paper 6: What Pragmatism Is," in *The Collected Papers of Charles Sanders Peirce: Electronic Edition*, edited by Charles Hartshorne and Paul Weiss, Vol. 5: Pragmatism and Pragmaticism, § 3, 417 (Charlottesville, VA: InteLex Corporation, 1994).

[8] Charles Sander Peirce, "Paper 7: Issues of Pragmaticism," in *The Collected Papers of Charles Sanders Peirce: Electronic Edition*, edited by Charles Hartshorne and Paul Weiss, Vol. 5: Pragmatism and Pragmaticism, § 1, 443 (Charlottesville, VA: InteLex Corporation, 1994).

[9] Charles Sanders Peirce, "Lecture 2: The Universal Categories" in *The Collected Papers of Charles Sanders Peirce: Electronic Edition*, edited by Charles Hartshorne and Paul Weiss, Vol. 5: Pragmatism and Pragmaticism, § 2, 51 (Charlottesville, VA: InteLex Corporation, 1994).

[10] Israel Scheffler. "In Praise of the Cognitive Emotions," in *In Praise of the Cognitive Emotions: And Other Essays in the Philosophy of Education*, pp. 2–13, 9 (New York: Routledge, 2010). Although Scheffler is focused on the cognitive experience of surprise, it is interesting to point out that Peirce relates the "irritation of doubt" to the "irritation of a nerve," suggesting that he may also have thought of surprise as potentially initiating a corporeal-existential experience. See also Kerdeman's discussion of the limits of Scheffler's idea of cognitive surprise; Deborah Kerdeman, "Pulled Up Short: Challenges for Education," in *Philosophy of Education 2003*, edited by Kal Alston, pp. 208–16 (Urbana, IL: Philosophy of Education Society, 2004).

[11] In his discussion of the "pragmatic maxim," Peirce qualifies his idea of "irritation of doubt" as not to be understood too strongly, such that he wishes to speak of doubt that arises even from minor indecision "however momentary"; in Charles Sanders Peirce, "Paper 5: How to Make Our Ideas Clear," in *The Collected Papers of Charles Sanders Peirce: Electronic Edition*, edited by

new beliefs.[12] Peirce calls this struggle "inquiry." Inquiry, specifically the scientific method of inquiry, does not ignore doubt, but rather investigates it as an opportunity to learn.[13] Peirce (just as later pragmatists) distinguishes the scientific method of inquiry from "the method of tenacity," "the method of authority," and the "a priori method" in a form that indicates it as a different way of dealing with doubt. Whereas the "method of tenacity" calls for blind adherence to one's existing beliefs, the "method of authority" arbitrarily forces one to take on the beliefs of others, and the "a priori method" resorts to believing what one is "inclined to believe." In contrast, the scientific method takes up the experience of doubt as indicative of a need to question and thoughtfully explore one's existing beliefs.[14]

Peirce's concept of doubt highlights the educative meaning of discontinuity in learning because it points not only to an experience of the limits of knowledge and ability, but also to the phenomena of one's "struggle" to move past these limits. This relates to what philosopher Sydney Hook emphasizes is characteristic of pragmatism, namely, a stress on "the efficacy of human ideals and actions and at the same time their inescapable limitations."[15] Whether one agrees with the pragmatists' emphasis on the scientific method of inquiry as a method for acquiring new ideas and beliefs, the point I wish to draw out is that Peirce is seeking a method for acquiring new

---

Charles Hartshorne and Paul Weiss, Vol. 5: Pragmatism and Pragmaticism, § 2, 394 (Charlottesville, VA: InteLex Corporation, 1994). These qualifications of how we are to understand how doubt comes about make clear that Peirce is talking about a much more common everyday phenomenon of doubt (as an example, he uses not knowing how to pay a fare for a horse-car) and not limited to extreme cases. Peirce also states that we can speak of "feigned hesitancy" as initiating scientific inquiry ("Paper 5: How to Make Our Ideas Clear" § 2, 394). However, Scheffler makes the important point that although Peirce notes that feigned doubt could be a starting point for inquiry, feigned doubt is not the same as real and living doubt; it would not have the same effect on us, for it would not invalidate the proposition in question in the same way; see Israel Scheffler, *Four Pragmatists: A Critical Introduction to Peirce, James, Mead, and Dewey*, pp. 68–69 (London: Routledge and Kegan Paul, 1974).

[12] Peirce, *FOB*, § 4, 374; see also Peirce, "Lecture 2: The Universal Categories" § 2.

[13] On this point, see also Nicholas C. Burbules, "Aporias, Webs, and Passages: Doubt as an Opportunity to Learn," *Curriculum Inquiry*, 30, no. 2, 2000: 171–87.

[14] Peirce, *FOB*, § 5, 377–87. Although I am looking at the process of moving from doubt to belief from the perspective of individual experience, it should be noted that Peirce saw collaboration as important to the process of scientific inquiry. I am grateful for my discussions with Naoko Saito, in which she pointed this out.

[15] Sydney Hook, *Pragmatism and the Tragic Sense of Life*, p. 4–5 (New York: Basic Books Inc., 1974). Hook calls this recognition of limitation a recognition of the "tragic sense of life." Although I do not adopt the term "tragic," the discussion surrounding the tragic sense of life is related, in the sense that it points to the idea of having limitation. The focus is more on the recognition *that* we do experience limitation, whereas my focus is on *how* we experience limitation. I return to this notion in Chapter 5.

knowledge that places significance on *doubt* (or, more generally speaking, the discontinuity and negativity of experience) as a productive moment within the process of learning. On this understanding, doubt marks a limit to our knowledge and ability, and, in that sense, locates a break with past belief and action that we can identify as a discontinuity in experience. Inquiry into doubt is a quest to learn from the experience of limitation. This idea of doubt and its connection to learning is an essential aspect of pragmatism that also arises in the thought of James, Mead, and Dewey.

James: On the Connection between Difficulty and Leading Ideas

In his 1907 lectures on pragmatism, William James develops a notion of "leading ideas" in a way that extends our understanding of the productive meaning of discontinuity in experience.[16] With the notion of a "leading idea," James seeks to answer the question of how we find an idea that gets us *out* of the troubling state of affairs we find ourselves in when faced with a new experience, such as encountering a new object, an unanticipated idea, or a perplexing moral question. James's concept of "leading ideas" begins to shed light on the notion of an exploratory space for learning between old and new ideas, one that is opened up by the interruptions in our experiences – a space that constitutes the in-between realm of learning.

What is significant to note in James's concept is that leading ideas directly relate to our experience of discontinuity. Leading ideas deal with the difficulty arising from those breaks in our experience that occur upon our encounters with the new and different. For James, we need these leading ideas when we are caught up or entangled in a difficult situation: leading ideas are "helpful in life's practical struggles."[17]

James's characterization of these moments of difficulty as problems of practice becomes more clear in his concept of "double-urgency." For James, in moments of encountering a new experience, we are faced with a "double-urgency", that is, we feel an urgency to get out of this situation that is based in

---

[16] William James, *The Works of William James: Electronic Edition*, edited by Frederick H. Burkhardt, Fredson Bowers, and Ignas K. Skrupskelis, Vol. 1: Pragmatism, pp. 1–176. (Charlottesville, VA: InteLex Corporation, 2008). I will use the term "leading" here to describe ideas that James characterizes using various terms, including leading, but also "ideas which carry us" (e.g., in Vol. 1, James, p. 36), or ideas that "guide us" (e.g., in Vol. 1, James, p. 102).

[17] William James, "Lecture II: What Pragmatism Means (1907)." In *The Works of William James: Electronic Edition*, edited by Frederick H. Burkhardt, Fredson Bowers, and Ignas K. Skrupskelis, Vol. 1: Pragmatism, pp. 27–44, 42 (Charlottesville, VA: InteLex Corporation, 2008).

our need to both "lean on old truth *and* grasp new fact."[18] James is thus drawing our attention to a pertinent question that arises for the individual caught up in a practical struggle: How do I bring together what I have learned thus far – the "old truths" I feel are established – with this new experience that contradicts what I have learned?

What James is identifying are those moments when our old ideas no longer suffice to deal with the present situation in which we find ourselves. In other words, as I have characterized this situation previously, we have reached a certain limit to our own knowledge and ability. A "leading idea," in James's account, enters into the space created by this encounter with a limit, the space between old ideas no longer deemed valid and the new ideas yet to be found. For James, ideas are true when they lead us in our experience, "stretching" it and serving as a "go-between," a bridge between an old idea – now "put to a strain"[19] by a new experience – and a new, different idea.[20] Such ideas help us make sense of something that does not immediately make sense to us.

James's characterization of the process of finding a leading idea that satisfies this double-urgency identifies a space of exploration that we can say lies between *the interruption* in experience (arising in our encounter with the new) and the development of a hypothesis about how to potentially move on. True leading ideas are not immediately presented to us; they do not suddenly emerge when we are in a difficult situation. Rather, they have to be sought out. The search that James describes is itself a process of trying to connect our new (as yet troubling) experience to a learning process.

The in-between realm of learning, as I am defining it, is a space for exploration of new possibilities for thought and action. James gives further indication of what residing in this in-between realm might look like when he points out that our search for a leading idea involves a look to an imagined future, or, more specifically, to imagined *future interruptions* in experience: an idea is true that "helps us *deal*, whether practically or intellectually, with either the reality or its belongings, that doesn't entangle our progress in frustrations."[21] He considers that the search for such an idea is a search for "what works best in the way of leading us, what fits every part of life best and combines with the collectivity of experience's demands," with the added

---

[18] Ibid., p. 36, emphasis mine.

[19] Ibid., p. 34.

[20] Ibid., p. 35.

[21] William James, "Lecture VI: Pragmatism's Conception of Truth (1907)," in *The Works of William James: Electronic Edition*, edited by Frederick H. Burkhardt, Fredson Bowers, and Ignas K. Skrupskelis. Vol. 1: Pragmatism, pp. 95–114, 102 (Charlottesville, VA: InteLex Corporation, 2008). On this point, see also Scheffler, *Four Pragmatists*, 109.

caveat that there is "nothing omitted" from our search, so that all possibilities are explored.[22]

James's description indicates that learning on account of an interruption in our experience requires more than simply overcoming a present difficulty or frustration; it entails imagining and anticipating future difficulties and frustrations (i.e., future interruptions in experience). In other words, when looking for a way out of a difficult situation, one must ask oneself, "How can I move on in a way that would prevent me from being interrupted in a similar way in the future?"

Although some have criticized James for saying that the search for a leading idea is a harmonious process of finding an idea we like best, this criticism is not entirely sound.[23] Just as Peirce considers the process of inquiry a *struggle*, James views the process of finding those leading ideas that have truly taken all possible future frustrations into consideration as "extremely difficult."[24] Leading ideas offer us something more than simply a quick-fix or patched-on solution to the present problem, or a way around the problem; *they must have the potential to change the way we think*. Thus, we can draw out from James's thought that learning not only involves finding a new idea that "works" (in a broad sense of the term), but, in doing so, it involves accounting for *what does not work*. That is, to find the leading ideas that help us truly grasp and come to understand the new and unfamiliar, we must explore and understand what has brought our experience to a strain – we must understand the interruptions in our experiences.

Although James gives important insight into what a space for exploration and learning might look like, I see two problems with James's account that blur the meaning of discontinuity in experience that I am developing here. For one, he does not go far enough in his characterization of encounters with the new. Rather, he focuses on ways that we can modify or "stretch" our old ideas by adding onto existing knowledge, to accommodate the new and unfamiliar object or idea, without a transformative experience.[25] Furthermore, James's account of what is entailed in our search for leading ideas remains subjective insofar as he leaves it, at least in part, up to the individual's subjective choice to decide to what extent he or she will engage in this process of searching for a

---

[22] James, "Lecture II: What Pragmatism Means," p. 44.

[23] Scheffler emphasizes that although James is not saying that truth is simply what is pleasant, he criticizes James on the point that, for James, "pleasantness" can be one evidence of truth. I agree with Scheffler when he writes: the fact that "a belief comforts the believer is no count at all in favour of its truth"; see Scheffler, *Four Pragmatists*, p. 108.

[24] James, "Lecture VI: Pragmatism's Conception of Truth," p. 104.

[25] See for example, James, "Lecture II: What Pragmatism Means," e.g., p. 35–36.

leading idea, and remain in an in-between state to explore present and future possible interruptions in experience, so as to continue to learn. In a moment, we will get to Dewey's thought on the intersubjective educational questions surrounding the transformational potential of interruptions in experience. But first, I introduce Mead's insights into the connection between individual experience and the social realm.

Mead: On Problems for Thought and the Breakdown of the World

George Herbert Mead develops a version of pragmatism that is grounded in an expanded idea of experience. More than Peirce and James, Mead explicates the idea that history and society mediate both our initial individual experiences of difficulty, as well as the solutions we find to those difficulties. Mead's explanation of the social character of experience demonstrates that an individual's problem or difficulty is always more than an individual issue; the problem has social purport.

What Mead terms a "problem for thought" is something that arises from one's experience of the common world, a world co-created and given meaning through human interaction and communication. According to Mead, the human being stands in an insoluble relation to the world and other human beings. Mead argues that the starting point of experience is a common world, a world that is "continually breaking down."[26] The breakdown of the world arises on the basis of a "conflict of meanings" that stop us in our tracks.[27] These create "problems for thought" that require a solution.[28]

On Mead's account, it is unavoidable that each individual experience has a "social character."[29] Accordingly, although each individual experience preserves a certain uniqueness or "exception," the experience can be shared with others in a way that it can become connected to a group's common experiences.[30] Mead provides the relatable example that one person's headache may be a unique experience of pain for him or her, but it can have common traits with others' experiences of headaches that allow one individual's experience

---

[26] George Herbert Mead, "A Pragmatic Theory of Truth," in *Selected Writings George Herbert Mead*, edited by Andrew J. Reck, pp. 320–45, 341 (Chicago: University of Chicago Press, 1964). Cited in the following as PTOT.

[27] Mead, PTOT, p. 328.

[28] Ibid., p. 322. In a way indicative of the pragmatic theory of Peirce and James, Mead's theory places emphasis on the fact that the solutions that we find cannot be arbitrary or predetermined by an external authority; rather, the solution must connect directly to our inquiry into the original problem arising in experience; Mead, PTOT, p. 331.

[29] Mead, PTOT, p. 340.

[30] Ibid., p. 341.

to be at the same time a shared common experience.[31] We can say that when an individual encounters a problem in her experience of the world and on that basis understands that she does not know something, then sharing this experience of "not-knowing" is itself a contribution; one individual's difficulty or problem can become part of our common human understanding of the difficulties that can arise in the world.

From Mead's insights, we can draw out two significant points about the role of individual experiences of discontinuity in social growth and understanding. First, Mead is making us aware that those solutions in the world that we have come to take for granted initially arose from discourse on problems in individual experiences. Before science found remedies to the common headache, there existed a common problem that needed a shared solution. In other words, the process of arriving at solutions entailed the discontinuity in individual experiences – that is, the rupture or break in individual experience. The structure of such development is common in social and historical movements large and small. Efforts to resolve transportation or housing issues to efforts to determine how to create ethical and democratic relations between groups arise from the recognition that something within the common world is not sufficient, but requires modification or reconstruction. These efforts indicate that, on the basis of individual experiences of difficulty – that is, individual encounters with the limits of thought and knowledge – the group as a whole recognizes its arrival at a limit to thought and knowledge that needs to be addressed.

Second, Mead's insights indicate that the world – and the solutions we find therein – is not final. The world is continually "breaking down," and old solutions prove insufficient to account for new problems, such that new social discoveries need to be made. In the context of these two points, we can understand Mead's emphasis on the productive meaning of what we might call a *negative* understanding of the world: "There is . . . no question that there is a profound meaning in seeing the world whole, but the most enlightening approach to its meaning is to be found in bounding it, that is, in discovering *what it is not*."[32]

Although Mead is not specifically addressing education, his insights into the social nature of experience point to the fact that knowing one's limits – that is, grasping the discontinuity and negativity of one's experiences – has educative value.[33] Mead is drawing our attention to the fact that a human

---

[31] Ibid.

[32] Ibid., p. 334, emphasis mine.

[33] For an interesting analysis drawing out Mead's thoughts on education, see Gert J. J. Biesta, "Mead, Intersubjectivity, and Education: The Early Writings," *Studies in Philosophy and Education*, 17, no. 2, 1998: 73–99.

being learns *already as* a social being in the context of a common world, but also learns *to become* social through his or her interaction with that common world by participating in it and sharing new problems and experiences with others. Further, we can conclude that education is not simply passing on finished packaged solutions, but entails sharing the ruptures and breaks within human experience – that is, the discontinuities of experience – with the next generation. These form the basis for creating social interconnections between human beings.

3   LEARNING "IN-BETWEEN"

The In-Between of Learning

Dewey develops a notion of reflective experience that further illuminates the in-between realm of learning and how it relates to an individual's ability to interact with the world. Dewey extends pragmatic notions of doubt and difficulty and, also, those notions of struggle in moral learning developed by Herbart. His discussion of experiences such as uncertainty, doubt, perplexity, and confusion demarcates indispensable moments within all learning experiences that point to the educational meaning of discontinuity and the negativity of experience (although he does not use the term negativity in the way I am using it here). Dewey's theory of learning delimits a space between the interruption in experience and our arrival at a way out of a difficult encounter with the world, a space I refer to as the "in-between realm" of learning. On this basis, discontinuity in experience proves to have vital meaning for the learning process: only by means of the learner's own exploration within this opening – or in-between realm – can she identify and potentially *change* her relation to herself and the world.

Dewey provides a description of what he terms "experience," expressing the idea that human beings are not just actors and constructors of the world and their environment; they are also receptive to the world. A central claim that permeates Dewey's work is that all experience involves both doing *and* undergoing.[34] For Dewey, undergoing describes the receptive side of the

---

[34] For example, see the following works: *DE* 146; John Dewey, "Experience and Education (1938)," in *The Later Works*, edited by Jo Ann Boydston, Vol. 13, pp. 1–62. (Carbondale: Southern Illinois University Press, 2008); John Dewey, "The Need for a Recovery of Philosophy (1917)," in *The Middle Works*, edited by Jo Ann Boydston, Vol. 10, pp. 3–48, 11 (Carbondale: Southern Illinois University Press, 2008); John Dewey, "Reconstruction in Philosophy (1920)," in *The Middle Works*, edited by Jo Ann Boydston, Vol. 12, pp. 77–202, 129 (Carbondale: Southern Illinois University Press, 2008); *AE* 47–48.

human being, which is essential for understanding how we experience the world and *learn* from it. We *receive* something from the world when it resists our attempts at interaction: we *undergo* or *suffer* the world. Dewey writes, "It is not experience when a child merely sticks his finger into a flame; it is experience when the movement is connected with the pain which he *undergoes* in consequence" (*DE* 146, emphasis added). In this description of a basic form of human interaction, Dewey reveals that the child learns only when he reflects on the *relation* between the pain and the consequent burn in such a way that is fruitful for guiding future experiences; he learns because, through reflection, he makes a connection that leads him to understand that "henceforth the sticking of the finger into the flame means a burn" (*DE* 146).[35]

This example highlights the meaning of *undergoing*. When we undergo the world through our encounters with the new, we learn that something or someone in the world has defied our expectations (such as when we find out for the first time that a flame can be harmful). On the basis of this encounter, we become open to the possibility of reconsidering our previous knowledge and actions and entering into a state of questioning what we know and how we behave. In these moments, we are not merely experiencing continuity with what we know and how we have acted. Rather, we are interrupted by the new: we experience discontinuity – a break with ourselves and thus a break with our ability to navigate the world.[36]

When our experience is opened up by interruption, by *undergoing* the world as *other*, such that our prior knowledge and ability is called into question, we enter into an in-between realm of experience and learning. Although, for Dewey, both doing and undergoing are equally part of experience, I place emphasis on the undergoing, receptive side of experience because that is the moment when something other resists us, or *counters* us in the *encounter*.[37] Dewey draws our attention to this countering force of a

---

[35] On this point, see also, James Garrison, "John Dewey's Philosophy as Education," in *Reading Dewey. Interpretations for a Postmodern Generation*, edited by Larry Hickman, pp. 63–81, 67 (Indianapolis: Indiana University Press, 1998).

[36] These ideas relate to concepts of self-reflexivity that I drew out in Chapter 1.

[37] Importantly, Robert Westbrook emphasizes that even "undergoing" for Dewey is not passive, citing Dewey's "The Need for a Recovery of Philosophy" (1917); see Westbrook, *John Dewey and American Democracy*, p. 127 (Ithaca, NY: Cornell University Press, 1991). As Westbrook points out, Dewey also calls undergoing "active." I believe there is some further needed clarification here, in that I interpret Dewey to be saying that we are not passive, in the sense of having no agency to respond to what we have undergone. But this does not imply that *in the moment* of undergoing we are *active*, in the same way that "active" in used in Dewey's term *doing*, as referring to the active side of experience. For my discussion, it is important to keep this distinction clear, for if we deem all aspects of experience "active," then we miss the significance of what we take in or "receive" from the world. I discuss this idea of receptivity further later.

learner's encounter with the new in his later work, *Art as Experience* (1934). There, he connects undergoing, learning, and the experience of resistance:

There is ... an element of undergoing, of suffering in its large sense, in every experience. Otherwise there would be no taking in of what preceded. For "taking in" in any vital experience is something more than placing something on the top of consciousness over what was previously known. It involves reconstruction which may be painful.[38]

In this context, Dewey locates a particular problem that hinders such "taking in" and learning from our interaction with the world: the problem is that if we only "do" and treat "resistance" as "an obstruction to be beaten down," we miss the opportunity to see it "as an invitation to reflection" (*AE* 51).

The moments of undergoing the world and experiencing resistance highlight the discontinuous moments in experience. They point to the fact that when the *world resists us*, it is "telling" us that we do not have control, we are not able to correctly anticipate, we do not have accurate foresight, and we are not able to calculate how our interaction with the world will unfold. Resistance tells us that routine and habit are not sufficient to engage the world, but that they are limited because the world is not how we thought it was. Dewey's notion of undergoing the world is a way of talking about the *new as other* that enters into all realms of life and learning; we must come to terms with it if we want to learn.

Dewey's notion of experience underscores the idea that there is always an unknown, unexpected element within experience. If we merely confirm existing belief through repetition and reiteration of what we already know and have already done, then, for Dewey, there is no experience had. Dewey (similarly to his fellow pragmatists) underscores the idea that, contrary to common sense, undergoing the world, being interrupted by it, and experiencing resistance does not hinder learning; rather, it *incites* learning. One might ask: In what sense does undergoing incite learning? Or, put another way, if undergoing is an experience of otherness, then how can we learn from the otherness of the world?

The Space of Reflection in Experience

Dewey's answer to how learning is possible is found in his notion of "reflective experience." On his account, reflective experience is different from a simple trial-and-error mode of experience. Both reflective and trial-and-error forms

---

[38] *AE* 47–48.

of experience have in common that they begin when we are interrupted by the new, that is, they begin when we have encountered the new and unfamiliar such that, as Dewey states, something becomes "uncertain," "doubtful," or "problematic" (*DE* 155). However, when we proceed by the method of trial and error (in contrast to when we proceed by the method of reflective experience), we are relying solely on learning from the success or failure of a particular attempt to do something in the world; we continue trying something new until we reach our aim.

What Dewey is pointing out is that the method of trial and error is limited in its ability to deal with uncertainty or a doubt-filled situation. Using trial and error, a learner may realize whether his or her attempt to change the doubt-filled situation has been successful or unsuccessful, but does not fully know *why*. One's thinking – and one's ability to learn – within the experience is limited in that this method only clarifies that one is no longer having a difficulty and thus is no longer stuck. However, it fails to tell one how to identify similar situations of difficulty, under what conditions one could avoid them entirely, or what decisions or circumstances need to be modified for one to better navigate similar situations in the future.

A reflective experience proceeds differently; it views the discontinuity in experience as a starting point for reflectively exploring our interaction with whatever new and unfamiliar things threw us off course. Reflection is the inquisitive form of thinking that holds us in "suspense," analyzes the limits of given knowledge, and develops new possible ways of seeing the world within this realm of uncertainty and difficulty (*DE* 155).[39] Through reflective thinking, the learner must remain in a state of uncertainty because she does not know where her exploration may lead. The learner is seeking something unknown, something "not at hand," which does not simply mean she is seeking new knowledge in the abstract (*DE* 155). Rather, the learner is seeking new knowledge that is connected to and arises out of her own inquiry into the *discontinuity* and *negativity* of her experience. With Dewey scholar Harriet Cuffaro, we can say that, for Dewey, reflection is "that pause in which we struggle to give form to what we sense and feel."[40] In other words, whatever it was that the learner *underwent* in his or her interaction with the world that brought upon a state of difficulty or doubt now becomes the object of inquiry (*DE* 155). It is in the process of searching that the learner finds herself in the

---

[39] See also Dewey, *HWT*, p. 121; see also Dietrich Benner and Andrea English, "Critique and Negativity: Toward the Pluralisation of Critique in Educational Practice, Theory and Research," *Journal of Philosophy of Education*, **38**, no. 3, 2004: 409–28.

[40] Harriet K. Cuffaro, *Experimenting with the World: John Dewey and the Early Childhood Classroom*, p. 63 (New York: Teachers College Press, 1995).

"twilight zone of inquiry," as Dewey phrases it, or in what I refer to as the in-between realm of learning (*DE* 155). In this realm, the learner has the opportunity to deal with problems of thinking and learning that lie *between* knowledge and ignorance, ability and inability.

Thinking reflectively on Dewey's account involves not merely seeking out our positive, established knowledge – that is, what we know – but simultaneously trying to clarify in what our perplexity consists – that is, what we do *not* know. Reflective experience, on Dewey's account, proceeds differently than trial and error in that it entails that we thoughtfully engage the uncertainty arising from our interaction with the world in an attempt to understand what went awry within that interaction. Reflection is sparked by the "confusion," "doubt," or "perplexity" that comes about in our experience of the unexpected and uncertain (*DE* 157). To reflect is to take recourse to the perplexity and analyze it: "The perplexities of the situation suggest certain ways out. We try these ways, and either push our way out, in which case we know we have found what we are looking for, or the situation gets darker and more confused – in which case, we know we are still ignorant" (*DE* 155–56). In other words, to reflect is to ask oneself, "Why am I confused, in doubt, or perplexed?"

It is in the process of reflectively searching that the learner finds himself in the in-between realm of learning, where he is trying to establish *connections* between what he has done and what he has undergone – that is, between self and world. It is by way of the idea of "reflection" that we can also understand Dewey's notion of continuity. Reflective thinking, for Dewey, creates a *connection* or *continuity* out of what was directly experienced as discontinuous and disconnected. Philosopher James Garrison underscores this meaning of continuity in Dewey's notion of experience: "We learn to establish connections between what we do and what we suffer as a consequence of our effort to coordinate our activity. This is continuity."[41] By understanding Dewey's notion of experience from this perspective, we can say with Sydney Hook

---

[41] Garrison, "John Dewey's Philosophy as Education," p. 67. Although Garrison does not use the term discontinuity in his explanation, his recognition of the significance of "suffering" the world, in Dewey's notion of experience, is a recognition of what I point to as the discontinuity or negativity constitutive of experience. In this context, Garrison also points out that many have misunderstood Dewey and mistaken his notion of experience as one connected with empiricism or logical positivism (Garrison, p. 65). Saito also emphasizes discontinuity as essential to understanding Dewey's notion of temporal continuity: "Dewey's idea of development in temporal continuity" is not "a linear progression" or "repetition . . . of what existed before. Rather it entails discontinuity." In Naoko Saito, *The Gleam of Light: Moral Perfectionism and education in Dewey and Emerson*, p. 114 (New York: Fordham University Press, 2005), see also p. 118. I return to Dewey's idea of continuity in the next chapter.

that "in Dewey's opinion, the term continuity is correlative with the term discontinuity . . . Both are found in experience."[42] Similarly, we can say that both positivity and negativity are part of experience, notions I continue to unfold in later sections.

My emphasis on discontinuity in Dewey's theory of experience and learning aims at demarcating the moment at which one enters the in-between realm of learning. This realm is a space for experimentation with new ideas and new potential choices for action, *prior to* and independent of overt action. Dewey's proposal for the general structure of a reflective experience provides a model of how the learner can move within the *in-between* of learning. The experimental method of science comes into play in Dewey's theory of a reflective learning experience as a way of structuring the process of experimentation with the new. In a reflective experience, the learner analyzes the negativity of her experience (an inquiry into the limits of her knowledge), seeks to explain it on the basis of theory, and thereby gains hypothetical insights for attempting something new with an increased possibility of attaining the desired outcome (*DE* 157–58). In this way, the learner attempts to reach her aim experimentally by revising expectations and modifying the conditions of action. *Learning*, on this account, means *learning to think* within the realm of the in-between, such that, as Dewey explains, "thinking" itself becomes an experience (*DE* 152). By delimiting this gray area between knowledge and ignorance, Dewey finds an answer to the question of how learning is possible and thereby succeeds in avoiding Meno's paradox, which only recognizes complete knowledge or complete ignorance (*DE* 155).[43]

Dewey's theory of reflective experience begins to identify that the discontinuity and negativity of experience – often revealed in our uncertainty, perplexities, and doubt – are constitutive of learning. His explanation demonstrates that a learner's negative experiences, such as perplexity, doubt, or confusion, cannot be overlooked in the learning process. These point to the learner's arrival at a *limit* of knowledge and ability, and these limits must be explored by the learner within the realm of the in-between in order for

---

[42] Sydney Hook, *John Dewey: An Intellectual Portrait* (1939), p. 215 (Westport, CT: Greenwood Press, 1971).

[43] Dewey's play on the opposition between knowledge and ignorance in *Meno* overshadows the important transitional phases of discontinuity and negativity of experience in the learning process as it is experienced by the learning slave boy. In *Meno*, the learning slave boy, who attempts to answer Socrates' questions, becomes disillusioned and perplexed about his own knowledge until he is led to eventually proclaim "I do not know." This experience of not knowing and knowing that you do not know is a precondition for the boy's search for knowledge. "Meno," in *Plato Complete Works*, translated by G. M. A. Grube, edited by John M. Cooper and D. S. Hutchinson, pp. 870–97 (Cambridge, MA: Hackett Publishing Company, 1997).

learning processes to unfold. This is not to say that established knowledge and ability is not useful; rather, it is to say that positive knowledge gains central meaning in light of its connection to the negativity of experience that we have undergone or suffered in our encounter with the world. Dewey's concept of undergoing shows that undergoing has an instructive force: although it is true that we must do something in the world as a necessary precondition for the possibility of encountering the new in experience, only when we undergo the world by truly encountering the new do we gain the possibility to *learn from experience*. Thus, the negativity of experience (marked by the fact that we have suffered the world) is itself an indispensable aspect of learning processes in two central ways: it both invites *and* provides a point of orientation for reflective thinking, a point where self and world (mediated by resistance) have en-*countered* one another.

What Is a Problem?: The Role of Problems in Reflective Experience

Is undergoing the world largely a cognitive experience? Certainly, Dewey's use of the terms "perplexity," "confusion," and "doubt" in his examination of experience in *Democracy and Education* (1916) seems to suggest as much. This may be at least one reason that Dewey's notion of learning gets characterized as merely a mode of problem solving (an idea often associated with pragmatism in general and with Dewey in particular). However, this characterization misses the central point of his notion of learning as reflective experience; it imposes an intentionality on the learning process and diminishes the meaning of the unintentional – of what we suffer and undergo when the new and unfamiliar confronts and interrupts us. The "problem-solving" characterization overlooks a central question underlying Dewey's inquiry into the process of learning, namely, why does the learner have what we are calling a "problem" in the first place. The question of what a problem signifies for Dewey thus comes to bear on our understanding of reflective learning processes. By turning to Dewey's analyses of "problems" in two of his later tomes, *How We Think* (1933) and *Logic: The Theory of Inquiry* (1938), we can gain a deeper understanding of the experience of discontinuity as something other than purely cognitive, namely, as an existential experience indispensable for reflective learning experiences. In these texts, we find his description of an existential moment that brings us closer to understanding as the sense of an *interruption* in experience that I am developing here.

In his discussion of reflective thinking in *How We Think*, Dewey explicitly points out that reflection does not begin with a problem. Rather, it begins as a search to understand *prereflective* situations of experience. Here, Dewey

distinguishes between *problems* and the states of perplexity, doubt, confusion, uncertainty, or trouble that arise in our experience *prior to* identifying the problem. He explains that problems are part of a phase of
reflective thinking, whereas perplexities and the like are part of *precognitive* processes that cannot, as such, be considered elements of reflective
thought (*HWT* 199–200). However, for Dewey, what is qualified as a
"problem" directly connects to our prereflective experience: problems
arise out of reflective inquiries into the nature of our prereflective experience (which we come to characterize as perplexing, doubt-filled, or
confused).

To further understand Dewey's distinction, it is necessary to grasp the
context in which "prereflective" perplexities and what we might call "reflective" problems[44] arise. Dewey distinguishes between "indeterminate situations," which include perplexities but not problems per se, and "problematic
situations" (*LTI* 109–12). Dewey's notion of the "indeterminate situation" tells
us that we experience the world in resistant ways prior to having a problem
and prior to reflective inquiry into our experience; our experience incites the
states of mind, like doubt or perplexity. From a pragmatist's perspective, such
states are initiators of reflection, or, more precisely, they can be, if we so
choose. For Dewey, to say one is perplexed or in doubt (or other related
cognitive states of being) implies that one has had a direct experience.[45] This
direct experience of interaction with the world has led to what Dewey also
calls a "disturbed situation" – a term he uses interchangeably with "indeterminate situation" – in light of which one now considers oneself perplexed
(e.g., *HWT* 200; *LTI* 109).[46]

Dewey terms situations "indeterminate" because something is uncertain
and troublesome, but we do not know exactly what it is (*LTI* 109–10). The
philosopher Günther Buck underscores Dewey's idea of this initial state of

---

[44] In an earlier essay, I termed these "post-reflective" problems (see English, "Interrupted
Experiences: Reflection, Listening and *Negativity* in the Practice of Teaching," *Learning Inquiry*,
1 [Special Issue "Listening and Reflecting," edited by Leonard J. Waks], no. 2, 2007b: 133–42.)
However, because Dewey uses the term "postreflective" to refer to a finished and determinate
situation (see *HWT* 200), I have changed my own terminology so as not to confuse readers.

[45] A "direct experience" for Dewey means that we have interacted with the world, we have done
something, and, in turn, undergone or suffered something, see *HWT* 194.

[46] Dewey uses various terms to refer to the process of reflective inquiry, including reflective activity
(*HWT*) and inquiry (*LTI*), the latter of which he defines as the "controlled or directed transformation of a indeterminate situation" into one that is "determinate" (*LTI* 108). I continue to use
the terminology of *reflective experience* as Dewey uses it in *DE*, to refer to the different
formulations of the processes of reflective inquiry.

experience, describing it as a state of disquietude (*Beunruhigung*).[47] Dewey scholar Richard Bernstein explains that, in such situations, there is "an immediacy, an awareness of a difficulty."[48] We can add to this that this is an embodied awareness, not a purely cognitive recognition. Along these lines, Cuffaro points to the experience of an indeterminate situation as an "encounter with the qualitative, the sensing and feeling of unsettlement."[49] She explicates further that "at this prereflective, preintentional point there is neither a problem nor inquiry."[50] We might say that the indeterminate situation describes the situation of being stuck in the muddy waters of experience, where things are not clear because we are not sure how we got there and are not sure how to leave.

Dewey's use of the term "disturbed" to describe indeterminate situations (he also uses other terms, such as "uneasy" or "perplexing") is significant because it points to a *disturbance* – or, in my sense, an interruption – in our experience. We might primarily think of being disturbed as something bad. Commonly speaking, we connect disturbance with the unsettling of a restful state. For example, our concentration is disturbed, we are disturbed by a loud noise while sleeping, or maybe we are disturbed by a dog while trying to read a good book in the park. But here, Dewey is drawing out the educational meaning of a disturbance in that it "arouses inquiry" and "incites reflection" (*HWT* 193).[51] For Dewey, the disturbance is not merely cognitive unrest; rather, it is an existential experience that is felt:

The indeterminate situation comes into existence from existential causes, just as does, say, the organic imbalance of hunger. There is nothing intellectual or cognitive in the existence of such situations, although they are the necessary condition of cognitive operations or inquiry. In themselves they are pre-cognitive.[52]

This embodied existential sense of the indeterminate situation is again emphasized by Dewey in a later essay "Inquiry and Indeterminateness of Situations" (1942), addressing his critics. In this work, he refines his earlier

---

[47] See Günther Buck, *Lernen und Erfahrung*, p. 72 (Stuttgart: W. Kohlhammer, 1969). Therein, Buck also emphasizes that the "negativity of experience" is part of the essence of experience for Dewey.

[48] Richard J. Bernstein, *John Dewey*, p. 105, see also p. 104. (New York: Washington Square Press, 1966).

[49] Cuffaro, *Experimenting with the World*, p. 63.

[50] Ibid.

[51] On this point, see also Gert J. J. Biesta and Nicholas C. Burbules, *Pragmatism and Educational Research* (Oxford: Rowman & Littlefield, 2003); and Joseph Margolis, *Reinventing Pragmatism: American Philosophy at the End of the Twentieth Century* (Ithaca, NY: Cornell University Press, 2002).

[52] *LTI* 111.

terminology and writes that his aim in using the concept "indeterminate" was to conjure up the sense of the "uncertain, not indeed in its cognitive sense, but in the sense in which it is said that a man's footing is unsure."[53] This notion of finding oneself on unsure footing gets us closer to an understanding of the existential experience that is at the outset of a reflective experience, namely, our experience of an interruption and our subsequent arrival in an indeterminate situation. To be interrupted means that we encountered something or someone in the world in an unexpected and unanticipated way. As philosophers Gert Biesta and Nicholas Burbules explain, "indeterminate situations in a sense simply 'happen,' the process of inquiry begins when we try to identify what is actually happening."[54] They also emphasize that there is a "disruption" based in "conflicting habits," such that "we do not know how to respond" to what has happened.[55] Philosopher Leonard Waks writes that, for Dewey, perplexing experiences are felt when "the smooth flow of social experience grinds to a halt in doubt."[56] Pragmatism scholar Joseph Margolis underscores that we arrive in indeterminate situations because we have encountered a "practical and unavoidable impasse."[57] Although these scholars do not use the term "discontinuity" in this context, descriptions such as theirs nonetheless identify the moment in experience when activity becomes disturbed or interrupted, and we are not capable of following our familiar patterns of activity.

The experience of interruption is itself prereflective, but it can be transformed into a reflective aspect of experience if it is consciously and thoughtfully addressed and not ignored. For this transformation to take place, we first must recognize the interruption as pointing to the negativity of experience; that is, it points to something beyond the limits of our present knowledge and ability. Only then can we begin to ask ourselves: What happened? What went wrong? What might I need to change? The interruption in our experience only says that something has become uncertain for us; however, it is not yet a

---

[53] John Dewey, "Inquiry and Indeterminateness of Situations (1942)," in *The Later Works*, edited by Jo Ann Boydston, Vol. 15, pp. 34–41, 40 (Carbondale: Southern Illinois University Press, 2008).

[54] Biesta and Burbules, *Pragmatism and Educational Research*, p. 60.

[55] Ibid. 58, see also, 59–60; see also Walter Feinberg on the connections between disruption in experience and Dewey's idea of community; Walter Feinberg, "The Conflict Between Intelligence and Community in Dewey's Educational Philosophy," *Educational Theory*, 19, no. 3, 1969: 236–48.

[56] Leonard J. Waks, "Reflective Practice in the Design Studio and Teacher Education," *Journal of Curriculum Studies*, 31(3), 1999: 303–16.

[57] Margolis, *Reinventing Pragmatism*, p. 113. Larry Hickman also underscores that the "existentially doubtful situation" initiates inquiry; see "Dewey's Theory of Inquiry," in *Reading Dewey. Interpretations for a Postmodern Generation*, edited by Larry Hickman, pp. 167–86, p. 184 (Indianapolis: Indiana University Press, 1998); see also Saito, *The Gleam of Light*, p. 73.

problem. A "problem," in Deweyan terms, is part of a "problematic situation," that is, a situation in which we have determined we need *to find* a problem and we attempt to do so (*LTI* 111–12).

Once we have identified and called something a "problem," this represents partial knowledge, or what we might call a form of positivity: "A problem represents the partial transformation by inquiry of a problematic situation into a determinate one" (*LTI* 112). Significantly, when we are talking about a "problem" in Deweyan terms, we are talking about something that is already guiding and *limiting* inquiry; it guides our search for solutions, limits what solutions we find, and limits what actions we take on the basis of these solutions. For example, if a teacher determines that a problem with her teaching is based in what textbook she is using, then she will seek out better textbooks. However, she may not investigate other factors, such as the classroom environment, learning differences among learners, or her methods of explaining the material.[58] On this account, to call something a problem is to reach a specific stage of reflective thinking; it assumes we have "intellectualized" our prereflective experience and *transformed* it into a "problem to be solved."[59] The existential experience of interruption is now cognized – made into a problem – and thus made an object of inquiry.

If we attempt to see learning as something that begins with problems, we miss the essential educative meaning of prereflective experience, and that of discontinuity. Thus, as Dewey's distinction between indeterminate and

---

[58] To take this further, we can say with Richard Bernstein that the limiting effect between problem and solution is reciprocal: "What we will subsequently accept and reject as possible solutions depends on how we formulate the problems; we could also say that the closer we come to a solution the clearer we become about what is the problem." Bernstein, *John Dewey*, p. 106. Taking the example mentioned, if, after a teacher determines that a problem with her teaching is based in what textbook she is using, and she tries a few different textbooks, she may then realize that the same or similar problems are occurring with the students' learning. Thus, she may then realize that it was not the textbook per se, but a particular issue raised in the book, or she may rule out the textbook as a problem and look for other factors to help resolve the situation. As Bernstein emphasizes, "finding the solution" helps us hone in on the actual problem and narrow or limit its scope. However, we must not overlook the fact that, even though finding the solution helps us redefine the problem, there is a new interruption that makes this possible, namely, the fact that what we thought was the problem is not leading us to the solution we desired. So, on account of something unexpected happening (i.e., not getting the desired results), we have to redefine the problem. What Bernstein does not state, but my view should be made explicit, is that the continued inquiry into the nature of the problem entails new interruptions that lead us "back" to reexamining the problematic situation anew.

[59] Dewey terms this process a transformation of the situation of uncertainty and indeterminacy, that is, the *indeterminate* situation becomes a *problematic* one (*HWT* 200–01). In the process of intellectualization, we analyze our prereflective state of being, grant it constitutive meaning for further inquiry, and seek to make it intelligible as a guide to action.

problematic situations makes clear, the prereflective interruption in experience is as necessary for learning to take place as the reflective inquiry into the
interruption itself. It is only on account of the prereflective, interrupted
experience that the possibility opens up of recognizing the limits of our
previously acquired knowledge and experience. In other words, we recognize
that our previous experiences and accrued knowledge and ability do not
suffice, yet we do not yet know what to change or even how to find out
what needs to be changed. When our experiences are interrupted, this space
opens up and opportunities arise for reflectively and intersubjectively exploring and experimenting with new ideas and new modes of practice.

Two Beginnings of Learning

Following the previous sections, we can conclude that *problems may be a
beginning of learning, but they are not the initiators of reflective experiential
learning processes.* Dewey's distinction between prereflective phenomena
(characterized as perplexities or confusions) and *problems* points to the idea
that there are *two* beginnings of learning. The first takes the form of what I call
a *prereflective beginning* that characteristically comes forth as a learner's
"perplexities," "confusions," or "troubles," arising within his or her interactions with the surrounding world. The second beginning of learning takes the
form of what I refer to as a *reflective-transformative beginning* of learning.
This marks a starting point to learning that occurs when the learner transforms a prereflective experience of interruption into a problem into which he
or she can reflectively inquire.

Both the prereflective and reflective-transformative beginnings of learning
point to two different forms of *negativity of experience* which are equally
constitutive and indispensable for learning to take place. Both beginnings
result in the learner finding herself in an in-between realm of learning.
However, they each demarcate different aspects of this realm of learning
between old and new knowledge and ability. The prereflective beginning of
learning marks a moment in experience when the learner is interrupted
within her interaction with the world; she undergoes a lived experience of
the world. In this realm of the in-between, the learner finds herself in an
indeterminate situation. In the words of philosopher of education Käte
Meyer-Drawe, we can characterize this realm of the in-between as a space
in which the new "is not yet understood" and the old "is no longer trusted."[60]

---

[60] Käte Meyer-Drawe, "Anfänge des Lernens" [Beginnings of Learning], *Zeitschrift für Pädagogik*,
49, 2005: 24–37, 32.

The prereflective experience of interruption that begins a learning process is an encounter that the learner *does not consciously choose to have*; it occurs in an unforeseen and unplanned way. However, although this experience is outside the realm of choice, we can describe it as a beginning of the learner's learning process because it opens up new and unforeseen opportunities for the learner to discover new choices for thought and action.

Prereflective beginnings of learning are necessary (although not sufficient) to incite reflective learning experiences because only by means of the interruption can the world become a *problem* for the learner; the world becomes *unique* to the learner because she undergoes something on the basis of *her* particular interaction with that world. Learning begins in a prereflective way when the learner encounters a limit to her thought and action. One's experience with the world, in this case, is not marked by the positive knowledge that one has gained; it is not marked by grasping a math problem, figuring out the meaning of a new word, or playing a game with a classmate that creates an understanding of friendship. Rather, one's experience is marked by one's own negative experience of the world, one's experience of one's own limits – the individual experiences things that she does not yet know, cannot yet do, and does not yet understand.

Reflective-transformative beginnings of learning are equally necessary for reflective learning experiences to take place because they locate a beginning of learning that the learner chooses for herself. She chooses *if, how,* and *to what extent* she will *transform* the interruption in her experience into a reflective experience. Put simply, one chooses to transform one's own confusion or perplexity into a problem that one can reflectively deal with. In other words, learning begins in a reflective-transformative way when the learner creates a "problematic situation" out of what was only an uncertain "indeterminate situation." When the learner starts to finds ways to reflectively transform her experience of limitation as interruption, then her encounter with a difficult math problem, a confusing word, or a strange interaction with a classmate becomes a focal point for the learner. In this process, the learner seeks to determine what her unique relation to the world consists in; the interruption in her experience sparks a desire to inquire and find new ways of relating to that world.

Reflective-transformative beginnings thus open up a different aspect of the *in-between* realm of learning: they open up a space in which the learner has identified a particular problem within her interaction with the world, but has not yet identified the way out or solution. The conscious decision to inquire into the negative forms of experience and to activate new learning processes cannot, however, secure the results of inquiry – it can only open up new possibilities for learning. By way of the transformation of prereflective inter-ruptions into questions and problems that require inquiry, the learner learns to move past simple trial-and-error forms of learning. Instead, the learner moves toward reflective learning experiences because she begins to learn the structure of learning processes – the learner begins to learn *how to learn*.

Dewey's thinking demonstrates an acute awareness of the fact that, without reflection into the moments of interruption in our experiences, opportunities to learn from the world may be intentionally ignored or arbitrarily over-looked. Prereflective experiences of interruption – which we can reflectively refer to as perplexing, difficult, confusing, irritating, or unsettling – point to the discontinuity and negativity of our experiences; they point to the moments of undergoing the world. If we bypass the *undergoing* phase of experience and learning, we also bypass the negative and discontinuous moments in learning and their educational significance. The conscious turn to the negativity of a perplexing experience opens up the opportunity *to learn* from experience. This conscious turn to inquire into the interruptions in our experiences and our relationship to the world is a choice. Just as for Herbart, also for Dewey, this choice to reflect and learn from experience cannot be left entirely to chance. Dewey's vision of the educator's role underscores that it is the responsibility of the educator to cultivate this choice through systematic education and instruction. As I will demonstrate in the next chapter, such cultivation entails what I call "teaching in-between."

Chapter 4

Teaching in the Openings of Learning

For Dewey, questions of how we learn – and thus questions of how to teach in ways that promote learning – are based in how we understand problems. As I explained in Chapter 3, on Dewey's account, genuine problems arise from an individual's questions about the nature of their prereflective encounters with the new and unfamiliar. Traditional schooling views problems as "ready-made," that is, determined independently of particular students who enter the learning environment. In such cases, as Dewey notes, the "problem" comes from the teacher or the book, and the teacher's interest in the child is focused around finding ways to get the child to solve *this* particular predigested problem or find predetermined correct answers to *this* particular predesigned question.

I argue that Dewey's theory of learning problematizes notions of teaching as the transmission of finished ideas and solutions. For, if learning begins with prereflective interruptions in experience, then teaching cannot begin with presenting learners with predigested problems and prepackaged thoughts. Rather, it has to begin by *interrupting* the learner's experience. For only on account of such interruptions will learners begin to think and to formulate their own questions and challenges to thought, and thereby enter into transformative learning processes.

Dewey's ideas present a vision of the teacher as one who challenges learners to arrive at their own limits – and ask questions about the nature of those limits. In this chapter, I address particular aspects of Dewey's theory of teaching in order to provide a way of seeing teaching as a reflective orientation on the discontinuity and negativity of learners' experiences. Teaching, on my account, is a reflective practice. I term this form of reflective practice *teaching-in-between*. In the first section, I discuss the notion of reflective practice developed by Donald Schön. I examine Schön's notion of the generalizability of the reflective practitioner to demonstrate that it is an important starting point for discovering what is *unique* about the reflective practice of teaching. I then return to Dewey's terminology to develop the idea of how teaching is unique and different from other forms of professional practice. In the second section, I consider certain aspects of the Deweyan classroom that relate directly to the idea of teaching as "teaching-in-between." In the third section, I address some implications of this theory for understanding teaching as a moral task. I conclude the chapter by examining how "teaching in-between" connects to Dewey's vision of democracy.

1 REFLECTIVE PRACTICE AS TEACHING IN-BETWEEN

Donald Schön's explanation of the idea of reflective practice has been very influential in educational discourse and serves here as a starting point for grasping the idea of teaching as a reflective practice. In his two major works on the reflective practitioner, Schön draws on Dewey and develops a theory of reflective practice that is meant to have validity for all realms of professional practice, including that of teachers.[1] Schön's broad focus on the structure of reflective practice across professions is important and tells us how teaching is connected to other professions in a particular. Namely, it points to the fact that the structure of teaching processes is also discontinuous (in a way that follows the structure of learning processes delineated in Chapter 3). Two ideas in Schön's conception of reflective practice contribute to understanding the uniqueness of teaching practice: the connection between uncertainty and reflection, and the concept of reflection-in-action.

Drawing on Dewey, Schön argues that uncertain situations are indicative of professional practice and need to be addressed through reflection. Schön explicates that unexpected and surprising events in experience and practice – which I have been referring to as interruptions – initiate reflective thought. Although Schön notes that unexpected or surprising situations arise not only in professional practice but in all forms of practice, he sets out specifically to delineate how professionals deal reflectively with such situations. For Schön, reflection begins in situations that he characterizes as "messy," "indeterminate," "problematic," and "swampy zones of practice."[2] The practitioner deems a situation in professional practice "messy" when it becomes

---

[1] Donald Schön, *Educating the Reflective Practitioner* (San Francisco: Jossey-Bass, 1987), and Donald Schön, *The Reflective Practitioner: How Professionals Think in Action* (Hants: Ashgate, 1983/2005).
[2] Schön, *Educating the Reflective Practitioner*, p. 3–7; Schön, *The Reflective Practitioner*, p. 16; see also 42.

uncertain, unique, or disordered, or when the practitioner's values have in some way come into conflict with each other.[3]

Schön develops a notion of reflection-in-action that he uses to describe how professionals deal with such uncertain, unsettling, or puzzling situations they encounter in practice. In describing what makes reflection-*in*-action particular to professional practice, Schön distinguishes this type of reflection from reflection-*on*-action. Both forms of reflection unfold out of puzzling or surprising situations and both attempt to understand what led the practitioner into that particular situation.[4] However, unlike reflection-on-action, reflection-in-action places emphasis on action continuing despite surprise (without ignoring it). Reflection-on-action involves thinking about what we have done in a particular puzzling situation after or independent of the situation at hand.[5] This can either involve contemplatively thinking about something after it has already come to completion (e.g., later in the day), or it can involve a pause to "stop-and-think" in the midst of action.[6] In contrast, reflection-*in*-action involves *thinking in the moment*, such that reflection occurs, as Schön explains, "in the midst of action, without interrupting it."[7] In this way, reflection-in-action seeks to allow action and thought to move forward interactively, in a way that relates to what Aristotle called *phronesis* (it also relates to what Herbart called "pedagogical tact," as I developed it in Chapter 2, although Schön does not mention this connection).

In a similar vein, although without clearly distinguishing, as Dewey does, between "indeterminate" and "problematic" situations, Schön makes clear that reflection in professional practice does not begin with a preformulated problem, but rather with the need to *set* a problem. For Schön, "problem-setting" is the precondition for problem solving and therefore the first stage of reflection-in-action.[8] In the process of setting the problem, practitioners seek to "make sense of uncertain situations" by selecting or "naming" what they

---

[3] Schön, *The Reflective Practitioner*, 15–16.; see also Schön, *Educating the Reflective Practitioner*, p. 6.

[4] Schön, *Educating the Reflective Practitioner*, p. 26.

[5] Ibid. On Schön's notion of reflection in action, see also Waks, "Reflective Practice in the Design Studio and Teacher Education," *Journal of Curriculum Studies*, 31, no. 3, 1999: 303–16.

[6] Schön, *Educating the Reflective Practitioner*, p. 26.

[7] Ibid. In an earlier essay, I argued that Schön did not place enough emphasis on the fact that action has been interrupted by the unexpected, unforeseen event, which reflection sets out to explain; see English, "Interrupted Experiences: Reflection, Listening and Negativity in the Practice of Teaching," *Learning Inquiry*, 1 (Special Issue "Listening and Reflecting," edited by Leonard J. Waks, no. 2, 2007b: 133–42). However, I have modified my earlier argument because it seems clear that implicit in Schön's idea of reflection-in-action is the significance of the break in experience that he locates with words such as "surprise" or the "unexpected."

[8] Schön, *The Reflective Practitioner*, p. 40.

will attend to and defining or "framing" the boundaries of the situation.[9] Once the context of the situation has been framed, reflection-in-action proceeds to solve the problem and experiment (in action) with the proposed solution.[10] As action and thinking proceed, Schön explains, the practitioner engages in a "reflective conversation" with the materials of the situation and can learn from the results of experimentation.[11] In line with Dewey's theory of inquiry, Schön emphasizes that the practitioner will not necessarily achieve the intended result, but rather, she may hear "back-talk" from the situation – which I contend can be conceived of as a new interruption in practice, creating a new messy situation. The back-talk informs the practitioner that she must think further.[12]

Schön's account of professional practice underscores the idea that teaching processes (just like other professional practices) share the structure of reflective learning processes developed by Dewey (which I addressed in Chapter 3). Teachers also experience interruptions – discontinuity and negativity within the experience of teaching – and come into uncertain situations in the practice of teaching; this uncertainty provides a basis for reflection.[13] When a teacher enters into an indeterminate situation, this means that she has become uncertain, but does not know exactly *why* she is uncertain. If the teacher begins to question the nature of her uncertainty, she begins to transform this uncertainty into a problematic situation and develop a question that she is trying to answer. For example, if the teacher determines that she became uncertain because a student in the back of the class looked confused by what was written on the board, the teacher may ask herself, "What should I do to address the student's confusion?"

In my account, the nature of interruption for teachers makes teaching as a professional practice *unique*, distinct from other professional practices (a distinction Schön's theory does not include). In the context of teacher-learner interaction, the interruption for a teacher is interconnected to the interruptions in the learner's processes of learning. This means that when a teacher's

---

[9] Ibid.; see also Schön, *Educating the Reflective Practitioner*, p. 4.
[10] Schön, *Educating the Reflective Practitioner*, p. 28–29.
[11] Ibid., p. 31, see also p. 73.
[12] Ibid.
[13] In their work, authors Biesta and Burbules, as well as Cuffaro, give examples of how teachers enter into indeterminate situations. Their examples underscore the idea that, for Dewey, the structure of reflective experience applies to both the structure of the teaching process as well as to the structure of learning processes. See Gert J. J. Biesta and Nicholas C. Burbules, *Pragmatism and Educational Research* (Oxford: Rowman & Littlefield, 2003); Harriet K. Cuffaro, *Experimenting with the World: John Dewey and the Early Childhood Classroom* (New York: Teachers College Press, 1995).

experience is interrupted in the context of teacher-learner interaction, such that the teacher becomes uncertain, the teacher's uncertainty with reference to *how to teach* is mediated by the problems and uncertainties the learner has with *how to learn*. This is what Dietrich Benner means when he writes that a teacher's experience is mediated by a twofold form of negativity of experience.[14] Put simply, this means that the learner's perplexity, problem, or difficulty (e.g., in understanding a mathematical formula, a strange new word, or a historical event) initiates the teacher's perplexity, problem, or difficulty of how to cultivate the learner's understanding of the subject matter at hand.

I argue that the interruption in the teacher's process of teaching points to the uniqueness of teaching as a reflective practice. When a teacher becomes uncertain and begins to reflect in the context of teacher-learner interaction, his or her reflective self-questioning is not only based in the broad question of "What do I do?" but more specifically in the question of "What do I do to initiate a reflective learning process for this particular learner?" Thus, as Schön emphasizes, teaching as a reflective practice is similar to other professional practices insofar as it involves uncertainty and reflective engagement with this uncertainty. However, teaching is also dissimilar to other professional practices: interruptions in teaching are interconnected to the interruptions in a learner's learning process (although the nature of the interruption for teacher and learner is not the same).[15] When the learner has been interrupted by the new and unfamiliar subject matter and has become uncertain about how to proceed, a teacher's uncertainty in this context is based in how to teach this learner, so that that learner can address his or her own uncertainty.

Thus, to recognize the interruption in the experience of teachers is to recognize the heart of the educational matter. When a teacher becomes uncertain in the context of teacher-learner interaction, this means the teacher

---

[14] See Dietrich Benner, "Kritik und Negativität. Ein Versuch zur Pluralisierung von Kritik in Erziehung, Pädagogik und Erziehungswissenschaft," *Zeitschrift für Pädagogik*, 46, 2003: 96–110; see also Dietrich Benner and Andrea English, "Critique and Negativity: Toward the Pluralisation of Critique in Educational Practice, Theory and Research," *Journal of Philosophy of Education*, 38, no. 3, 2004: 409–28.

[15] Without explicating the difference between reflection in the practice of teaching and in other professional practices, Schön does provide examples of reflection in teachers' practices that indicate that a teacher begins to reflect (and thereby potentially change her methods or materials of teaching) when she identifies a learner is having difficulty with learning the material at hand. See Schön, *The Reflective Practitioner*, for example, pp. 331–38. Such examples are in line with the argument I am making here, that teacher's interruptions in the experience of teaching are interconnected to learner's interruptions in their experience of learning.

is faced with a *choice* to change her teaching practice to facilitate learning for a particular learner. Although the teacher operating on a model of teaching-as-transmission may also experience an interruption – for example, a student may ask an unexpected question that indicates his or her confusion about the subject matter at hand – the aim of that teacher in addressing this interruption is to fill the learner's "gap" in knowledge with a predevised solution or answer. In this context, the learner's uncertainty or confusion – which points to the negativity of the learner's experience – is considered a sign of failure to learn, and not as an essential part of the learning process itself. On the model of *teaching-in-between* that I am developing here, the reflective teacher recognizes that the interruption in her experience indicates that she may need to modify her teaching method or the content of what is being taught, and direct it toward the needs of a particular learner who is now lost or stuck in an uncertain situation.

The notion of teaching-in-between is a way of describing reflective practice as it is unique to the profession of teaching or educating another human being. When a learner's experience is interrupted (thus initiating the learner's confusion or frustration and landing her in an indeterminate situation), a teacher's experience of teaching is also interrupted insofar as the teacher could not entirely foresee exactly when and how the learner would become frustrated with or confused by the material. The openings in the learner's learning process – the points of confusion and the like – provide openings for the teacher to teach in the spaces *between* a learner's given knowledge and what the learner is still trying to grasp, between the learner's given ability and what the learner is still figuring out how to do. According to the concept of teaching-in-between, these openings are points of orientation for the teacher to begin to reflectively question not only the learning process of that particular learner, but also her own process of teaching. Such self-questioning can include: "What is it that this learner does not yet understand?"; "What resources might I need to help the learner ask questions about how to get at the new and unfamiliar?"; "Have I considered that this learner may be seeing things in a way that I do not yet understand?"; "What questions can I ask this learner to understand where she is coming from?"; "Do I need to modify the aim of this task?"

These are just a few questions a teacher may think about. The point here is that the reflective teacher who teaches in-between recognizes the gray zones of thinking and learning as productive for the learner; in these gray zones, the learner can begin to think and ask questions. The aim for the teacher, then, is not merely to get the learner to a predetermined outcome, but to see that, in the process of a learner's interaction with the world, the desired outcome for this learner may change. This not only means that the teacher has to assess whether the learner has been over- or underchallenged, but also whether the aim of the challenge should be changed because the learner has brought in a perspective that the teacher did not previously foresee or imagine.

To clearly identify what is specific to teaching-in-between as a notion of reflective teaching, I return to the terminology surrounding Dewey's notion of reflective experiential learning processes discussed in Chapter 3. According to the notion of reflective teaching I present here, teaching orients itself on initiating and identifying prereflective and reflective-transformative beginnings of learning. Prereflective beginnings of learning are initiated by creating situations for learning in which learners can find themselves in uncertain "indeterminate" situations, begin to recognize their own limits, and begin to question given knowledge and understandings. To do this, the teacher must create situations for learning in which learners are productively interrupted and become uncertain. This occurs, for example, when learners begin to question whether they have found a contradiction between two readings about a historical event, when they become confused about the meaning of a poem, or when they are perplexed when asked to apply a math formula to a real-world problem. Reflective-transformative beginnings of learning are initiated when teachers support learners in asking questions and finding resources that serve to locate ways out of the indeterminate situation and into a problematic situation. To do this, teachers must support each learner's search for his or her unique problem of thought or understanding and encourage the learner's experimentation with various resolutions to this problem.

By initiating these beginnings of learning, the work of the reflective teacher resides in productively interrupting the learner in order to find ways to dwell in the in-between *with* the learner. This movement within the in-between of a learner's learning experience is difficult; it requires that the teacher not rush the learner to arrive at a predetermined outcome, but also not leave the learner settled in the comfort of existing knowledge and ability. The teacher who teaches in-between is thus always asking two central questions:

- Is the learner moving *between* her own prereflective beginning of learning toward a reflective-transformative beginning? Put another way, the teacher attempts to find out if the learner is asking questions about the nature of her own confusion, difficulty, or doubt – is the learner trying to explore the interruption in her experience?
- Is the learner moving *between* her own reflective-transformative beginning of learning and her determined solution or way out? Asking this

question means that the teacher attempts to determine whether the learner has transformed her initial confusion into a question that she is trying to answer.

This model of teaching (which I discuss further in the context of classroom practice in the next section) requires an understanding of teaching as productively interrupting the learner's learning process.[16] Only by means of an interruption can the learner enter into the realm of the in-between and seek out new perspectives and understandings of herself and the world.

But this idea that learning processes begin with an interruption in experience brings up a dilemma for the teacher: there is no way to predict exactly when and how a learner will be interrupted, will get lost and become uncertain, will locate a problem in thought or action, or will arrive at a solution. Thus, at each phase of the learner's learning process, moments occur when the teacher will be caught off guard, taken by surprise by the learner's questions, comments, ideas, and aims. Something *unexpected* will happen within the teacher-learner interaction that the teacher could not plan for or entirely foresee: at these moments, the teacher's experience is *interrupted*.

The deeper sense of being interrupted as a teacher can be understood with reference to philosopher Israel Scheffler's comment on the ambiguity of the term "unexpected."[17] He writes that "the concept of unexpectedness" could mean that something "has simply not been anticipated" but is still within the realm of the thinkable, or it could mean that something encountered was "positively ruled out by anticipation."[18] Although Scheffler is not referring to the experience of teachers, his distinction proves crucial to understanding the vital meaning of teaching as a reflective practice. These two "types" of encounters with the unexpected occur for the teacher and interrupt his or her experience of teaching in differing degrees. For example, a teacher may simply not anticipate that a particular learner who is learning fractions will be confused by the fact that although 8 is more than 4, 1/4 is greater than 1/8. That learners may have this difficulty is not unthinkable for the teacher, even though she did not expect that this particular student would have this difficulty. However, some encounters with the unexpected in the context of teaching are not foreseeable. A good example of this can be found in the documentary

---

[16] In Chapter 7, I elaborate on this notion of teaching, relating it to contemporary theories of teaching currently discussed in philosophy of education, and I provide a diagram showing the interaction between teacher and learner described here.

[17] Scheffler, "In Praise of the Cognitive Emotions," in *In Praise of the Cognitive Emotions: And Other Essays in the Philosophy of Education* (New York: Routledge, 2010).

[18] Ibid, p. 9.

on Matthew Lipman's Philosophy for Children entitled "Socrates for 6-Year-Olds."[19] In the film, a class of young children discuss whether we can think without a brain. A young girl, in retort to her fellow classmates who believe that it would be *impossible* to think without a brain, states, "I think it could be possible [to think] without your brain, because you have a heart and the heart can beat and it could think that it's beating."[20] The surprise a teacher might experience at such a thought from a learner demonstrates a form of interruption in teaching that stems from the newness of this learner's perspective, a newness existing outside the teacher's realm of the thinkable prior to this encounter.

When a teacher allows herself to be interrupted, this means that she is open to the learner as other: the teacher is open to the idea that the learner may be lost in a way that could never have been anticipated; the learner may present a perspective that the teacher had never considered; the learner may find a problem or a path to a problem that the teacher did not previously see as possible; or the learner may find an answer that the teacher could not have previously imagined. When a teacher is interrupted, she begins to think and enter into her own realm of the in-between as a teacher and thus can seek out new ways of teaching. Thus, in the moments of interruption, the teacher learns something *new*, something about the learner and about herself as a teacher. With Dewey we can say that, in these moments of teacher-student interaction, "the teacher is a learner, and the learner is, without knowing it, a teacher" (*DE* 167).

2 THE CLASSROOM: A SPACE FOR INTERRUPTING EXPERIENCE

Dewey's vision of the classroom as a space for learning provides a way of understanding how teachers can initiate educative reflective learning experiences. For Dewey, as I have stated, learning processes that promote thinking and inquiry cannot begin with a finished idea. Taken from the perspective of Dewey's theory of learning, we can say that such prepackaged "ideas" represent the finished learning processes of others. They can be considered the end or product of learning, but not the starting point. If the classroom is thus not a space for transferring or transmitting finished products to learners, then how are we to envision it? By viewing Dewey's critique of transmission-style teaching as not only identifying a *limit*, but simultaneously *a possibility* of

[19] *Socrates for Six Year Olds*, DVD, 1990, UK, produced by SAPERE, 2010.
[20] *Socrates for Six Year Olds*, 11:49–11:57.

what the teacher is capable of, then we can understand the classroom as a space for teaching in a new way. Although teachers cannot directly transfer ideas to students, teachers *can* and *should* create environments in which learners can discover their own new ideas. On my account, this entails envisioning the classroom as a space for *interrupting* students' experiences. Here, I consider two important aspects of such a space: the role of difficulty and the role of learning by doing.

For Dewey, each individual must engage in his or her own learning process in order to come to a *new* idea – an idea that may not be new for the teacher, but is new for the learner – and such engagement requires encounters with "difficulty." The traditional classroom setting of rows of desks facing forward is, for Dewey, symbolic of the type of learning based in passive listening. The learner is required to absorb what he or she hears or reads and thus absorb a series of prepackaged truths determined to be worthwhile by the school and teacher. In Dewey's vision, the classroom is a space for learner's direct experience of perplexity, frustration, and confusion, not ready-made or mock problems. Through the real encounter with *genuine* problems based in prereflective interruptions, the learner can uncover the limits of her thought, knowledge, and ability. The learner learns only when she can discover her own limits and seek new ways of dealing with the negativity of her experience. In the context of a plea for genuine problems of learning, Dewey poses a critical question to educators regarding the creation of classroom learning environments: "What is there [in schoolrooms] that is similar to the conditions of everyday life which will generate real difficulties?" (*DE* 162; see also *DE* 169 and 188).

Dewey's call for a connection between the classroom and the everyday life of the child is not to say that the classroom is a space for reiterating everyday life experiences. Rather, he is suggesting that when there is a space for direct experience and doing, then this space generates opportunities for the learner to undergo the world, to experience disruption with what he or she knows or does, and thus be interrupted by the other (this directly relates to the connection between doing and undergoing drawn out in Chapter 3). In this sense, Dewey's focus on real difficulties connects to his underlying learning-theoretical claim that all learning involves a struggle.[21] The struggle incites

---

[21] On this point in Dewey, see the argument for changing our conception of what we deem mistakes in education in Nathaniel Klemp, Ray McDermott, Jason Raley, Matthew Thibeault, Kimberly Powell, and Daniel J. Levitin, "Plans, Takes and Mis-Takes," *Critical Social Studies*, 10, 2008: 4–21; without directly connecting to Dewey, Spychiger et al. also argue that schools must develop a space for making mistakes; see Maria Spychiger, Fritz Oser, Tina Hascher, and Fabienne Mahler, "Entwicklung einer Fehlerkultur in der Schule" [Developing 'A Culture of Error'

independent thought, so that the learner can begin to think on his own about the situations of uncertainty that he encounters. Accordingly, only those forms of thought that arise in the context of a struggle can be part of educative learning processes:

Only by wrestling with the conditions of the problem at first hand, seeking and finding his way out, does he think . . . If he cannot devise his own solution . . . and find his own way out he will not learn, not even if he can recite some correct answer with one hundred per cent accuracy.[22]

This *struggle*, in which learners seek their own way out of perplexing situations, is an indispensable aspect of all reflective learning processes; it is constitutive of learning.[23]

But what is the teacher's role in this process of the learner's struggle? What might it mean to create difficulty for a learner, to create struggle? The teacher is not a passive bystander, even though his or her role is limited because, as I stated before, interruptions in a learner's experience cannot be planned. Neither the learner nor the teacher can be certain when the learner will be interrupted and enter into an uncertain "indeterminate" situation. This is precisely the point: *The classroom is a space for discovering at what point a student will be interrupted in his or her interaction with the new objects and ideas encountered therein.* The classroom must be viewed as a place for learning processes to productively begin with prereflective experiences. This is precisely why, on Dewey's model, "doing" must be the starting point for learning in classroom learning environments.

Although Dewey's emphasis on activity and his call for situations of "learning by doing" is well known, it is less well considered that this call

in Schools] in *Fehlerwelten-vom Fehlermachen und Lernen aus Fehlern* [Worlds of Error – On Making and Learning from Mistakes], edited by Wolfgang Althof, pp. 43–70 (Opladen: Leske und Budrich, 1999). This also relates to the argument of learning as painful, involving learning *that* we do not know and *what* we do not know; see Maria Spychiger and Fritz Oser, *Lernen ist Schmerzhaft. Zur Theorie der Fehlerkultur und zur Praxis des Negativen Wissens.* (Learning is Painful. The Theory of "A Culture of Error" and the Practice of Negative Knowledge) (Weinheim: Beltz, 2005).

[22] *DE* 167; see also *DE* 188.

[23] Philosopher of education Paul Standish makes the interesting point that the tradition of liberal education as developed in the Anglophone tradition by R. S. Peters and others, although correct in certain criticisms of strongly child-centered education, has overlooked the importance of gaining knowledge by direct acquaintance, which led to overlooking the connection between knowing a subject well and understanding how it "resists" us. As Standish suggests, to be familiar with something, or to have learned, involves knowing "the characteristic kinds of resistance that [the material one works with] presents", that is, the problems it could present to us under certain circumstances; Paul Standish, "Moral Education, Liberal Education and the Voice of the Individual," in *Education in the Era of Globalization*, edited by Klas Roth and Ilan Gur-Ze'ev, pp. 33–50, 48–49 (Dordrecht: Springer, 2007).

implies that teachers are creating the possibility for learners to encounter prereflective discontinuities in experience. To create situations for a learner to actively engage with the subject matter of learning means that the learner is presented with something "new (hence uncertain or problematic)," and yet "connected to existing habits," to call out a response that is beyond the "routine or capricious" (*DE* 161). The teacher is thus creating an environment for learners to undergo the world and struggle through their encounters with new objects, new ideas, and new ways of interacting with others.

The significance of Dewey's connection between learning and active "doing in the world" can be illustrated with an example from Rousseau's *Emile*. Rousseau advises educators to allow the child to learn how to make judgments about the world on his or her own. Rousseau relates in an example that such direct learning necessarily involves making mistakes:

If, for example, [Emile] is deceived about the appearance of the broken stick, and to show him his error you are in a hurry to pull the stick out of the water, you will perhaps undeceive him. But what will you teach him? Nothing but what he would soon have learned by himself. Oh, it is not that which has to be done! The goal is less to teach him a truth than to show him how he must always go about discovering the truth. In order to instruct him better, you must not undeceive him so soon.[24]

In a way that seems to influence Dewey, Rousseau is demonstrating that, as human beings, we must experience certain forms of negative experience (such as perplexity) based in our own effort to engage with the world; only then do we learn of our own limits and abilities. Philosopher of education David Hansen emphasizes this point when he writes that Dewey, like Rousseau, advocates the learner's self-activity, pointing to the fact that both thinkers promote indirect teaching.[25] Hansen underscores that indirect teaching for Rousseau entails creating an educational setting that teaches learners "that there are limits to their powers."[26] Hansen's point is significant; it tells us that learners cannot find such limits when teachers try to transfer ideas directly to learners. Rather, learners must be "active" in order to find and define such limits for themselves.

---

[24] Jean-Jacques Rousseau, *Emile or On Education*, translated and edited by Allan Bloom, p. 205. (New York: Basic Books, 1979).

[25] David T. Hansen, *Exploring the Moral Heart of Teaching: Toward a Teacher's Creed*, p. 65 (New York: Teachers College Press, 2001).

[26] Ibid, p. 65 ; see also Avi I. Mintz, "The Happy and Suffering Student? Rousseau's Emile and the Path Not Taken in Progressive Educational Thought," *Educational Theory*, 62, no. 3, 2012: 249–65.

To take this idea further, we can say that the central point of Dewey's thought on "doing" in learning is that situations of actively doing are necessary so that the learner can experience discontinuity – which may take the form of frustration, perplexity, doubt, and the like. Only when teachers create learning environments that support learners' own active interaction with the material of learning will the learner encounter prereflective discontinuity of experience – encounters that open up possibilities for reflective thought. For Dewey, only by means of prereflective experiences – that is, by means of undergoing the world on account of an interruption – can learners run up against and recognize their own limitations and, in turn, reflectively seek to address them.

This point is relevant to the theory of teaching that I am advancing here for two central reasons. First, when we understand the classroom as a space for actively doing, then, as educators, we need to recognize that the reason for such activity is to provide learners with a space to encounter difficulty and *choose* to learn. Such choice involves the reflective transformation of one's own encounter with the new in a way that leads beyond the "trial-and-error" mode of experience of everyday life. Only insofar as "learning by doing" initiates "real difficulties" in the learner's experiences does it serve as the starting point for reflective learning processes in classroom settings. Thus, significantly, as Dewey scholar Meinert Meyer explains, "the slogan 'learning by doing' does not mean Dewey is of the opinion that a person learns *just* by doing. Rather the idea is a command: Learning is to be constructed such that that which is happening around us and what one does oneself, makes increasingly richer experiences possible."[27] Learning by doing thus describes neither the aim of learning nor its general method, but rather a starting point for those types of learning processes that can initiate reflective learning processes in the classroom.

Second, the significance of prereflective interruptions in classroom learning is that the prereflective discontinuity in a learner's experience is not only a starting point for the learner; it is also a starting point for the *teacher*. For the learner, the prereflective interruption in experience represents a starting point of the learning process; the learner enters an in-between realm of learning and

---

[27] Meinert A. Meyer, "John Deweys Vorstellungen bezüglich der Inhalte des Unterrichts – Eine Untersuchung zur Historischen Curriculumtheorie" [John Dewey's Idea of the Content of Instruction: An Investigation of Historical Curriculum Theory], in *Modernisierung von Rahmenrichtlinien*, edited by J. Keuffer, pp. 49–80, p. 57 (Weinheim: Deutscher Studien Verlag, 1997), translation mine, emphasis mine; see also Meinert A. Meyer, "Stichwortartikel: Alte oder Neue Lernkultur" [Keyword: Old or New Learning Culture], *Zeitschrift für Erziehungswissenschaft*, 1, 2005: 5–27.

has the chance to reflectively engage the interruption in his or her experience (as I described in Chapter 3). For the teacher, the learner's prereflective interruption in experience is a starting point for teaching in the form that I call *teaching in-between*. Thus, the learner's interruption in experience tells the teacher where an *opening* exists in the learner's experience for a reflective learning process to unfold. When a learner is interrupted, the teacher learns, at least tentatively, where the learner needs to go next in the learning process. The teacher learns, in Dewey's words, to understand the learner's "needs and capacities" that emerge in the "interplay" with the subject matter of learning (*DE* 191). That is, the teacher learns what questions the learner has, what questions the learner still needs to ask of herself, and what resources the learner may need to answer those questions.

However, by identifying a learner's interruption in experience as the starting point for both learner and teacher, I do not seek to imply that the learner and teacher are experiencing or proceeding from this starting point in the same way. Whereas the learner is asking herself, "What happened?," "What went wrong?," "Why am I confused?," the teacher is asking, "How do I support this learner's learning process?," "How do I cultivate this learner's experience of difficulty or perplexity so that she begins to reflect and transform her uncertainty into a question or problem into which she can inquire?" In theoretical terms, the teacher is asking herself, "How to I support the learner in transforming her prereflective beginning of learning into a reflective-transformative beginning of learning?"

But what kind of difficulties, what kind of interruptions, allow for such openings? So far, we have not answered this question. Just as it is important to recognize the need for creating situations that present the learner with difficulty, it is equally important to qualify what counts as an *educative* difficulty. Dewey underscores that educators must seriously consider the nature of the difficulty that the learner is encountering. He writes that, although "a difficulty is an indispensable stimulus to thinking," significantly "not all difficulties call out thinking. Sometimes they overwhelm and submerge and discourage" (*DE* 163). Dewey's distinction here is indispensable to understanding the teacher's task in creating an environment for learning: only those difficulties that "call out thinking" are pedagogically legitimate.[28]

---

[28] With Egon Schütz, one can argue against a narrow behaviorist conception of Dewey's concept of a situation. Schütz explains that "if Dewey understood the phenomena of the situation merely as a pattern of stimulus-response and saw in this pattern a causal necessity, to which man was helplessly subjected, then it would not be possible for Dewey to grant the teacher influence on the objective conditions of educative situations" (p. 199). As he goes on to emphasize, the educational situation for Dewey is, however, "a situation of extraordinary influence." See Egon Schütz, *Freiheit und*

Those difficulties (or other forms of negative experience, such as perplexity, confusion, etc.) that overwhelm the learner and hinder thinking cannot be considered part of educative learning environments that support reflective learning processes. In this sense, Dewey considers "the art of instruction" as the art of finding the sort of difficulties that make "new problems large enough to challenge thought, and small enough so that, in addition to the confusion naturally attending the novel elements, there shall be luminous familiar spots from which helpful suggestions may spring" (DE 164).

One might ask: What about continuity? Should teachers not be concerned with the continuity of learning? Dewey's aim, in my view, is to demonstrate that *if* a learner does not have the discontinuity of her own experience – her own perplexities, resistance, or existential uncertainty – as her reference point, then the connections or continuities that the learner establishes through thought cannot truly be her own. In other words, as I emphasized in Chapter 3, reflective thought, sparked by the discontinuity of experience, creates continuities or connections out of what has been experienced in the world as discontinuous. In this sense, we can understand Dewey's emphasis in "Experience and Education" on *two* principles of educative experiences: continuity (or experiential continuum) and interaction.[29] Continuity connects our formation of attitudes or habits, but Dewey reiterates that the principle of continuity connotes change (not stagnation or merely fixed habit formation): "The principle of continuity of experience means that every experience both takes up something from those which have gone before and modifies in some way the quality of those which come after."[30] This change has a transformative effect, in that "every experience enacted and undergone modifies the one who acts and undergoes, while this modification affects, whether we wish it or not, the quality of subsequent experiences. For it is a somewhat different person who enters into them."[31]

These two principles of educative experiences are indispensable to one another for Dewey. The principle of continuity rests on the fact that we have *interacted* with the world (and are continuing to interact with it). This interaction is defined as an "interplay" of "objective and internal conditions," or an interplay between self and

---

Bestimmung. Sinntheoretische Reflexionen zum Bildungsproblem (Freedom and Determination: Theoretical Reflections on the Problem of Bildung), p. 203 (Ratingen: Henn, 1975).

[29] John Dewey, "Experience and Education (1938)," in *The Later Works*, edited by Jo Ann Boydston, Vol. 13, pp. 1–62, 10 and 17 (Carbondale: Southern Illinois University Press, 2008).

[30] Ibid., p. 19.

[31] Ibid., p. 18; on educative experiences, see also James Garrison, "John Dewey's Philosophy as Education," in *Reading Dewey. Interpretations for a Postmodern Generation*, edited by Larry Hickman, pp. 66–68. (Indianapolis: Indiana University Press, 1998).

world.[32] Equally true for Dewey is that the principle of interaction rests on the fact that something has been reflectively "taken up" from prior experience into the new experience. Interaction with the world allows us to gather the material for reflective thinking; the continuum of experience established by reflective thinking changes our framework of anticipations and thereby changes our perspective on what is possible and what is desirable. Thus, with Garrison's emphasis that, for Dewey, "interaction" is meaningless "in itself" (i.e., without continuity),[33] it can be equally emphasized that establishing continuity without interaction in the world is also meaningless (if not impossible).

If teachers are to help learners understand the connections and continuities of forms of knowledge and experience, it is *not* by manufacturing a linear step-by-step model of progression from ignorance to new knowledge and ability. Rather, it is by cultivating educative reflective experiences, mediated by the discontinuity and negativity of experience. What Dewey refers to as a "miseducative experience" is "any experience ... that has the effect of arresting or distorting the growth of further experience."[34] These are had in those classrooms that fail to initiate difficulties that *call out thinking* and that fail to allow the learner's *individual* difficulties to arise from her interaction with the world and others; such classrooms thereby fail to encourage the learner's reflective engagement with such difficulties. These environments fail to provide opportunities for the learner's reflection to be initiated by engaging and undergoing the world in a way that changes the learner's perspective on herself and the world. Environments that do provide such opportunities enable learners to discover the connections between things and also enable them to create new connections.

Thus, the sharp dichotomy between Dewey's idea of the classroom and traditional models of the classroom is found in the role given to a learner's experience of difficulty – more specifically, in the role given to *educative experiences of discontinuity* in learning. With Dewey scholar Fritz Bohnsack, this central difference can be stated in the following way: whereas the traditional school orients learning on "the bit by bit anorectic force-feeding of unsolicited chunks of knowledge," Dewey views "thinking and learning" as arising "out of the need stemming from a [learner's] encounter with a

---

[32] Dewey, "Experience and Education," p. 25. Dewey uses the term *interaction* here, although in other contexts he uses *transaction* to refer to the same interplay of self and world. I will continue to use interaction.

[33] Garrison, "John Dewey's Philosophy as Education," p. 67–68.

[34] Dewey, *Experience and Education*, p. 11.

difficulty, [and his] reflection upon the best way towards its overcoming."[35] As we saw in Dewey's learning theory (discussed in Chapter 3), difficulty arises from an encounter with the unexpected – an interruption in experience. The aim of creating situations for interruption in learning environments is not to leave learners stuck in the in-between, stuck without any way to discover "luminous familiar spots" that move them beyond the interruption in experience.

In attempting to convey completed thoughts to learners, traditional education leaves no room for learners' direct experiences – it leaves no room for interruptions in experience from which genuine problems arise for the learner. Without this personal experience of *undergoing*, which is expressed in difficulty, frustration, and alienation, learners do not acquire the inquisitive attitude connected to forming what Dewey calls "reflective habits." Rather, they only acquire a strategic attitude toward learning that is aimed at figuring out how to answer the teacher's question *without* making that question their own (*DE* 163). On this view, the learner is considered a "pupil," that is, a student who is absorbing prepackaged information for memorization. Without encountering genuine difficulties arising from direct experience, "the pupil's problems are not his; or, rather, they are his *only as* a pupil, not as a human being" (*DE* 163). In this way, for Dewey, traditional schooling facilitates strategic forms of learning aiming to quickly arrive at right answers; however, it does not facilitate the sort of transformation of self and world that we encounter as human beings through lived experiences.

The classroom, in my view, must be seen as a space for both teacher and learner to discover what the learner knows and is able to do, as well as what she does not yet know and is not yet able to do; simultaneously, the classroom must provide the learner with opportunities to question what she thinks and knows through her encounters with the otherness of the world. In this context, "not knowing" or "ignorance" is not the enemy of knowledge. Rather, we can consider it "the inevitable shadow of knowledge."[36] Such notions of connections between knowledge and ignorance, ability and inability, entail an understanding of teaching in which the teacher is open to

---

[35] Fritz Bohnsack, *Demokratie als erfülltes Leben. Die Aufgabe von Schule und Erziehung. Ausgewählte und kommentierte Aufsätze unter Berücksichtigung der Pädagogik John Deweys* [Democracy as Fulfilled Life: The Task of School and Education. Selected Essays, with Commentary on John Dewey's Pedagogy], p. 33 (Bad Heilbrunn: Klinkhardt, 2003), translation mine.

[36] Nigel Blake, Paul Smeyers, Richard Smith, and Paul Standish, *Education in the Age of Nihilism*, p. 210 (London: Routledge, 2000). See their chapter on "Taking Ignorance Seriously" for a further discussion.

exploring the gray areas of learning with the learner. For such exploration to take place in a fruitful way, the teacher must recognize that there may be unknowns in what the learner knows, and there may be knowns in what the learner does not to yet know. To teach in-between, teachers must be open to discovering the possibilities that lie within this experimental realm of learning; if teachers do not view the interruptions in a learner's experience as openings, then it is difficult (if not impossible) for learners to see these as openings.

Teachers *close* the openings in learner's experiences (without necessarily recognizing them as openings) when they merely tell the learners what they *should* know and then test for successful or failed knowledge acquisition. On such models, the school and the teacher are implicitly asking learners to passively accept the judgments of others, judgments concerning both the worthwhile content of instruction as well as what is deemed right and wrong in epistemological and moral terms. They are not asking learners to think critically about their relations between self and world, or, in Dewey's terms, between doing and undergoing. The productive questioning of one's own self-understanding, as well as one's understanding of the world, occurs when learners are provided with opportunities to be interrupted by the new and engage in a struggle with the new in a way that incites confusion, doubt, or uncertainty, but also the excitement of inquiry.

3   TEACHING AS A MORAL TASK

Reflective teaching must entail creating an environment that cultivates difficulties that "call out thinking" and supports learners' struggles to engage these difficulties – that is, to engage the negativity and discontinuity of their experiences. In this view, teaching in-between is a moral task in the sense that it aims to teach learners to think and choose to learn from the other. Teaching in-between makes us ask critical questions about the environment we are creating for learning: Do these conditions foster an environment in which learners are challenged to discover the limits of their own knowledge and ability through interruptions in experience? Do these environments provide learners with the necessary resources to reflectively inquire into and transform the uncertain situations they have landed in? According to this concept of teaching in-between, teaching does not amount to simply feeding learners into a certain system of existing practices, behaviors, or beliefs. Rather, it entails encouraging and motivating learners to think critically about ways to move beyond the status quo, to attempt to change it via experimental practice, and to continually discover the new – and its constitutive negativity – in thinking and practice.

Dewey views reflective experience as a way of being in the world that is distinct from moral understandings that bind morality to particular conduct, independent of mode, or which bind morality to principles of action, independent of the consequences of action. Dewey instead connects morality to the process of experience. This process involves the interaction between thought and action, in which both the self *and* the world change. This process of experience follows the method of reflective experience, which is, for Dewey, the only productive method of searching and finding action-oriented ways of dealing with the discontinuity and negativity of experience. It is a path that we wander along and that allows us to change our habits by encountering new and unfamiliar objects and ideas that indicate to us that the value of our fixed habits need to be called into question. Dewey's notion of learning as reflective experience thus takes on moral meaning; it forms the basis of what might be called an experimental morality that is neither moral absolutism nor moral subjectivity. Experimental morality seeks out prereflective negativity of experience in order to learn from otherness.

Reflective experience connects to morality insofar as it informs us of the path we traveled to come to a particular consequence. This awareness of the path gives us the opportunity to change ourselves, the conditions of our actions, or both the next time we engage with the world and others.[37] Thus, reflective experience for Dewey is the method that *connects intelligence and character*. It is akin to what he deems the *experimental* method of intelligence, which grounds his philosophy of education. The experimental method of intelligence makes the experimental nature of human thought and action into a conscious aspect of all decisions to act: "it takes honest account of the fact of contingency ... [It] thus teaches us how to deal with doubt."[38]

Forms of teaching that support the learner's awareness of the path of reflective experiences also cultivate the learner's "reflective habit," that is, the habit of *making reflection a habit*. In this way, teaching is cultivating the learner's ability to choose to learn rather than just the ability to learn something specific. On Dewey's model; moral education is not simply a series of lessons about morals; it does not amount to teaching particular virtues and duties. Rather, moral education involves supporting learners' experiences

---

[37] Compare *DE* 280 ff; see also John Dewey and John L. Childs, "The Underlying Philosophy of Education (1933)," *The Later Works*, edited by Jo Ann Boydston, Vol. 8, pp. 77–103 (Carbondale: Southern Illinois University Press, 2008).

[38] Dewey and Childs, "The Underlying Philosophy of Education," p. 95; see also p. 89 and pp. 92–94.

of self and world toward becoming self-questioning beings. Douglas Simpson, Michael Jackson, and Judy Aycock note that the artistry of the teacher, for Dewey, lies in the teacher's ability to transform the student's "inclinations and interests" into "intelligently conceived and planned purposes."[39] This entails "knowing when and how to get the student to stop and consider the consequences of thinking, feeling, and behaving in certain ways," that is, to "stop and think."[40]

By engaging learners so that they are interrupted by the world and *stop and think* – not only in situations of direct moral concern, but in all areas of knowledge and learning – teachers play an essential role in learners' development of moral selfhood, of the ability to recognize and learn from the experience of the other. From the dilemmas of an ethic of duty or an ethic of interest, Dewey draws a conclusion that connects learning theory and ethics: anyone who acts according to principle in ignorance of a given difficulty does not know how to "learn from experience" (*DE* 363). On this account, *learning from experience* means explicitly addressing and analyzing the negativity of one's experience (by analyzing the given difficulty or perplexity), seeking to understand it as a sign of the necessity to reorient action, and finding new solutions for problems one has identified. It is in this vein that Dewey asserts that one who is truly interested in doing his duty is one who is "able to stand temporary discouragement, to persist in the face of obstacles, to take the lean with the fat: he makes an interest out of meeting and overcoming difficulties and distractions" (*DE* 363).

The concept of "learning from experience," which Dewey also calls "plasticity," demarcates Dewey's concept of perfectibility (or *Bildsamkeit* for Herbart, as I discussed in Chapter 1). Plasticity is not to be understood as a simplistic idea of growth determined from without (*DE* 57-58). Rather, as Dewey scholar Naoko Saito underscores, it is growth without a final end; Dewey's concept of plasticity is ateleological.[41] As Cuffaro emphasizes, for Dewey, "plasticity is the ability to retain from one experience that which will be of use in coping with the difficulties and newness of later situations. It is the

---

[39] Douglas J. Simpson, Michael J. B. Jackson, and Judy C. Aycock, *John Dewey and the Art of Teaching: Toward Reflective and Imaginative Practice* p. 20 (London: Sage Publications Inc., 2005).

[40] Ibid., p. 21.

[41] Compare Naoko Saito, *The Gleam of Light: Moral Perfectionism and Education in Dewey and Emerson*, p. 140 (New York: Fordham University Press, 2005). Saito specifically speaks of Dewey's ateleological concept of growth and "the idea of perfection without final perfectibility" (p. 140). But it should be noted that Saito uses the term "perfectibility" slightly differently than I am using it. Her term "perfection" is in line with how I have been using the term "perfectibility" (and related terms "plasticity" or *Bildsamkeit*).

ability to modify and coordinate actions on the basis of results gained in other experiences."[42] Plasticity or perfectibility points to the grounding interplay of self and world; it says that the essence of what it means to be human is that we can always learn from newness, from the unfamiliar, from otherness, and become "instructed" by the other:

To "learn from experience" is to make a backward and forward connection between what we do to things and what we enjoy or suffer from things in consequence. Under such conditions, doing becomes a trying; an experiment with the world to find out what it is like; the undergoing becomes instruction – discovery of the connection of things.[43]

By learning to address interruptions in experience, learners learn to recognize the other in all realms of life.

If, as educators, we overlook the moments of interruption in learner's experiences or judge these as bad and as signs of failure, we gravely miss Dewey's point. In *Art as Experience* (1934), Dewey's remarks on the value of moments of resistance in our experience:

Life itself consists of phases in which the organism falls out of step with the march of surrounding things and then recovers unison with it – either through effort or by some happy chance. And, in a growing life, the recovery is never mere return to a prior state, for it is enriched by the state of disparity and resistance through which it has successfully passed. If the gap between organism and environment is too wide, the creature dies. If its activity is not enhanced by the temporary alienation, it merely subsists.[44]

Taken as a warning to educators, Dewey's remarks tell us not to forget that the experience of limitation is an inherent part of the human being's capacity for self-transformation. What Dewey refers to as falling out of step, disparity, resistance, and alienation reveals itself to have both productive and destructive meaning. If learners are left to deal with moments of limitation on their own, without educators or guides, they may remain feeling overwhelmed or submerged, without the possibility for educative transformation. In this case, undergoing the world becomes destructive, and not productive or educative, because the learner remains lost. Equally true, however, is that if learners do not experience the sort of alienation felt on account of the interruption of an encounter with the world, they merely sustain themselves without change or growth (*alienation* here implies not only an estrangement from our

---

[42] Cuffaro, *Experimenting with the World*, p. 17.
[43] DE 147.
[44] AE 19–20.

environment, which is not responding to us in ways we expected, but also an alienation from self). Thus, *doing* must also be enhanced by *undergoing* and reflecting on the connections between the two. Dewey's criticism of persons who just "do" by following routine and fixed habits without the change of falling out of step is a criticism of the egoist, who Herbart also warned against, the one who cannot or refuses to learn from the other. Such a person does not live in a way that entails seeking out ways to learn from otherness and contribute to ideas of the new within the social realm.

4 DEMOCRACY AND THE END OF EDUCATION

Dewey views reflective experience and learning as simultaneously leading to and providing a medium for democracy. His concept of democracy calls for the critical examination of both the extent to which every individual's experiences with the world and with others are mediated by the negativity of experience in all areas of human practice and the extent to which the results of each individual's learning processes are allowed to influence decisions about the future of the community. In light of his view of the central role of what I have called discontinuity and negativity of experience in education, we can locate a central connection between education and democracy, one that concerns learning. Specifically, Dewey's critical notion of democracy can be conceived as a measure for determining whether *reflective experiential learning processes* are helped or hindered in any particular area of practice.

Dewey's quest to make democracy be seen not merely as a political system but "as a way of life" (*DE* 93) goes hand in hand with his quest to make education be seen not merely as the transmission of predetermined knowledge and skills but as the transformation of self. Both education and democracy evolve and grow through exchanges among human beings who have the option of seeing the world otherwise. A self-determined, critically thinking human being is one who can imagine alternatives – an idea that Herbart sees in the multifaceted person. As Maxine Greene eloquently states, "When people cannot name alternatives, imagine a better state of things, share with others a project of change, they are likely to remain anchored or *submerged*, even as they proudly assert their autonomy."[45]

For Dewey, as I stated earlier, *mis*educative experiences overwhelm, submerge, and thus hinder a person from transformations of self and world. As philosopher of education Egon Schütz describes, the task of a Deweyan view

---

[45] Maxine Greene, *The Dialectic of Freedom*, p. 9 (New York: Teachers College Press, 1988), emphasis mine.

of education is to "awaken and encourage" a person's capacity for self-transformation, a capacity Schütz refers to as a person's ability "to transformatively reposition oneself to the world" (*Umzudisponieren*).[46] Such change and self-transformation resulting from varied interactions between members of society with diverse interests, opinions, and varied experiences of the new and unfamiliar are accordingly only possible in open – namely, democratic – societies. Democratic forms of society, in the Deweyan sense, are created in such a way that they continually provide individuals with new opportunities for acting in and *undergoing* the world by interacting with it in new ways. As Sydney Hook emphasizes, democratic societies create "a richness of co-operating diversities that contrasts sharply with the fixed patterns stamped on the minds, even on the bodies, of individuals in regimented societies."[47] Furthermore, as democratic forms of society enable new means for social interaction, they in turn permit new forms of perplexities, frustrations, and resistance – new forms of discontinuity in experience – to present possibilities for renewed learning processes.

Forms of teaching and educating that are oriented on cultivating discontinuity as a productive moment in learning processes prepare individuals for critical participation in democratic ways of life, without attempting to form particular positivist concepts of citizenship. This requires a notion of democratic education that, as Roland Reichenbach states, reflects the ambiguity of the outcomes of educational processes and thus [is] understood, in accordance with John Dewey, as "experimental."[48] On this account, processes of education reflect the openness of democratic communities in that they are "processes of transformation with unknown outcomes," not teleological "processes of perfection."[49] Reichenbach makes clear that what is characteristic of democratic forms of living is their ability to foster an environment open to the "*possibility* of self-deception."[50] As I defined in the foregoing chapters, to be open to self-deception means that individual members of the community are open to discontinuity and negativity of experience in

---

[46] Egon Schütz, *Freiheit und Bestimmung*, p. 212, translation mine.

[47] Sydney Hook, *John Dewey: An Intellectual Portrait* (1939), p. 224 (Westport, CT: Greenwood Press, 1971).

[48] Roland Reichenbach, "On Irritation and Transformation: A-Teleological Bildung and its Significance for the Democratic Form of Living," *Journal of Philosophy of Education*, 36, no. 3, 2002: 409–19, 412–13; see also 417.

[49] Reichenbach, "On Irritation and Transformation," p. 411; on this point, see also Bohnsack, "Demokratie als erfülltes Leben," p. 23, and Fritz Bohnsack, *Erziehung zur Demokratie: John Deweys Pädagogik und Ihre Bedeutung für die Reform unserer Schule*, p. 72–78 (Ravensburg: Otto Maier Verlag, 1976).

[50] Reichenbach, "On Irritation and Transformation," p. 417.

individual and social experiences – they are open to fallibility, to the experience of disillusionment and interruption that occurs when arriving at individual and social limits of thought and ability.

Education can change the way individuals can participate in society when it provides them with the means and experiences to choose the other and to choose the otherness within themselves – that is, to reflect upon themselves and their relation to the world and, on that basis, make decisions for action. The aim, then, of such education is to support individuals in their process of confrontation with the new so that they begin to see opportunities to seek out the challenges accompanying encounters with the new and unfamiliar.[51] On this view, it is the right and duty of members of democratic communities to engage in dialogue with one another, in order to seek out possible misconceptions and false judgments. For the investigation into misconceptions and misjudgments to be educative, it must be promoted by forms of education and educational institutions that recognize the experiences of doubt, fear, or frustration – or more broadly, discontinuity and negativity of experience – as constitutive of all human learning processes. It is precisely such experiences that incite learners to engage in critical self-reflection, to begin the search for new habits, new thoughts, and new modes of action, and to initiate processes of self-transformation.

---

[51] On this point, see Richard Bernstein, *John Dewey*, p. 105 (New York: Washington Square Press, 1966). Hilary Putnam connects the idea of seeking out challenges and difficulty to Peirce's pragmatism, when he writes, "Before Karl Popper was even born, Peirce emphasized that very often ideas will not be falsified unless we go out and actively *seek* falsifying experiences. Ideas must be put under strain, if they are to prove their worth; and Dewey and James both followed Peirce in this respect," in Hilary Putnam, *Pragmatism: An Open Question*, p. 71 (Wiley-Blackwell, 1995).

Chapter 5

Conclusion: Morality, Democracy, and Pluralist Society

1 DEWEY: A BREAK IN THE HISTORY OF EDUCATIONAL PHILOSOPHY?

Both Herbart and Dewey begin their reflection on education with a critical question: Wherein lies the real possibility of education that promotes self-determination? For both authors, education toward self-determination presupposes forms of learning that are mediated by perplexity, confusion, disillusionment, and self-critique. Furthermore, both thinkers recognize that the ways out of seemingly aporetic and question-filled situations cannot be predetermined by the educator; rather, these must always be sought and found by the learner herself.

In the previous four chapters, I have sought to make clear that Herbart's and Dewey's concepts of education are connected in that they both distance these concepts from indoctrination and dogmatic-absolutist concepts of teaching. Although education must always contend with the paradox that self-determination is cultivated through determination by another, dogmatic forms of teaching seek to determine the learner in a way that makes her dependent on the judgments of others, not self-determined and critical. However, despite their critiques of such concepts, neither Herbart nor Dewey goes so far as to say that we should give up on the possibility of education. Rather, they each develop concepts of education and teaching that are oriented on the critical and self-reflective experiences of learners. They delimit ways for educative interactions to occur between teacher and learner that aim at creating paths for the learner to reflect on the limits of her interaction with the world – her difficulties, problems, or uncertainty – and engage in productive interplay with the discontinuity and negativity of experience.

The task of the educator, for Herbart as well as for Dewey, is found in identifying and developing ways for learners to recognize and respond to the other in judgments and actions. Teachers and learners working together can seek out ways for responsible, self-determined interaction with the world through experimental learning processes that take account of the dimension of the unknown future. Such learning processes are not aimed at one particular outcome and, as such, must reflect the fact that the new, other, unfamiliar, and unexpected are constitutive of all learning processes; the negativity of our experience of encounters with the new and unexpected should not be ignored, but rather directly engaged.

Using the concept of discontinuity and negativity of experience, I have drawn out underlying connections between the theories of Herbart and Dewey. Both authors recognize moments of negativity in the learning processes of both teachers and learners; both assign the moment of discontinuity of experience an indispensable, meaning in that it can make one aware of the limits of one's own previous thought and experience in a way that points to the need for the expansion of one's horizons of thought and experience; and both interpret the significance of negative experiences, such as doubt or struggle, as pointing to the fact that customary and habitual modes of action can never prove to have unlimited application – there is always a chance we will encounter something new that cannot be accommodated by established concepts and habits.

Essential to such an understanding of education is the idea that both teachers and learners must develop a critical self-relation through which old ways of interacting with the world can be analyzed and problematized and new modes can be drafted. Both Herbart and Dewey underscore the idea that the whole of education takes on moral meaning in that it aims to support learners' ability to "pause" and cultivate their ability to acquire a self-critical relation to their own ideas, motives, and experiences. For teachers to be able to support learners' ability to reflect, critique, and analyze the negativity of their experiences, teachers themselves must learn to reflect, analyze, and critique the experiences they have with learners. This is a task of teacher education that I address further in Part Two.

From these authors' works, I have developed the notion that the experience of discontinuity – an encounter with the other that interrupts our flow of thought and action – opens up an in-between realm for new, fruitful learning processes. We find in these moments that our customary mode of action and our dulled routines of thought have reached a – perhaps initially indescribable – limit: we are in-between, we have not yet arrived at a zone of thought and action that allows for renewed freedom of movement. This *in-between* is an opening, a space, for experimenting with different relations between theory and practice. Experimentation offers us a way to reorient ourselves toward the existing predicaments and seemingly aporetic situations that have entangled us. To admit the necessity of experimental practice in the in-between is to admit that, despite our newly revised expectations, the world and others can surprise us, interrupt us, and force us into a new in-between. To admit the necessity of experimental practice is also to admit that a simple return to the old way of doing things cannot possibly satisfy our need to break out of the old, reflect upon it, and place judgment upon what needs to be changed.

For Herbart, educative interaction with the in-between involves moral self-evaluation, in which an individual's subjective side prevents her objective side from unreflective action. On account of this break with oneself, the individual begins to question herself, so that she considers the multifaceted interests that she has developed through educative instruction and then projects new possibilities for action. This break with oneself entails what Hannah Arendt calls the *two-in-one*, the "*duality* of myself with myself that makes thinking a true activity, in which I am both the one who asks and the one who answers. Thinking can become dialectical and critical because it goes through this questioning and answering process."[1] For Dewey, the in-between is a space that invades all realms of learning; it provides a space for reflectively considering new pathways that lead from old to new, as yet unconsidered, forms of thought, judgment, and action. Although Dewey does not articulate as clearly as does Herbart the idea of the self-self break in the moment of interruption or disruption by the other, his notions of uncertainty and reflection point to such forms of self-alienation as inherent in his conception of reflective experience. The teacher must be able to interrupt the learner's learning process in order to productively initiate the learner's self-reflection – reflection upon her negative experiences – and facilitate the learner's navigation through the in-between, so that she does not remain stuck. With this approach, education leads to the learner's self-determination, and teaching seeks out its own end.

2   READING HERBART WITH DEWEY – READING DEWEY WITH HERBART

Like Dewey, Herbart has genuine regard for the need for instruction to give learners the opportunity to encounter a world beyond their direct, immediate, everyday life experiences. But Herbart conceives of the learner's path in cognitive learning as primarily a continuous development without

---

[1] Hannah Arendt, *The Life of the Mind*, p. 185 (New York: Harcourt Brace Jovanovich, 1981).

discontinuity and disruption. Dewey correctly criticizes Herbart's method of instruction, although his critique does not extend to Herbart's theory of moral guidance and moral learning. Although Dewey's critique applies more to the work of Herbart's followers (e.g., Ziller, who emphasized more rigid adherence to following formal instructional steps)[2] than to that of Herbart himself, Dewey is right to identify that Herbart does not fully take account of the role of the new in learners' learning processes in instructional situations (*DE* 77). In other words, Dewey sees that Herbart's emphasis on the teacher's ability to draw on and expand on the learner's existing knowledge overshadows the role of the "genuinely novel and unforeseeable" in the learner's experiences (*DE* 77).

In the twenty-first century, it may seem strange to look all the way back to Herbart for insights into education in a pluralist society. Writing in the early nineteenth century, Herbart had not experienced the twentieth century's increasingly inclusive democracies, nor its atrocities. But, ahead of his time, Herbart makes a remark that foregrounds the difference between education in pluralist and authoritarian societies in a way still vitally relevant today:

Education discourages everything . . . that fosters conceit and selfishness . . . The child, the young boy and the adolescent – at *every* age, must be accustomed to bear the *Censor*, which moves him, so long as it speaks justly and comprehensibly. It is a cardinal tenet of moral guidance to ensure that the general voice of the environment, just like public opinion, allows the *Censor* to be rightly heard . . . If the teacher is the only one representing the general voice, or if he must outright contradict it, he will have trouble demonstrating the value of the *Censor*.[3]

---

[2] On this point, see Muth, who discusses, for example, Ziller's more methodical version of Herbart's stages of instruction, Jakob Muth, *Pädagogischer Takt. Monographie einer aktuellen Form erzieherischen und didaktischen Handelns* [Pedagogical Tact: Monograph of an Actual Form of Educative and Instructive Action] (Heidelberg: Quelle und Meyer, 1967)); see also Johannes Bellmann, "Re-interpretation in Historiography: John Dewey and the Neo-Humanist Tradition," *Studies in Philosophy and Education*, 23, no. 5, 2004: 467–88; Joop W. A. Berding, "War John Dewey ein (neo)Herbartianer. Die Debatte zwischen den 'alten' und der 'neuen' Erziehung," in *Herbart und Dewey: Pädagogische Paradigmen im Vergleich*, edited by Klaus Prange, pp. 7–18. (Jena: IKS Garamond, 2006); and Robbie McClintock, "On (Not) Defining Education: Questions about Historical Life and What Educates Therein." Theoretical Perspectives on Comprehensive Education: The Way Forward. Hervé Varenne and Edmund W. Gordon, eds. (Lewiston, NY: The Edwin Mellen Press), 2009, pp. 27–60. See also the chapters on Herbartianism in Harold B. Dunkel, *Herbart and Education* (New York: Random House, 1969) and *Herbart and Herbartianism: An Educational Ghost Story* (Chicago: University of Chicago Press, 1970).

[3] Herbart, *SE* 247, translation modified. Special thanks to Dietrich Benner for conversations on some ambiguity in this passage. I concluded from our discussions that this translation coincides with the tone and content of other passages in Herbart's work.

This statement reveals that self-critical thinking of the type required for moral action presupposes a public that allows for critique. In other words, the teacher cannot be asked to be the mouthpiece of social norms, nor can he be allowed to pass on his personal views to the learner. Both of these situations reduce the teacher's listening to what we can call listening for the learner's conformity to an external authority. For the learner to be able to truly recognize the educative discontinuity represented by his own inner censor as meaningful, he must be confronted with differences of perspectives and allowed to engage in social critique. Only in such encounters with otherness and difference do we become interrupted by the other in an educative way: the other calls on us to respond in such a way that we become self-critical of our taken-for-granted modes of being in the world.

Although Herbart did not experience the political form of democracy we know today, in the quoted passage he expresses that a certain form of the public realm was an essential precondition for successful education. In his time, however, he saw a conflict between the aims of politics and economics and those of education, and he leaves his audience with a certain skepticism about the possibility of the creation of public institutions that educate individuals toward multifacetedness: "I do not believe that in our current world meaningful public institutions leading learners towards conscious action can be found" (*AP* 105).

At the beginning of the twentieth century, Dewey was more optimistic about the possibilities of interplay between education and the social realm. Admittedly, Dewey's optimism about our ability as human beings to solve the particular difficulties and crises we may at times confront gives the impression that reflective experience will always take us on a path toward the Better. However, Dewey's emphasis on uncertainty and its role in our endeavors to interact with and understand the world makes explicit the negativity of our experience as an indispensable part of our understanding of experience and learning. His notion of uncertainty underscores the idea that we do not have control over the future, that we can always be blindsided, that the connections we may have found could prove erroneous, such that things may remain disconnected and unintelligible. Reflective experience as a method of intelligence means not simply a look forward, but a look back on what went wrong, what we did not have control over. This points to the fact that Dewey considered what has been called by philosophers "the tragic sense of life," which is a recognition of the idea that the contingency of life hinders us from control or even accurate foresight in our attempts to interact with the world.[4]

---

[4] On this notion of the "tragic sense of life," see Sydney Hook, *Pragmatism and the Tragic Sense of Life* (New York: Basic Books, Inc., 1974); see also other authors who have discussed Dewey's tragic

Our experience of the world is fraught with frustration, doubt, or difficulty arising from our encounters with the unexpected. From the viewpoint of the tragic sense of life, we must consider the fact that taking such a reflective look back at what happened to us, what defied our expectations, does not ensure progress toward our aims or ideals the next time we try, *despite* intelligence. As Dewey states in his 1940 text "Time and Individuality":

Development and evolution have historically been eulogistically interpreted. They have been thought of as necessarily proceeding from the lower to the higher, from the relatively worse to the relatively better. But this property was read in from outside moral and theological preoccupations. The real issue is . . . : Is what happens simply a spatial rearrangement of what existed previously or does it involve something qualitatively new? From this point of view, cancer is as genuinely a physiological development as is growth in vigor; criminals as well as heroes are a social development; the emergence of totalitarian states is a social evolution out of constitutional states independently of whether we like or approve them.[5]

Although Dewey has been criticized for not having a radical conception of evil, his thoughts here suggest a view of human beings as capable of undemocratic and inhumane developments, even despite our best attempts to prevent them, as individuals and as a society. We cannot assume that the method of intelligence will ensure an unrelenting march toward the Better, toward democratic ideals. Even though we can and should learn from the past, as Dewey says, the world in some sense always remains "opaque," "a mystery," "the source of development both creative and degenerative."[6] To account for

---

sense: Nicholas Burbules, "The Tragic Sense of Education," *The Teachers College Record*, 91, no. 4, (1990): 469–79; and Naoko Saito, *The Gleam of Light: Moral Perfectionism and Education in Dewey and Emerson* (New York: Fordham University Press, 2005). Raymond Boisvert offers a counter-position, contending that Dewey did not sufficiently recognize the tragic sense of life. However, I do not believe that Boisvert adequately takes into consideration Dewey's attention to uncertainty, as my foregoing argument suggests. See Raymond, D. Boisvert "The Nemesis of Necessity: Tragedy's Challenge to Deweyan Pragmatism," in *Dewey Reconfigured: Essays on Deweyan Pragmatism*, edited by Casey Haskins and David I. Seiple, pp. 151–68 (Albany: State University of New York Press, 1999). My discussion here developed in part owing to a response I was asked to give to an inspiring paper on Dewey's notion of intelligence by Carl Anders Säfstrom, "Intelligence for More Than One: Reading Dewey as a Radical Democrat," in *Philosophy of Education 2012*, edited by Claudia Ruitenberg, pp. 418–426 (Urbana, IL: Philosophy of Education Society, 2013). My response is entitled "Intelligence and The Unexpected: Considering Dewey's Tragic Sense," in *Philosophy of Education 2012*, edited by Claudia Ruitenberg, pp. 427–429 (Urbana, IL: Philosophy of Education Society, 2013).

[5] John Dewey, "Time and Individuality (1940)" *The Later Works*, edited by Jo Ann Boydston, Vol. 14, pp. 98–114, 108–09 (Carbondale: Southern Illinois University Press, 2008).

[6] Ibid, p. 112.

such opaqueness in a notion of intelligence and learning, we must consciously consider and openly discuss the role of the unexpected – of the negativity of experience exposed in our encounters with it – in individual and social experience.

From my discussion in Part One, three concepts emerge to highlight the role of the unexpected in its connection to our experience of discontinuity: *learning in-between, pedagogical tact,* and *perfectibility*. In Part Two, I continue to draw out these concepts, further connecting my foregoing discussion of Herbart and Dewey to concepts within the current discourse on the philosophy of education (in both German- and English-language discussions). In doing so, I aim to suggest ways that we can continue to articulate the meaning and significance of discontinuity in educational processes. The next chapter (Chapter 6) focuses on learning and Chapter 7 turns to discuss teaching and tact. In the final chapter (Chapter 8), I return to the concept of perfectibility with which this book began and relate it to how we conceive of the teacher's task.

PART TWO

TEACHING AND LEARNING FORGOTTEN?

Chapter 6

Revisiting Learning In-Between and *Umlernen*

1   FORGOTTEN LEARNING, OR REMEMBERING PLATO'S CAVE

Learning, considered as a transformational process, takes place *between* or *beyond* right and wrong; it also changes how we conceive of right and wrong. As I argued in Part One, with reference to Herbart and Dewey, inquiring into the process of learning involves uncovering the discontinuity, disruptions, and interruptions constitutive of learning, and the perplexity, frustration, and irritation that characterize the learner's experiences and those of teachers, as well. These aspects of learning relate to the negativity of experience and have consequences for how we understand teaching and how we understand what it means for a teacher to recognize and give voice to the difference and otherness of the learner. In this first chapter of Part Two, I readdress the concept of "learning in-between" that I developed in Part One and tie this concept to the German notion of *Umlernen*, which describes learning as a complex transformative experience. In this way, I draw connections between contemporary German and Anglo-American philosophical inquiries into learning, with the hope of reinvigorating cross-cultural educational discourse around learning as a transformational process.

The term "negativity of experience" (as defined in Part One) points to our experience of the unfamiliar, different, strange, and unexpected that we experience as an interruption. This interruption in experience identifies the moment when the world in some way defies our expectations. Both Herbart and Dewey, albeit to differing degrees, thematize this vital gap in our experience of the world, a gap that exists in the moment between an encounter with the unexpected and the discovery of a new path that may lead out of the disorienting experience. This gap in experience marks the moment when we do not know how to move on. In Part One, I developed the idea that this gap, or "in-between," is an important opening created by the interruption in our experiences, an opening for new judgments and new choices to be made with respect to how we think and act, and that it therefore has consequences for learning.

This kind of opening is more than a mere crossroads. The notion of coming to a crossroads limits our thinking about the meaning of interruption in experience because it implies distinct paths that are *known* (even if we do not know where they might end up). A crossroads can too easily connote a simple pause in our experience, a hiccup along the road toward making a decision, which, once made, completes the overarching continuity of our experience. In contrast, the notion of interruption reminds us of the discontinuity of experience, that experience is also negative, and that our initial encounters with something unexpected are at first *felt*, as Dewey points out, and thus experienced in the full sense of the word. An interruption is a physical, emotional, and existential moment when situations do not take a planned (or necessarily desired) course. This experience is prereflective; it occurs prior to our cognitive processing of known paths and prior to any decision about what path we might want to take. When one is interrupted in this way, there are no immediately known paths that necessarily recommend themselves as options to move forward.

Thus, this break or interruption in experience is an opening that implies a turning point in our experience. This turning point is initially experienced as disorientation and as disillusionment about our taken-for-granted modes of thought and action. When our experiences are interrupted, we can say that a space has opened up, and we find ourselves between old and new. In this space, opportunities arise for reflectively exploring and experimenting with new ideas and new modes of practice. As a turning point in the learning process, this gap cannot simply be skipped over if it is to become part of a transformational learning experience; rather, it must be addressed reflectively, or we remain stuck.

So, one might ask: To what extent are we forgetting learning (as the section title suggests)? I contend that the transformational nature of learning processes has been forgotten in educational policy, where the concept of learning has been limited to the continuous step-by-step achievement of predefined outcomes. As philosopher of education Horst Rumpf emphasizes, this limited definition of learning relativizes the process of learning to its results, and thereby closes off the openings created by negativity and discontinuity in learning.[1] Moreover, it is exactly this negativity and discontinuity in learning

---

[1] Horst Rumpf, "Lernen als Vollzug und als Erledigung – Sich einlassen auf Befremdliches oder: Über Lernvollzüge ohne Erledigungsdruck" [Learning as an open process or for completion – Engaging with the strange: On Learning Processes without the Pressure of Completion], in *Dem*

processes, namely, the learner's negative experiences of frustration, doubt or difficulty, which bring the voice of the learner to the fore. As educational theorists have underscored, an outcomes-based idea of learning and education fails to recognize the uniqueness and individuality of learners.[2] Such a one-size-fits-all idea of learning seeks to preemptively close the gaps in the learner's learning process before they have been opened and explored. Thus, if we continue educational discourse on learning in the manner of certain current educational policies, there is an increasing likelihood that the transformational meaning of learning will be entirely forgotten.

Examining connections between negativity and learning opens up the possibility of grasping meaningful differences between *learning as mere correction of error* and *learning as transformation of self and world*. Using the German term *Umlernen* to examine these connections in this chapter, I illustrate further ways that we can discuss learning not as a smooth transition from ignorance to knowledge, but as a discontinuous process that involves struggle and can be painful. This struggle arises from disorienting interruptions in our experience. I also point out how we might broaden our understanding of the nature of the educational relationship between teacher and learner.

But there is another reason that I suggest a connection between learning and forgetting. The negativity of experience in learning is difficult to conceptualize. Part of the reason for this difficulty is that, after one has learned something, one forgets the difficulties encountered along the path of learning.[3] Once one learns to read, one forgets the fear and difficulty involved in the process. Once one understands the principle of multiplication, one forgets the frustration involved in arriving at this understanding. Once one learns to swim, one forgets the anxious feeling of losing air or the utter discomfort of inhaling water. In other words, the negativity of our experience of learning is forgotten. Before turning to the analysis of the concept of *Umlernen*, I will first illustrate how we can conceptualize what it means to forget the negativity of our experience with reference to Plato's Cave Allegory.

Lernen auf der Spur, edited by Konstantin Mitgutsch, Elizabeth Sattler, Kristin Westphal, and Ines M. Breinbauer, pp. 21–32 (Stuttgart: Klett-Cotta, 2008).

[2] See, for example, Gert J. J. Biesta, *Beyond Learning*, pp. 73–74 (Boulder, CO: Paradigm, 2006); Robert Boostrom, "Teaching by the Numbers," in *Teaching and Its Predicaments*, edited by Nicholas C. Burbules and David T. Hansen, pp. 45–64 (Boulder, CO: Westview Press, 1997); James Garrison, "Teacher as Prophetic Trickster," *Educational Theory*, 59, no. 1, 2009: 67–83; Claudia W. Ruitenberg, "Giving Place to Unforeseeable Learning: The Inhospitality of Outcomes-Based Education," in *"Philosophy of Education 2009"*, edited by Deborah Kerdeman, pp. 266–74 (Urbana, IL: Philosophy of Education Society, 2010).

[3] On this point, see Bernhard Waldenfels, "Die Macht der Ereignisse" [The Power of the Events], in *Aesthetik Erfahrung, Interventionen*, edited by Jörg Huber, pp. 155–70 (Wien: Springer, 2004).

One might recall the experience of the liberated prisoner in the cave. On his path out of the cave, the prisoner experiences the pain of being blinded by the light outside the cave.[4] Then, when he is asked to differentiate the objects he sees, he becomes perplexed, because he had previously only seen the objects as shadows on the cave wall and thinks they were truer than the objects presently before his eyes. Slowly, he is able to examine brighter objects until he can finally look to the sun. This image reveals the negativity of experience that arises for the prisoner in his confrontation with the new and unfamiliar. But it also gives insight into the problem of the *forgotten* negativity of experience. In the allegory, the reader is asked to imagine what it would be like for the prisoner, who has now grown accustomed to the light, to suddenly be taken out of the light and returned to the darkness of the cave. Upon his return, the prisoner can no longer relate to the other prisoners, who have never left the cave. Whereas the other prisoners still believe the shadows on the wall are the truth, the liberated prisoner now sees these shadows differently. The liberated prisoner's return to the cave demonstrates that, in learning, one forgets the frustration and pain of first leaving the cave – one forgets the path of learning and its constitutive negativity. This points to the fact that, in learning, what was once familiar becomes strange, and what was once new and strange becomes familiar.[5]

2   REMEMBERING LEARNING AS A TRANSFORMATIONAL PROCESS: ON *UMLERNEN*

To remember the transformational potential of learning, we have to analyze learning as a process, not simply as a product. Only by inquiring into learning as a process can we understand how the interaction between self and other becomes educative. For educators, it is tempting to grasp learning solely as a product because we can see when a child has learned; learning reveals itself as an observable event in the world.[6] In other words, teachers, parents, and

---

[4] Meyer-Drawe underscores this point in her reading of Plato's cave, stating that Plato, more than any other, highlighted the "painful" aspect of learning and pointing out that "the beginning of learning is not equivalent to beginning to see"; rather, it begins, for Plato, "in the disruption of sight"; see Käte Meyer-Drawe, "Anfänge des Lernens" [Beginnings of Learning] *Zeitschrift für Pädagogik*, **49**, 2005: 24–37, 32, translation mine.

[5] See, in particular, passages 515b–517b of Plato, "The Republic," in *Plato Complete Works*, translated by G. M. A. Grube and C. D. C. Reeve, edited by John M. Cooper and D. S. Hutchinson (Cambridge, MA: Hatckett Publishing Company, 1997).

[6] Compare Klaus Prange, "Lernen im Kontext des Erziehens. Überlegungen zu einem pädagogischen Begriff des Lernens" [Learning in the Context of Educating: Reflections on a Pedagogical Concept of Learning], in *Dem Lernen auf der Spur*, edited by Konstantin Mitgutsch,

educators see that learning has happened when a child knows how to answer a math problem or is able to do something, such as play scales on a piano, or anything the child was not able to do before. An attempt to examine learning processes proves difficult in practice because when we observe the learning processes of others, we do not know if learning is taking place until it is done and then reveals itself in some, at least tentative, positive result. Similarly, it seems that one cannot witness one's own learning processes because there is something about learning that involves being "in the moment" and not knowing you are learning prior to coming to the point at which you realize you have grasped something new. So, how can we grasp what that experience of learning is like for the one experiencing it? By turning to contemporary German-language philosophical inquiries surrounding the concept of *Umlernen*, and related discussions of learning in the English-language discourse, we can show that philosophical examination of the connection between experience and learning reveals something otherwise hidden about the structure of learning. Namely, it reveals the negativity of experience that is constitutive of all learning processes.

In his work *Lernen und Erfahrung* (*Learning and Experience*),[7] the German philosopher Günther Buck draws on Aristotle, Kant, and Herbart, but also on twentieth-century traditions of phenomenology and hermeneutics, such as Husserl and Gadamer, in a way that has influenced present-day discourse surrounding the topic of discontinuity and learning. His approach in this work leads to a fruitful understanding of the term *Umlernen*. In analyzing the connection between learning and experience, he first points to some common understandings of experience that help illuminate the meaning of "negativity" in experience. He points out, for example, that the experiences we tend to call "instructive" or "learning experiences" are those that we were resistant to and happened to us in ways contrary to expectations.[8] He argues, however, that this connection alone is too simplistic because it only allows us to see learning

---

Elizabeth Sattler, Kristin Westphal, and Ines M. Breinbauer, pp. 241–48 (Stuttgart: Klett-Cotta, 2008).

[7] Günther Buck, *Lernen und Erfahrung* (Stuttgart: Kohlhammer, 1969).

[8] Ibid., p. 16, translation mine; Buck here is connecting to Gadamer, who in *Truth and Method* also speaks of experience as "negative." Gadamer writes that when we speak of experience, we are referring both to "the experiences that conform to our expectations and confirm it and the new experiences that occur to us." But he adds, "this latter – 'experience' in the genuine sense – is always negative." Gadamer relates this to learning, stating that, on account of new experiences, we realize we have not seen the object "correctly" and come to "know" an object "better" such that we can say "the negativity of experience [has] a curiously productive meaning." Hans-Georg Gadamer, *Truth and Method*, Second revised edition, translation revised by Joel Weinsheimer and Donald G. Marshall, p. 353 (New York: Continuum, 2000); on this point, see also Koch, *Bildung und Negativität*, pp. 28–31.

as a "possible consequence" of experience, not as an "immanent consequence" of experience.[9] Buck explains that the deeper connection between
learning and experience can be grasped when we think about those experiences we call a "life experience" (*Lebenserfahrung*).[10] We only consider something a life experience once we have drawn out the consequences of the
experience and realize we have learned something from it. In this sense, "an
experience, without consequences, from which one learned nothing, is not an
experience."[11] As Buck writes, experiences that are instructive appear to be
both "negative" and "positive": they are negative because we "learned the hard
way (*Lehrgeld bezahlt*)"; they are "positive" because we learned.[12]

Learning that is connected to experience in this way is what Buck describes
as *Umlernen* (a term formed from the German verb *lernen*, meaning "to
learn," and the prefix *um-*, which indicates movement or change). Buck's use
of the terms *negative* and *positive* plays on the pejorative meanings of the
terms as they are used colloquially, but the term *negativity* has a deeper
educative meaning in learning. The term *Umlernen* implies that all genuine
learning involves struggle, disillusionment, or suffering because it involves
encounters with something new, such as a new concept, a different perspective, or an unfamiliar activity that we are trying to get to know and understand. Experiences of the new and unfamiliar, and therefore unexpected, are
part of everyday life. They are part of the contingency we live with that allows
us – and often forces us – to experience our own limitations. No amount of
planning can take into consideration all possible unexpected circumstances.
When the world defies our expectations, we experience an *interruption*: a
disruption, an opposition, or a resistance from things or other human beings
that counteracts our attempts and implicitly tells us that what we thought,
did, or said does not suffice to deal with the situation at hand (as I covered in
Part One).

It is important to note that, on the meaning of interruption that I have
drawn out in this book, an interruption in experience is not an immediate
feeling of knowingly lacking something or of making a quantifiable mistake,
such as getting a wrong answer on a test. Because it is not immediately felt as a
lack, it does not immediately indicate to us a step forward in the form of a
simple acquisition of knowledge that could fill the void. Rather, the experience of interruption is an experience of one's own limitations. As such, it is an

---

[9] Buck, *Lernen und Erfahrung*, p. 17.
[10] Ibid., p. 18.
[11] Ibid., pp. 17–18.
[12] Ibid.

experience of opposition and resistance that Käte Meyer-Drawe calls *Widerfahrnis*, or a "counter-happening," in which a human being breaks with him- or herself and opens up to new ways of being in the world.[13] The term *Umlernen* is necessary because it takes account of the fact that the experience of *receptivity* – of something happening to us, of suffering and undergoing, of becoming disoriented – is as indispensable a part of the process of learning as the attempt to *actively* orient ourselves through action in the world. The fact that we are receptive and not just active as human beings makes our experiences unavoidably discontinuous, negative, and contradictory, and not solely continuous, positive, and affirmative.

Using the German terminology, we can differentiate transformative learning processes, or *Umlernen*, from "additive" learning processes, or *Dazulernen*. Whereas the latter concept assumes learning is a continuous process of "adding onto" (*dazu*) existing knowledge on the path toward the accumulation of knowledge, the former recognizes the educative meaning of negativity and discontinuity in learning:

Umlernen ... is not simply the correction of this or that idea that one had about something; it also means an alteration of one's "disposition," that is, of one's entire horizon of experience. He who learns as "umlernen" is confronted with himself; he becomes conscious of himself. It is not only that certain ideas change, rather, the learner himself changes. On account of this essential negativity, the process of learning is the *history* of the learner himself.[14]

When learning brings about true change in the sense of a transformation, as Meyer-Drawe points out, it is experienced as a "painful turn-around" (*schmerzhaften Umkehr*) in which one breaks with one's prior knowledge, but also with oneself as a person.[15] Meyer-Drawe calls this experience of one's

---

[13] Käte Meyer-Drawe, "Anfänge des Lernens," p. 31, translation mine. See also Konstantin Mitgutsch, *Lernen durch Enttäuschung – Eine pädagogische Skizze* [Learning from resistance – A pedagogical outline] (Vienna: Braumüller, 2009). On the idea of learning as "difficult" and "negative," see also Nigel Tubbs, "Philosophy of the Teacher," *Journal of Philosophy of Education* 39, no. 2 (Special Issue) 2005, e.g., p. 320.

[14] From the original German: "Umlernen aber, das ist nicht nur die Korrektur dieser und jener Vorstellungen, die man sich über etwas gemacht hat; es bedeutet auch einen Wandel der 'Einstellung', d.h. des ganzen Horizontes der Erfahrung. Wer umlernt, wird mit sich selbst konfrontiert; er kommt zur Besinnung. Nicht nur gewisse Vorstellungen wandeln sich, sondern der Lernende selbst wandelt sich. Kraft dieser prinzipiellen Negativität ist das Geschehen des Lernens die *Geschichte* des Lernenden selbst." (Buck, *Lernen und Erfahrung*, p. 44, translation mine, emphasis in original.)

[15] Käte Meyer-Drawe, *Diskurse des Lernens* [*Discourses on Learning*], p. 206 (München: Wilhelm Fink, 2008); see also Käte Meyer-Drawe, "Von Anderen lernen. Phänomenologische Betrachtungen in der Pädagogik" [Learning from the Other: Phenomenological Observations

limits a "confrontation with one's own experiential history."[16] When our experience breaks with itself, then we can learn in a way that is not just a matter of adding on or correcting the content of our thought, or exchanging one aspect of knowledge for another. Rather, this negativity and discontinuity make a different type of learning possible: learning becomes *Umlernen*, a transformative restructuring of one's entire horizon of foregoing and possible experience.[17]

Without using the term *Umlernen*, Anglo-American philosophers have similarly discussed the transformative sense of learning that can emerge from our encounters with the unexpected and unforeseeable. Philosopher of education Deborah Kerdeman, drawing on the work of Hans-Georg Gadamer, emphasizes, for example, that our encounters with unexpected events "interrupt our lives," making us aware of our otherwise hidden "attitudes, qualities, and behaviours" embedded in our prereflective understandings.[18] Kerdeman says that, in these instances, we are "pulled up short" by our encounter with the unfamiliar and our "blind spots" are exposed.[19] Being pulled up short, as Kerdeman underscores, is thus a transformative form of challenge to oneself connected to "a new level of insight."[20] Kerdeman points out that, from this type of self-challenge, educative forms of self-questioning and doubt can arise. However, this is not the same as the type of self-questioning that occurs

in Education] in *Deutsche Gegenwartspädagogik*, Vol. 2, edited by Michele Borrelli, and Jörg Ruhloff, pp. 85–98, 89–90 (Baltmannsweiler: Schneider Verlag Hohengehren, 1996).

[16] Käte Meyer-Drawe, "Phänomenologische Bemerkungen zum Problem des Lernens" [Phenomenological remarks on the problem of learning], *Vierteljahresheft für wissenschaftliche Pädagogik*, 58, no. 4, 1982: 520–21.

[17] Ibid., p. 522; See also Dietrich Benner, "Kritik und Negativität," *Zeitschrift für Pädagogik* 46, 2003: 96–110; Dietrich Benner and Andrea English, "Critique and Negativity," *Journal of Philosophy of Education*, 38, no. 3, 2004: 409–28; Konstantin Mitgutsch, "Lernen durch Erfahren: Über Bruchlinien im Vollzug des Lernens" [Learning from Experience: On the Fault Lines in the Process of Learning], in *Dem Lernen auf der Spur*, edited by Konstantin Mitgutsch, Elizabeth Sattler, Kristin Westphal, and Ines M. Breinbauer, pp. 263–77 (Stuttgart: Klett-Cotta, 2008); Rumpf, "Lernen als Vollzug und als Erledigung." See also my discussion of this concept in the context of connections between the German tradition and the work of education philosopher Richard S. Peters in Andrea English, "Transformation and Education: The Voice of the Learner in Peters' Concept of Teaching," *Journal of Philosophy of Education*, 43, Issue Supplement s1 (Special Issue "Reading R. S. Peters Today: Analysis, Ethics and the Aims of Education," edited by Stefaan Cuypers and Christopher Martin) 2009: 75–95.

[18] Deborah Kerdeman, "Pulled Up Short: Challenging Self-Understanding as a Focus of Teaching and Learning," *Journal of Philosophy of Education*, 37, no. 2, 2003: 293–308, 296; see also, Kerdeman, "Pulled Up Short: Challenges for Education," In *Philosophy of Education 2003*, edited by Kal Alston, 208–16 (Urbana, IL: Philosophy of Education Society, 2004).

[19] Kerdeman, "Pulled Up Short: Challenging Self-Understanding as a Focus of Teaching and Learning," p. 296; see also, Kerdeman, "Pulled Up Short: Challenges for Education."

[20] Kerdeman, "Pulled Up Short: Challenging Self-Understanding as a Focus of Teaching and Learning," p. 297.

on the basis of one's conscious choice to challenge one's own beliefs.[21] Whereas the latter, although also important, arises out of a will to challenge oneself and one's beliefs, the former arises out of an existential need to understand what happened, a need to move on, which opens up the possibility for learning in ways we had not previously foreseen.

Nicholas Burbules offers a further way of understanding our encounters with the unfamiliar and unexpected. He uses the term *aporia* to describe "an experience that affects us on many levels at once: we feel discomfort, we doubt ourselves . . . Aporia is a crisis of choice, of action and identity, and not just of belief. When I have too many choices, or no choice; I'm stuck. I do not know how to go on."[22] In these moments in our experience, we are "lost," as Burbules states, and this sense of being lost can lead to a different kind of doubt than the doubt that arises merely as a transitional phase between a wrong answer and a predetermined right answer. This different kind of doubt is part of the experience of the "movement towards an unknown destination."[23] As he suggests, this sense of being lost makes a different kind of growth possible; it engenders new inquiries, exploration, and the posing of "questions that make a new understanding possible."[24] This experience of being lost points to the space of the in-between of learning (as I have described throughout this book), a space that allows for learning in ways we could not have imagined without this experience.

3   THE INWARD AND OUTWARD TURN OF LEARNING

Two interconnected implications can be drawn out from my discussion of *Umlernen* and other related conceptions of learning. First, that there is a beginning of learning that cannot be consciously self-initiated; rather, it is *felt* in the prereflective experience of negativity. That is, the beginning of learning is experienced as a break with ourselves, our habitual modes of being, our assumptions, our taken-for-granted perspectives – a beginning that I termed the *prereflective beginning of learning* in Chapter 3. These breaks or gaps in experience cannot be closed simply by attaining new knowledge, but they *can*

---

[21] Ibid., p. 294.

[22] Nicholas C. Burbules, "Aporias, Webs, and Passages: Doubt as an Opportunity to Learn," *Curriculum Inquiry*, 30, no. 2, 2000: 171–87, 173 ; see also Nicholas C. Burbules, "Aporia: Webs, Passages, Getting Lost, and Learning to Go On," in *Philosophy of Education 1997*, edited by Susan Laird, pp. 33–43 (Urbana, IL: Philosophy of Education Society, 1998).

[23] Burbules, "Aporias, Webs, and Passages: Doubt as an Opportunity to Learn," p. 175. Burbules delineates this point with reference to Plato's *Meno*.

[24] Ibid. p. 183; see also pp. 175 and 182.

be productively dealt with through reflection and inquiry.[25] In these moments of interruption, something or someone takes hold of us before we become aware that something has happened. In such moments, we are entangled in the situation, held in suspense, not knowing – even if only for a split second – what happened or why it happened. The interruptions in our experiences that leave us wandering and exploring choices within the *in-between* realm of learning make possible new relations to the world and others around us.

Second, in my account, discontinuity in learning is something more than a moment within an all-encompassing continuity. So, as German philosopher of education Friedhelm Brüggen points out, we must take the idea of discontinuity in learning a step further than does Buck, by acknowledging both continuity and discontinuity, without subordinating one to the other.[26] In doing so, we can grasp the transformative meaning of prereflective beginnings of learning. The prereflective beginning of learning is a response to the otherness of the world, to the difference we have encountered in our interaction with those around us. It brings to the fore that the world and others outside ourselves matter; the other affects us, and we are changed by the encounter. Bernhard Waldenfels illuminates the meaning of this responsivity in our experience of the other when he writes that our response to the other does not begin with speaking; rather, it begins "inescapably" with "listening and looking."[27] This means that responding to the other is initially *taking in*

---

[25] On this point, see Bernhard Waldenfels, *Das Zwischenreich des Dialogues* (*The In-Between of Dialogue*) (Den Haag: Martinus Nihoff, 1971), and Bernhard Waldenfels, *Bruchlinien der Erfahrung* [*The Fault Lines of Experience*] (Frankfurt am Main: Suhrkamp, 2002).

[26] Compare Friedhelm Brüggen, "Lernen-Erfahrung-Bildung oder Über Kontinuität und Diskontinuität im Lernprozess" [Learning-Experience-Education or on Continuity and Discontinuity in Learning Processes], *Zeitschrift für Pädagogik*, 34, no. 3, 1988: 299–313; see also Benner, "Kritik und Negativität," and Benner and English "Critique and Negativity." On Buck's description of continuity in relation to discontinuity, see, for example, Günther Buck, *Hermeneutik und Bildung* [Hermeneutics and Education] pp. 54–58 (München: Wilhelm Fink Verlag, 1981).

[27] Bernhard Waldenfels, "Antwort auf das Fremde. Grundzüge einer responsiven Phänomenologie" [Response to the Other: Essential Features of a Responsive Phenomenology], in *Der Anspruch des Anderen, Perspektiven phänomenologischer Ethik*, edited by Bernhard Waldenfels and Iris Daermann, pp. 35–50, 44 (München: Fink, 1998). It is worth noting that the word "response" is translated from the German word *Antwort*. In following typical translations of the German term *Antwort*, I have translated this word as "response," although the meaning also relates to the word "answer." However, the term should not be equated with a behaviorist idea of response to stimulus. Waldenfels differentiates between *Antwort* as "answer" to mean something akin to an acceptable answer to the question that fills the gap left by the question, and an *Antwort* as "response" that is not filling a gap, rather is "searching for" and "inventing" a possible response to the open "offering" left by the call (*Anspruch*) of the other, Ibid. This search on my account is a search in the in-between realm of learning. On learning as response see also Meyer-Drawe, "Anfänge des Lernens," p. 34, and

the other - it entails listening, looking, and feeling – and this connects to our search in the in-between, our search for the difference between what we anticipated (from another person, an object, or ourselves) and what is revealed in the moment when those expectations break down. When we begin to think about the role of discontinuity and negativity in learning in the ways discussed, we can begin to see the significance this understanding of learning has for the teacher-learner relation. The breaks and gaps in a learner's experiences are also openings, and the teacher must be *open to* these breaks and gaps in learners' experiences in order to understand how these can become educative.

Before examining the teacher-learner relation in the next chapter, I would like to turn to the autobiography of African-American author Richard Wright to illustrate the connection between negativity, learning, and transformation discussed thus far and in turn hint at connections to teaching. In writing about his life, Wright takes his readers to painful moments in his childhood. Growing up in the early twentieth century in the racially segregated South of the United States, Wright was unjustly denied the opportunity to receive continuous formal schooling. Despite this, he explains that his curiosity for words and his desire to read began at an early age. He describes one formative experience when he received some initial encouragement from his mother:

In the immediate neighborhood there were many school children who, in the afternoons, would stop and play en route to their homes; they would leave their books upon the sidewalk and I would thumb through the pages and question them about the baffling black print. When I learned to recognize certain words, I told my mother that I wanted to learn to read and she encouraged me. Soon I was able to pick my way through most of the children's books I ran across. There grew in me a consuming curiosity about what was happening around me and, when my mother came home from a hard day's work, I would question her so relentlessly about what I had heard in the street that she refused to talk to me.[28]

The text that baffled him and confronted him with his own limit became the source of possible new ways of seeing the world, a horizon of new, unanswered questions. However, throughout his life, Wright did not continuously have an active guide or teacher to cultivate his learning process. The individuals around him and society at large often discouraged him from asking more

Meyer-Drawe, *Diskurse des Lernens*, e.g. 188–190; see also Biesta, who connects this idea of learning to Levinas:, Gert J. J. Biesta, *Beyond Learning*, for example, pp. 27 and 68.

[28] Richard Wright, *Black Boy. A Record of Childhood and Youth*, p. 29 (New York: Perrennial Library, 1989).

questions, from inquiring into their possible answers, and from continuing to transform as a learning being, despite his impetus to do so.

Although unavoidable and necessary for transformational learning to take place, the breaks, interruptions, or ruptures in our experiences are not sufficient to incite a reflective transformative learning processes; the interruption is not in itself *educative*. One might ask, in what sense is it not educative? The term "educative" here is used in the sense of the Latin *education*, "to pull forth," or in German *erziehend*. As such, the interruption does not pull us forth. The interruption is, however, always *formative*, or in German, *bildend*. As in the example from the life of Richard Wright, learners can be left stuck in the in-between, alone and incapable of exploring new possibilities for self-discovery and discovery of the world. The interruption still takes on meaning for us, it forms us, but it becomes a moment in life in which we remember the harsh experience of being discouraged, stuck, stifled, submerged, or suffocated, without seeing further possibility for self-transformation, for increased complexity, for turning toward self and other, and for learning. Thus, rather than being seen as an opening, the interruption could be viewed as a *closure* by the individual who has endured the experience. Our confrontation with our own limits, whether early in life, such as when we begin to read or write, or later in life, when grappling with difficult concepts or complex social relations, is always an *opening* for changed and different modes of being in the world. But it is initially *only* an opening and, as such, does not necessarily contribute to self-cultivation until we move past the confrontation with otherness to the meaningful exploration of questions such as What is missing in my understanding?, How does this experience relate to my prior knowledge?, What might this mean for the choices I have made and for those yet to be made?

To help learners answer these questions requires a teacher who recognizes the learner as a learning being and thus sees the learner as someone who can learn from the negativity of experience. Such a teacher also must recognize the difference between *productive, educative* interruptions in experience and *destructive* interruptions in experience. Productive or educative interruptions I define as those that call forth and call out thinking and inquiry in the learner, whereas destructive interruptions in experience I define as those that hinder the learner's capacity for self-cultivation and transformation.

Remembering the moments of negativity and discontinuity in the structure of learning processes helps us understand how transformational learning processes take place. In other words, it helps us answer the question: How is it that one opens oneself up to something new, something different and unfamiliar? This is a central question of how we learn, a question that, as humans, we all have a stake in answering. For learning as a transformation of self to take place, the process of learning always necessitates an *inward* and *outward turn*. The *inward turn* happens when one begins to reflectively think about the prereflective interruption in one's experience and thereby to make it into a conscious moment to be examined. The *outward turn* refers to the changed outlook on the world that arises out of coming to understand oneself – one's wishes, one's capabilities, one's questions, one's needs, one's feelings, and one's difficulties – and the world differently or otherwise than before the learning experience. This new understanding is not necessarily a gain or a loss, although it can feel like either or both; it is primarily a different way of seeing and being in the world, including how we feel, think, act, and interact. In this way, the negativity of experience in learning has many implications for teacher-learner interaction, the topic of the next chapter.

Chapter 7

Pedagogical Tact: Learning to Teach "In-Between"

[I]t is quite consistent to rate the instructional planning process highly, while at the same time recognizing that, in the end, each and every lesson holds in store a myriad of unforeseeable possibilities and that the openness of teachers' minds to new situations, impulses, and the difficulties arising from the moment is a criterion of their pedagogical competence.

         – Wolfgang Klafki, 1958[1]

As we advance into the twenty-first century, it is upon us to recognize the intersubjective space "between" teacher and learner, where teachers recognize how learners *co*-constitute the pedagogical situation. As Käte Meyer-Drawe writes, "the child sees not 'nothing,' he also doesn't see everything, he sees things otherwise."[2] To grasp that the child sees things otherwise involves recognition that the voice of the learner is one that educators, at times, have to help him find. In this chapter, I further my examination of *pedagogical tact*, which I discussed in Chapter 2, in relation to Herbart. Pedagogical tact is a form of judgment that aims to cultivate the voice of the learner by initiating and supporting his or her transformational learning processes. Pedagogical tact in teaching refers to the ability to make wise decisions in the moment that are both oriented toward the individual learner – that is, toward his or her needs, abilities, challenges – and toward the principles of the profession – that

---

[1] Wolfgang Klafki, "Didaktik Analysis as the Core of Preparation of Instruction (1958)," in *Teaching as a Reflective Practice: The German Didaktik Tradition*, edited by Ian Westbury, Stefan Hopmann, and Kurt Riquarts, pp. 139–60 (Mahwah, NJ: Lawrence Erlbaum Associates, 2000). Reprinted with permission from the publisher © Lawrence Erlbaum Assoc, Inc. 2000.

[2] Käte Meyer-Drawe, "Die Belehrbarkeit des Lehrenden durch den Lernenden – Fragen an den Primat des Pädagogischen Bezugs" [The Ability of a Teacher to Learn from the Learner: Questions on the Primacy of the Pedagogical Reference], in *Kind und Welt: Phänomenologische Studien zur Pädagogik*, edited by W. Lippitz and K. Meyer-Drawe, pp. 63–73, 72 (Frankfurt am Main: Athenaeum, 1987).

is, the theoretical notions of what is right and good to do to promote learning and growth.

To understand pedagogical tact, it is helpful to initially ask: What might it mean for a teacher to help the learner find his voice? To begin, I would like to answer this question using an illustrative passage from literary theorist Edward Said's autobiography. He paints the picture of his memorable experience with a high school English teacher, Baldwin, as follows:

During the first weeks Baldwin assigned us an essay topic of a very unpromising sort: 'On Lighting a Match.' I dutifully went to the library and proceeded through encyclopedias, histories of industry, chemical manuals in search of what matches were; I then more or less systematically summarised and transcribed what I had found and, rather proud of what I had compiled, turned it in. Baldwin almost immediately asked me to come and see him during his office hours, which was an entirely novel concept, since VC's [Victoria College's] teachers never had offices, let alone office hours. Baldwin's office was a cheery little place with postcard-covered walls, and as we sat next to each other on two easy chairs he complimented me on my research. "But is that the most interesting way to examine what happens when someone lights a match? What if he's trying to set a fire to a forest, or light a candle in a cave, or, metaphorically, illuminate the obscurity of a mystery like gravity, the way Newton did?" For literally the first time in my life, a subject was opened up for me by a teacher in a way that I immediately and excitedly responded to. What had previously been repressed and stifled in academic study – repressed in order that thorough and correct answers be given to satisfy a standardized syllabus and a routinized exam designed essentially to show off powers of retention, not critical or imaginative facilities – was awakened, and the complicated process of intellectual discovery (and self-discovery) has never stopped since.[3]

The teacher here brings the student out of the type of strategic learning he has become accustomed to, which has only involved looking for the prescribed and predefined right ways of doing things according to the teacher's and the school's preconceived notions of correctness. His teacher is now asking him to think in some way differently than he had before, to find a voice that is different than the one he had grown accustomed to expressing. In this case, the voice he has been accustomed to expressing has been restricting and confining his way of thinking about the world. The student learns through this interaction in a way that involves the negativity of experience as the experience of *disillusionment*, of the sort that opens up

---

[3] Edward Said, *Out of Place: A Memoir*, p. 231 (New York: Vintage Books, 1999).

and liberates thinking. He experiences discontinuity in a way that rearranges, restructures, and transforms his entire thinking about what is possible in literary imagination, in self-understanding, and within the teacher-learner relation.

The passage not only tells us something about the experience of learning, but also about the experience of teaching. Teaching that cultivates growth and transformation in learners is not a series of preplanned steps for action made independently of learners and the situations of learning. Rather, it is an improvisational practice, one that requires recognizing where a learner has become stuck, has in some way retreated to the comforts of habit, or has lost the desire to move on past taken-for-granted ways of seeing and being in the world. Pedagogical tact is the learned ability to judge how to turn these situations around for the sake of the learner.

A concept of teaching that views the task of the teacher as one of recognizing and helping the learner find her voice means understanding teaching as *initiating* and *engaging* interruptions in the learner's experience of learning. On this view, teaching is teaching *in-between* (an idea developed in Chapter 4), a process of *interrupting experience*. A teacher who can productively interrupt the experiences of a learner is one who is receptive to the learner's *different* way of seeing the world. The teacher's task is to make judgments about what is pedagogically good and right to do on the basis of understanding that difference.

Pedagogical tact is the complex concept that addresses this existential experience of teachers responding to the call of the other – the learner. In the first section, I examine this notion in its connection to the teacher's experience as one that necessarily involves risk and improvisation. In the second section, I further highlight the receptive side of teaching by examining the role of listening as a central part of developing pedagogical tact in teaching. Listening as a topic of educational philosophy has been largely overlooked until recently.[4] In teaching, listening plays a vital role in helping the teacher gauge and understand the learning process of students, which is a vital aspect of being attuned to learners' experiences and able to interrupt them in an educative way. In closing, I present a model of "Reflective Teacher-Learner Engagement" that illustrates how the concepts I have developed throughout this book relate to a teacher's reflective practice.

---

[4] Throughout the chapter, I will discuss in detail some of the various connections between listening and education that have been made in recent education philosophical inquiries.

1   IMPROVISATION AND RISK

The pedagogical activity that develops in practice but is guided by theory is what Herbart refers to as "pedagogical tact" (*pädagogischer Takt*, addressed in Chapter 2). For teachers, pedagogical tact requires making judgments about the educational situation that take into account the learning beings who stand before them. Judgments about what is needed to cultivate transformational learning processes cannot be entirely preplanned. Rather, as Wolfgang Klafki emphasizes, pedagogical competence requires not only planning, but also being open to respond to the "unforeseeable possibilities," the "new situations, impulses and difficulties" that arise "in the moment."[5] The complexity and difficulty of the type of pedagogical judgment that is made in the moment can be easily underestimated by those outside the practice of teaching. Teachers are embedded in educational situations and lived experiences with learners. A teacher can only connect to the individual learner by finding out where the learner is in her thinking, what questions or problems she has, or where she has become stuck, and, on that basis alone, decide how to bring the learner to somewhere new and perhaps unfamiliar. Every act of teaching that is educative is directed toward an individual and involves being open in a way that makes teachers vulnerable to the call of the other. Pedagogical tact is a concept that addresses the existential experience of teachers as one that necessarily involves risk and improvisation.

To examine more closely the connection between tact and teaching as an improvisational practice, we first have to grasp the need for improvisation in teaching. We have to look to the nature of the educational situation and examine in what way it is "always changing," as Max van Manen emphasizes.[6] First, we can see that if a situation is educational, then the learners are learning and changing within themselves. But the changes in the learner do not happen in isolation. The pedagogically tactful teacher is observing, anticipating, and initiating changes in the learner's situation, such that the teacher is also changing; changing how she views the learner, views the appropriateness of her own lesson plan, and perhaps – a point I will return to later – how she views herself as a teacher. It might seem that if a teacher could only learn to anticipate the learner's next step in the learning process, then these changes could be planned for and there would be little need for risk and improvisation in teaching. Of course, this would be to miss the point that

---

[5] Wolfgang Klafki, "Didaktik Analysis as the Core of Preparation of Instruction."
[6] Max van Manen, *The Tact of Teaching: The Meaning of Pedagogical Thoughtfulness*, p. 187 (London: Althouse Press, 1991).

the *change* is what makes the situation *educational*. Despite planning, teachers perpetually find themselves faced with the unexpected and unforeseeable in their practice, both in the context of and outside of specific predesignated questions of curricular content. The unforeseeable may come as a learner who is frustrated with an art assignment, a student who expresses anxiety about a class trip, or a young girl who feels left out of a class activity because of her gender or the color of her skin. Students and teachers bring their lives to the classroom. The teacher is faced with the task of responding in an educative way, a task that calls for risk.

The complexity, innovation, and risk involved in teaching can be illustrated by an example from author and teacher Frank McCourt's memoir *Teacher Man.*[7] Therein, he recounts his experiences as a high school English teacher in New York, in the 1970s. He describes a particular dilemma he faced with his students, who are consistently forging parent excuse notes for their absences from class. McCourt realizes he cannot simply confront the students and accuse them of lying because it would only lead to "strained" relationships.[8] He also realizes that he could simply ignore the situation since forging notes is "just part of school life."[9] Then, as he begins to read the notes, he suddenly sees the writing talent of his students that he had never seen before:

Isn't it remarkable, I thought, how they resist any kind of writing assignment in class or at home. They whine and say they're busy and it's hard putting two hundred words together on any subject. But when they forge excuse notes they're brilliant. Why? I have a drawer full of excuse notes that could be turned into an anthology of Great American Excuses or Great American Lies.[10]

McCourt does decide to confront his students, but he confronts them as learners, not simply as excuse-makers or liars. He hands the whole class the notes with the names omitted and has the students read them. The students in his class are shocked. They are suddenly forced to think about something that they took for granted, namely, that they could lie and get away with it and that they could avoid *learning* to write. McCourt then turns the situation into a creative writing assignment on the topic "An Excuse Note from Adam [or Eve] to God."[11]

The situation shows how teachers can make an unanticipated and even unwanted situation into a pedagogically fruitful experience for both learner

---

[7] Frank McCourt, *Teacher Man* (New York: Scribner, 2005).
[8] Ibid., p. 84.
[9] Ibid.
[10] Ibid.
[11] Ibid., p. 87.

and teacher. This requires a teacher who can judge the situation using the art of pedagogical tact, the art of skillfully opening up learning opportunities when and where they are lacking. The teacher can never fully plan for these situations; they are part of the discontinuity and negativity of the *teacher's* experience that arises because of the call of the other. Jakob Muth describes this aspect of the educational situation as follows:

In the continuous flow of activity a discontinuous moment breaks in. And this makes apparent that we have to understand that tact cannot be planned in two respects: Unplanned is every discontinuous moment that breaks into and thwarts the ordinary flow of activity in school; unplanned is also the action the teacher will take in this moment, a moment which demands quick judgment and decision.[12]

When teachers open themselves up to the new and unexpected within the teacher-learner relation, they open themselves up to the voice of the learner that breaks into and breaks open the educational situation with an unexpected question, a frustrated look, an expressed difficulty with a concept, or a paralyzing fear to move on. In this sense, the pedagogical tactfulness in teaching, as I define it here, means *engaging* the learner's interrupted experiences by initially being open to the learner's frustrations and doubt about how to move on in the learning process. To engage the interruption in a learner's experience also means that the teacher, in light of this moment, must suspend judgment and initiate reflection regarding what to do. In this moment, the teacher asks herself, "How can I transform this moment in the learner's experience in a way that cultivates the learner's self-reflection and learning?"

Pedagogical tact requires that teachers judge on the basis of looking, listening to, and taking in students' questions, difficulties, and frustrations – that is, moments in students' learning experiences that point to the negativity of their experiences – in dealing with the material at hand. To do this is to recognize that educational situations are never fully in the hands of the teacher, and therefore it is an essential part of the educational atmosphere

---

[12] In the original German, the term for "discontinuous" is *unstetig* and for "continuous" *stetig*: "In einen an sich stetigen Ablauf bricht ein unstetiges Moment. Und das macht wiederum deutlich, dass die Nichplanbarkeit des Taktes in einer doppelten Weise gesehen werden muss: Nichtplanbar ist jenes unstetige Moment, das in den Handlungsablauf der Schule einbricht und ihn durchkreuzt; nichtplanbar ist aber auch das Handeln des Lehrers in dieser Situation, die schnelles Beurteilen und Entscheiden fordert," in Jakob Muth, *Pädagogischer Takt. Monographie einer aktuellen Form erzieherischen und didaktischen Handelns*, p. 77–78 (Heidelberg: Quelle und Meyer, 1967), translation mine. On the discontinuous (*unstetige*) moments in teaching processes, see also Otto Friedrich Bollnow, *Existenzphilosophie und Pädagogik* (Stuttgart: Kohlhammer, 1965).

that there remain what philosopher Otto Friedrich Bollnow calls "necessary tensions" (*notwendige Spannungen*) between the teacher's expectations of learners and what the learners actually reveal about themselves in practice.[13] The alternative to a fully controlled environment is not chaos in teaching; rather, for the teacher, it is thoughtfully planning ways to make learning happen, while at the same time remaining open to disappointment and having to rethink one's efforts.[14] To be open in this way as a teacher means to be open to the experiences of unease about your choices, to the fear of not knowing how to respond, to getting lost, to the frustration of balancing innovation with the requirements of the curriculum, and, most significantly, to the sense of despondency that comes with not knowing if you are reaching students.

When the voice of the learner breaks open the learning situation, teachers can feel thrown off course and thereby vulnerable and potentially afraid. If teachers do not understand the educative potential of these moments, it can hinder their ability to move on in teaching. The definitions of productive and destructive interruptions in experience (given in Chapter 6) thus also apply to teacher's experiences. Teachers are susceptible to destructive interruptions in experience, those that hinder their ability to teach, as well as to productive interruptions in experience, those that *call out thinking* and are seen as an invitation to innovate their practice. As I discussed in Chapter 4, the discontinuity and negativity of experience of teachers and learners are interconnected; the moments of discontinuity in learning that arise as frustration or perplexity in the learner's experience become moments of discontinuity in teaching because they are unexpected and unforeseeable and can lead to the teacher's frustration and doubt about how to move on in teaching.[15] These

[13] Otto Friedrich Bollnow, *Die pädagogische Atmosphäre: Untersuchungen über die gefühlsmäßigen zwischenmenschlichen Voraussetzungen der Erziehung* [*The pedagogical atmosphere: Investigations into the emotional-relational Conditions that make Education possible*], p. 54 (Essen: Die blaue Eule, 2001). Related to this, Nicholas Burbules speaks of "keep[ing] the tension alive" in teaching when faced with a dilemma. See "Teaching and the Tragic Sense of Education," in *Teaching and its Predicaments*, edited by Nicholas C. Burbules and David T. Hansen, pp. 163–74, p. 71–72 (Boulder, CO: Westview Press, 1997). See also Biesta, who calls the space of intersubjectivity between teacher and learner "troubling" but "necessary," in Gert J. J. Biesta, *Beyond Learning*, p. 53 (Boulder, CO: Paradigm, 2006).

[14] On this point, see Klaus Prange, "Die Funktion des pädagogischen Takts im Lichte des Technologie Problems der Erziehung" [The Function of Pedagogical Tact in Light of the Problem of Technology], in *Urteilskraft und Pädagogik*, edited by Brigitta Fuchs and Christian Schönherr, pp. 125–32 (Würzburg: Königshausen und Neumann, 2007).

[15] This point also relates to David Hansen's idea of the "predicament" that teachers get into when they do not follow routine. He underscores that this predicament is associated with "uncertainty" and "anxiety" as part of the practice of teaching; see "Being a Good Influence," in *Teaching and Its Predicaments*, edited by Nicholas C. Burbules and David T. Hansen, pp. 163–74, p. 163 (Boulder, CO: Westview Press, 1997).

moments can have productive, educative potential in that they present the teacher with opportunities to create a new path together with the learner. Tact is the ability to create this new path so that the learner feels recognized – not by leaping onto the learner's path, but by using the learner's path to take the learner somewhere new and undiscovered.[16]

Through pedagogical tact, the teacher creates an educational atmosphere that is dialogic and dialectical. Thus, the teacher both responds to the learner and, beyond that, also creates educational situations in which a response to the learner is necessary. To do this means that teachers have to take the risk of *interrupting* and *disrupting* student's taken-for-granted ways of seeing and being in the world by making the familiar strange. On this account, efficacy in teaching lies in the ability to make judgments about how to cultivate situations in which learners become productively confused, perplexed, or what John Passmore referred to as making learners "puzzled."[17] The aim of initiating interruptions in learners' experiences is always to create openings in which they can explore new ways of thinking and acting reflectively. Interrupting learners' experiences is indispensable in teaching if genuine transformative learning (or *Umlernen*) is to take place. When a teacher productively interrupts a learner's experience, the learner breaks with herself; only then can the learner realize that she can decide how she thinks and acts and who she wants to become.

2 LISTENING AND THE VOICE OF THE LEARNER

As I have discussed thus far, pedagogical tact entails recognizing and being attuned to the discontinuity and negativity of experience constitutive of the learner's experience in order to make judgments about learning on that basis. The underlying idea of teaching I have presented is one in which teachers are receptive to the learner's negative experiences and orient their practice toward initiating *productive, educative* interruptions in learner's experiences. This requires recognizing experiences such as confusion, perplexity, frustration, or doubt – also surprise and awe – that accompany learners' experiences of the new and unfamiliar. These moments of confusion or awe occur between the wrong and right answers, in the gray zones of thinking and

---

[16] On this point, see Jakob Muth, *Pädagogischer Takt* (Heidelberg: Quelle und Meyer, 1967) and van Manen, *The Tact of Teaching*.

[17] John Passmore, "On Teaching to Be Critical," in *The Concept of Education*, edited by Richard S. Peters, pp. 192–212 (London: Routledge and Kegan Paul Ltd., 1967); see also William Hare, "Reflections on the Teacher's Tasks: Contributions from Philosophy of Education in the 20th Century," *Educational Research and Perspectives*, 27, no. 2, 2000: 1–23.

learning. In this way, a central responsibility of teaching is examining the *process* and not simply the results of learning. This requires the ability to be receptive to the learner in a particular way, with the aim of understanding *if* the learner is thinking and *how* the learner's ideas relate to the results of learning. To better understand this receptive side of teaching, I examine the central role of listening in teaching, furthering my discussion of the three principles of critical listening that I discussed in Chapter 2 (on Herbart). Listening to the learner, although it is not the only way a teacher is receptive to the learner's experiences, plays a significant role in the experience of teaching; it can also help further illuminate the notion of pedagogical tact.

Author Grace Paley remarks that it is useful for writers to have two ears, "one for literature, and one for home."[18] A similar remark can be made about teachers. Teachers need two ears, one for teaching, and one for – in this case – everything else. The ear of the teacher comes into focus when we consider the role of listening in cultivating learning. Through listening, teachers can become open to difference and otherness that arise in the teacher-learner relation. When listening to the learner is aimed at initiating and engaging interruptions in the learner's experience, it becomes *educative*. The teacher's listening is educative when the teacher is engaged in listening for signs that a productive struggle is taking place in the learners' experiences, and simultaneously, for ways to support learners' transformation of this struggle into aspects of reflective learning processes. On this account, when teachers are engaged in educative listening, they are particularly attuned to interruptions in their own experience that can be indications of interruptions in the learner's experiences. When these interruptions are mediated by what the teacher hears, they can come forth as any unexpected response from a student to the material presented, such as a difficult question, a challenging viewpoint, or a confusing reply. On the basis of the interruption, the reflective teacher exercises pedagogical tact to formulate a response that promotes the student's thinking and learning.

Before more closely examining the educative sense of listening, I will briefly analyze a contrasting idea, namely, a form of listening in teaching that is not aimed at cultivating transformational learning experiences, and therefore could be termed *uneducative* listening. Uneducative listening in teaching can be described as listening in teaching that is normative, confined to mechanically filtering right and wrong answers. For the normative teacher, teaching is largely characterized by the motto "the teacher teaches, the student learns." In practice, this generally amounts to "the teacher speaks, the student

---

[18] Grace Paley, *The Collected Stories*, p. x (New York: Farrar, Straus and Giroux, 1994).

listens." Dewey identifies this shortcoming in traditional models of instruction, in which the teacher provides "ready-made subject matter and listens to the accuracy with which it is reproduced."[19] For example, the teacher may didactically present the "fives" of the multiplication tables on the board and then ask the class "What is five times five?" If a student's answer is "ten," it is deemed wrong and the teacher may listen on, but only to wait for a student to arrive at the right answer. This framework for a teacher's questions is reserved for confirming the acquisition of specific knowledge, so that interruptions, such as differences of opinion or unexpected responses in the classroom, are classified as a lack of understanding, nothing more than "wrong answers." In this context, interruptions inform the teacher only in a limited sense about the learning student, only in terms of how the student compares to the predefined outcomes of learning set by the teacher or the book. Learning is conceived of here as a linear model of moving from point A to point B, or, more broadly speaking, from ignorance to knowledge. This "teacher-centered" model of teaching, and the corresponding normative mode of listening, does not further the student's learning process in a transformative way.

What is different about how the pedagogically tactful teacher engages the interruption? For such a teacher, interruptions in listening are central to the educational process. Interruptions point out the differences in the ways of thinking between the teacher and student, and also between the various students in the classroom. On this model, the teacher aims to ask questions to interrupt the learner's flow of experience, cultivating the learner's *struggle* with understanding the material and listening to see if this *struggle* is taking place. Although this may seem like an abstract approach, we can take the earlier arithmetic example and imagine a plausible dialogue between a teacher and students that shows how the pedagogically tactful teacher might guide a class through the material in this way. Such a dialogue might look something like this:

TEACHER: "Who can tell me what five times five equals?"
STUDENT 1: "Ten."
TEACHER: "OK, how do we get to ten? How many fives are there in ten?"
STUDENT 2: "Two."
TEACHER: "OK, so if we take two 'fives' and add them together, five *plus* five equals ten, right?"
The students understand addition and have no objections.

---

[19] *DE* 167. Waks draws out Dewey's criticism of this form of listening and clarifies the idea of transactional listening in Dewey's work, in Leonard J. Waks, "John Dewey on listening and friendship in school and society," *Educational Theory* 61, no. 2, 2011: 191–205.

TEACHER: "So how many fives do we need to add together in five *times* five?"
STUDENT: "Five."
The teacher asks the student to write it out on the board and add them together:
5 + 5 + 5 + 5 + 5 = 25.
TEACHER: "Good. So five *times* five equals twenty-five. Now let's go back to look at the number ten. We said five *plus* five is ten, so five times what number equals ten? What number is missing?"

The significance of this example is that the teacher expected that the students would be able to answer the first question about multiplication, but when an unexpected (and, in this case, incorrect) answer is heard, it is drawn on to explore *differences* and *connections* between what the students already have learned and what the teacher is now trying to teach them. The teacher thereby shows the students ways of understanding the connections between addition and multiplication. Of course, there are many possible questions and answers that could lead to a different dialogue, depending on what level of knowledge the students already have, and depending on whether there are specific right or wrong answers to the questions at hand.

Independent of the subject matter, pedagogical tact in teaching involves working out the student's frustrations and difficulties dialogically. Accordingly, teaching entails helping the students discover the similarities and differences between what they know and what they still can learn. This is a process that involves both questioning and listening. This notion of teaching entails what Gert Biesta calls the *educational responsibility*, a responsibility that lies in asking "difficult questions," those with "the potential to interrupt" learners in their being.[20] It also entails listening to see if students are *thinking* beyond what they already know – that is, thinking about what they do not know or do not understand – and thus trying to grasp something new. By listening to the students, the tactful, reflective teacher is implicitly asking herself, "What do I need to hear so that I know that thinking and learning are taking place?" The answer to this question is never straightforward, regardless of the subject matter. In teaching, it is a difficult task to decipher whether a

[20] Compare Biesta, *Beyond Learning*, p. 150; see also p. 29–30. Biesta connects this idea to what he comes to call a pedagogy of interruption that he develops in connection to Levinas. On the significance of questions in teaching, see also the work of German education philosopher Sandy Kolenda, who describes how questions can open up experience and our perspective, and open up otherwise closed minds; Sandy Kolenda, *Unterricht als bildendes Gespräch: Richard Rorty und die Entstehung des Neuen im sprachlichen Prozess* (Instruction as an Educative Discussion: Richard Rorty and the Emergence of the New in the Language Process) (Opladen: Barbara Budrich, 2010); see also Ann Chinnery, William Hare, Donald Kerr, and Walter Okshevsky, "Teaching Philosophy of Education: The Value of Questions," *Interchange* 38, no. 2, 2007: 99–118.

student really is thinking about the material. The teacher might wonder if the student gave a right answer only as a repetition of what was read in the book or if the right answer truly demonstrates understanding. A similar dilemma may arise in considering if a student's wrong answer is just an arbitrary guess, or if it represents a genuine attempt to grasp the material.

Using judgments of tact in teaching, the teacher seeks to listen *between* right and wrong answers, in the *gray zones* of students' thinking and learning, which are revealed in the interruption. The notion of pedagogical tact *turns on its head* the idea that teaching consists in quickly getting learners to arrive at new knowledge and abilities without the unwanted interference of the gray zones marked by experiences such as doubt, confusion, uncertainty, or struggle. Instead, it says that the student's arrival at new knowledge and abilities is a transitional phase, and that what the teacher is after is the productive phases of doubt and perplexity – and other forms of negative experience – that signal that the student is thinking and thus that learning is *going on*. Although the tactful teacher anticipates certain potential answers in virtue of knowing the learners' level, at the same time, the teacher understands that this can never amount to knowing exactly what to expect from learners' responses. For the pedagogically tactful teacher, the unexpected *interrupts* the experience of teaching in a way that causes hesitation, suspense of judgment, and reflection on what to do. Philosopher of education Sophie Haroutunian-Gordon has examined interruptions in listening and importantly emphasizes that the interruptions in listening are central to the process of changing one's beliefs.[21] This manifests itself in dialogue with others who have differing beliefs such that "the nature of the interruption determines the direction of the shift in subsequent listening."[22] Genuine interruptions signal *blind spots* in a teacher's own thought and knowledge that make her consider

[21] Sophie Haroutunian-Gordon, "Listening – in a Democratic Society," in *Philosophy of Education 2003*, edited by Kal Alston, pp. 1–18 (Urbana, IL: Philosophy of Education Society, 2004).

[22] Sophie Haroutunian-Gordon, "Listening – in a Democratic Society," p. 13. See also Sophie Haroutunian-Gordon, *Learning to Teach Through Discussion: The Art of Turning the Soul* (New Haven, CT: Yale University Press, 2009); Sophie Haroutunian-Gordon, "Listening and Questioning," *Learning Inquiry* 1, no. 2 (Special Issue "Reflection and Listening," edited by Leonard Waks), 2007: 143–52; and Leonard J. Waks, "Listening and Questioning: The Apophatic/Cataphatic Distinction Revisited," *Learning Inquiry* 1, no. 2 (Special Issue "Reflection and Listening," edited by Leonard Waks), 2007: 153–61. See also Schultz's study on listening and how teachers can create listening communities in classrooms, in which teachers listen to students and students begin to listen and learn from each other: Katherine Schultz, *Listening: A Framework for Teaching Across Difference* (New York: Teachers College Press, 2003) and Elizabeth Meadows, "Transformative Learning through Open Listening: A Professional Development Experience with Urban High School Students," *Learning Inquiry* 1, no. 2 (Special issue "Reflection and Listening," edited by Leonard Waks), 2007: 115–23.

a perspective she has never considered before. When the teacher becomes aware of her own blind spot through a student's question or response in classroom interaction, and the teacher addresses and inquires into the nature of this blind spot, then the teacher learns and the student is, as Dewey puts it, "without knowing it, a teacher" (*DE* 167).

When a teacher is attuned to interruptions arising within teacher-learner interaction, she is listening to the otherness and difference of the learner, with the risk and even the desire to break with her ideas about teaching and learning, and about human beings. As philosopher Maxine Greene relates, "If I and other teachers truly want to provoke our students to break through the limits of the conventional and the taken for granted, we ourselves have to experience breaks with what has been established in our own lives; we have to keep arousing ourselves to begin again."[23] The process of teacher-student dialogue is transformative insofar as both teacher and learner begin to hear *how* they are being heard by each other; on this basis, they can seek out ways of learning from one another. Nicholas Burbules and Suzanne Rice make an illuminating point about all dialogue across difference, one that proves essential for understanding educative teacher-student dialogue: "As a process, dialogue requires us to re-examine our own presuppositions and to compare them against quite different ones; to make us less dogmatic about the belief that the way the world appears to us is necessarily the way the world is."[24] By listening to oneself as a teacher, teachers can become aware of their process of teaching and, in turn, aware of the fact that this process can be changed by their decisions.

When listening is educative, teachers learn how to guide learners – not simply toward predefined answers, but toward figuring out what questions to ask, or more generally, how to productively engage with the struggle of learning. If learners are to engage in discussion in classroom learning and

---

[23] Maxine Greene, *Releasing the Imagination: Essays on Education, The Arts, and Social Change*, p. 109 (San Francisco: Jossey-Bass, 1995); see also on this point, Barbara Stengel "Facing Fear, Releasing Resistance, Enabling Education," *Philosophical Studies in Education* 39, 2008: 66–75, and Deborah Kerdeman, "Pulled Up Short: Challenging Self-Understanding as a Focus of Teaching and Learning," *Journal of Philosophy of Education* 37, no. 2, 2003: 293–308, on the concept of being "pulled up short" (which I discussed in Chapter 6), as it applies to teachers.

[24] Nicholas Burbules and Suzanne Rice, "Dialogue Across Difference: Continuing the Conversation," *Harvard Educational Review* 61, no. 4, 1991: 393–406, 405; see also Nicholas Burbules, *Dialogue in Teaching. Theory and Practice* (New York: Teachers College Press, 1993); Megan Laverty, "Dialogue as Philosophical Inquiry in the Teaching of Sympathy and Tolerance," *Learning Inquiry* 1, no. 2 (Special Issue "Reflection and Listening," edited by Leonard Waks), 2007: 125–32; and Michelle Forrest, "Sensitive Controversy in Teaching to Be Critical," *Paideusis* 18: 1, 2008: 80–93.

not become passive listeners, then teachers must learn how to differentiate what they hear. They must seek to understand how a student's response relates to how that particular student is thinking about the subject matter. This idea of educative listening in teaching thus relates to what William Hare calls "being a good listener." Hare points out that being a good listener involves judgment of what is heard and knowledge of "how to take things and what to listen for."[25] This type of knowledge and judgment must itself be learned. Hare's discussion of the good listener makes clear that a certain interrelationship must exist between the listener and the speaker in order for listening to be generative for both. According to Hare, a good listener is one who is open-minded and willing to listen to the ideas and thoughts of the other person in such a way that allows those heard ideas to potentially change the way the listener thinks.[26]

For teachers to begin to understand themselves as critical, reflective, educative listeners, they must first understand how to become open to learning within the teacher-learner relation. For prospective teachers and in-service teachers to learn to listen in such a way that, through their listening, they are figuring out the limits of the student's knowledge and ability as well as their own, they have to learn to understand that listening involves becoming open to another person and to new ideas. As Jim Garrison points out, the openness required by listening to the other involves taking a risk and becoming vulnerable: "Remaining open is awkward. We must be willing to live with confusion and uncertainty about both ourselves and the other person we are attempting to understand."[27] An essential part of what it means to be a

---

[25] William Hare, "Has Listening Had a Fair Hearing," *Agora* 3, no. 1–2, 1975: 5–13, 9.

[26] Ibid.; see also William Hare, *Open-mindedness and Education* (Montreal: McGill-Queen's University Press, 1983). This idea of being open to changing one's beliefs relates to Michael Katz's definition of integrity in teaching. He importantly points out that integrity in teaching is not maintaining a fixed sense of self, but rather requires that "we continually remain open to examining how our actions may sometimes not be aligned with our preexisting value commitments" and are able to modify our beliefs. See Michael S. Katz, "Teaching with Integrity," in *Philosophy of Education 2008*, edited by Ronald Glass, pp. 7–11, 7 (Urbana, IL: Philosophy of Education Society, 2009). Also, a connection here can be made to a recent study in educational psychology, which demonstrates that open-mindedness in teachers makes them more likely to provide adaptations in instruction for learners with learning and behavioral difficulties (LBD); see Nezihe Elik, Judith Wiener, and Penny Corkum, "Pre-Service Teachers' Open Minded Thinking Dispositions, Readiness to Learn, and Attitudes about Learning and Behavioural Difficulties in Students," *European Journal of Teacher Education* 33, no. 2, May 2012: 127–46.

[27] James Garrison, "A Deweyan Theory of Democratic Listening," *Educational Theory* 46, no. 4, 1996: 429–51, p. 433; see also Pádraig Hogan, who underscores that to engage in teaching that combines "attentive listening with self-critical reflection and generous but critical response" is "to *live with risk*"; Pádraig Hogan, "The Integrity of Learning and the Search for Truth," *Educational*

teacher is learning how to take this risk and, in the process, begin to define yourself in terms of the other, the learner.

Although formulated in an earlier era, Herbart's notion of pedagogical tact is, perhaps unexpectedly, still relevant today. Pedagogical tact is a form of judgment that is important for furthering educational discourse because it is based in the teacher's ability to notice difference in the learning processes of each particular learner; it takes into consideration both the particular learning individual *and* what is required to cultivate transformative learning processes. Pedagogical tact is also a disposition, one that characterizes the teacher who takes discontinuity in teaching seriously, makes it a point to learn about the learner through each interaction, attempts to understand where the process of learning is headed and to recognize wherein its potential lies, and, ultimately, seeks to determine how to challenge the learner beyond his or her normally achieved standard. *This* standard is not defined by a test, but by the teacher and learner through their interactions. Teachers must come to know this standard, one that is in the process of changing as the learner changes and grows. Knowing this standard is important for teachers, not simply so that they can compare it with the expected norms of achievement measured by standardized tests, but rather so that they can use it to evaluate externally imposed standards in comparison to the abilities and potential of their students. So, although some might be solely concerned with the fact that a student failed a test, the pedagogically tactful teacher is able to determine whether or not *the test also failed the student*.

Being attuned to strangeness and difference, which continually interrupts the experience of teaching, means listening for and finding differences in each learner's learning process, recognizing that each learner is different. By understanding the process of teaching, we can see that the negativity of experience involved in learning is also part of teachers' experiences. In teaching, teachers are confronted with the interruptions in learners' experiences that interrupt their own process of teaching. In other words, teachers' experiences are mediated by a twofold form of the *negativity of experience* (as I discussed in Chapter 4). This means the *problem for the learner* regarding how to learn ("How do I learn something new?") becomes a *problem for the teacher* regarding how to teach ("How do I teach this new thing in a way that

Theory, 55, no. 2, 2005: 198; see also Mordechai Gordon, "Listening as Embracing the Other: Martin Buber's Philosophy of Dialogue," *Educational Theory* 61, no. 2 (Special Issue on "Listening," edited by Sophie Haroutunian-Gordon and Megan Laverty), April 2011: 207–19; and on listening in education and learning from difference, see also Sharon Todd, *Learning from the Other: Levinas, Psychoanalysis, and Ethical Possibilities in Education* (Albany: State University of New York Press, 2003).

the learner will understand it?"). When teachers begin to reflect on the interruptions in their own practice – that is, the unexpected questions and challenges that arise within their interaction with learners – they begin to learn about themselves as teachers and, in turn, learn how to teach.[28] They learn where the learners' experiences need expansion or modification and how to help learners find ways out of indeterminate and problematic situations.

A central part of educating is taking into account that the otherness of the world and the negative experiences that learners encounter are not *necessarily* educative. Resistant factors may thwart the child's attempts to learn about the world and potentially change it. To make the world educative, teachers have to help learners take it apart and explore realms that otherwise may be arbitrarily ignored or intentionally avoided out of fear or lack of interest. To do this, teachers have to learn to cultivate uncertainty in productive ways, so that learners begin to question their knowledge and beliefs and those of others. Productively interrupting learners' experiences means creating openings in the learners' experiences through which learners can make new choices. When construed in this form, teaching is an inherently moral practice; through the teacher's questions, learners begin to question their own beliefs, think critically, and begin to search for new knowledge.[29]

Ultimately, this form of teaching recognizes the voice of the learner and directly opposes the two prevailing models of teaching: the traditional model, which sees the teacher's task as "pouring in" knowledge to a passively receptive learner, and the progressive model, which sees the learner as the primary arbiter of what counts as worth doing.[30] A central problem with both of these models of educating is that they do not recognize the productive meaning of discontinuity and negativity in learning processes. The former

---

[28] See, on this point, Nicholas C. Burbules, "Aporias, Webs, and Passages: Doubt as an Opportunity to Learn," *Curriculum Inquiry* 30, no. 2, 2000: 171–87; see also Käte Meyer-Drawe, "Die Belehrbarkeit des Lehrenden durch den Lernenden."

[29] Nietzsche's *Lectures on Education* illuminate a similar understanding of the aporetic quality of education. Therein, the lecturer's aim can be viewed as provoking his listeners (or readers) to question how to distinguish between *truth* and *deception*, without promising them an answer. In doing so, the lectures make the audience conscious of the idea that the possibility of deception – that is, the possibility that our judgments were misjudgments; our knowledge, ignorance; our morals, immoral – is at the root of all inquiries; it renders such inquiries educative. Friedrich Nietzsche, "Über die Zukunft unserer Bildungsanstalten," in *Friedrich Nietzsche: Sämtliche Werke, Kritische Studienausgabe*, edited by Giorgio Colli and Mazzino Montinari, Vol. 1, pp. 643–752 (München: Deutscher Taschenbuch Verlag, 1988).

[30] This distinction relates to the dominant ideas of education in German educational discourse as *Führen* ("leading"), or as *Wachsenlassen* ("letting grow"). For a critique of these two models, see Bollnow, "Existenzphilosophie und Pädagogik."

"teacher-centered" form of educating sees the child's frustration and difficulty as the child's failure and therefore as a halt in the learning process. The latter "child-centered" form of educating does not remedy the problem either; the child's errors or confusions are given little meaning and, if anything, attempts are made to ameliorate such difficulty through strategies of coddling and safety.[31] On my account of teaching with pedagogical tact, being attuned to the voice of the learner means understanding how to cultivate discontinuity in the learner's thoughts and experiences, with the aim of supporting the learner's self-transformation – *without* a specific notion of what this transformation will look like.

We can understand pedagogical tact as the form of judgment in teaching that seeks to cultivate discontinuity without the intention of leaving learners lost or abandoned, but rather with the aim of making them responsible for participating in their own education. By listening to learners, teachers make possible this shift in learners' experiences: the shift from being passive recipients of knowledge to being active participants in their educational process. Philosopher of education Paolo Freire highlights the paradox of listening in teaching with his point that only "by listening to learners" can teachers learn to "talk with learners," and, in turn, "teach the learners to listen to them as well."[32] Freire's point makes clear that when teachers acknowledge the difference and otherness brought by learners to the educational situation, then learners in turn *desire* to listen – not because an authority compels them, but because they begin to view listening as a path to their own learning and growth. To take this idea seriously, we must consider that if we value cultivating transformative educational experiences for learners, then we must create opportunities for listening that stem from their desire to learn rather than from a dutiful or forced obedience.

3   REFLECTIVE TEACHER-LEARNER ENGAGEMENT

The question of how to productively interrupt a learner's experience is not always clear; a welcome challenge to one student may be an overwhelming,

---

[31] For a critique of progressive education's view of safety and an analysis of the productive meaning of fear in education, see English and Stengel, "Exploring Fear", *Educational Theory*, 60, no. 5, 2010: 521–42; see also Barbara Stengel, "The Complex Case of Fear and Safe Space," *Studies in Philosophy and Education* 29, no. 6, 2010: 1–18. On fear and teacher's experiences, see also Mary Jane Harkins, Michelle Forrest, and Terrah Keener, "Room for Fear: Using Our Own Personal Stories in Teacher Education," *Journal of Teaching and Learning* 6, no. 1, 2009: 15–23.

[32] Paulo Freire, *Teachers as Cultural Workers: Letters to Those Who Dare to Teach*, p. 115 (Boulder, CO: Westview Press, 2005).

destructive interruption for another. Educators must consistently ask themselves how to perceive *productive* interruptions in teacher-learner relations and how to clearly define what counts as a *destructive* form of interruption in a learner's experiences. A definition of teaching as a profession must entail an understanding not only of how to plan for the unexpected, but also of how to make judgments in the midst of practice when the truly unexpected arises. This requires judgments of pedagogical tact that are part of reflective teaching as "teaching in-between" (defined in Chapter 4). The model of *Reflective Teacher-Learner Engagement* (Figure 1) shows how teacher-learner interaction unfolds when teaching is understood as teaching in-between, that is, as teaching that entails initiating and engaging interruptions in the learner's experience of learning:

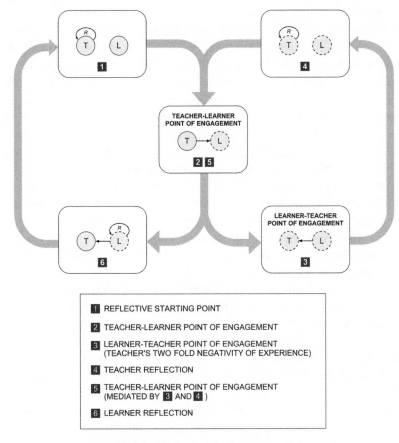

FIGURE 1 Model of Reflective Teacher-Learner Engagement

This model identifies central moments of reflective experiential learning processes within teacher-learner interaction. Underlying the model is the notion that the educational relation is based in initiating productive interruptions and reflection in the learner's learning process. This requires a teacher who can challenge the learner such that the learner's mind opens to the new and unfamiliar and the learner begins to think and ask questions. Thus, what I call the "Teacher-Learner Point of Engagement" (points 2 and 5) identifies the point at which the teacher's challenge (T → L) *interrupts* the learner in an *attempt* to initiate the learner's openness to the new (the dashed circle indicates the state of interruption). Here, a challenge is defined as any question, activity, or assignment presented to the learner that calls out the learner's thinking. In these moments, the teacher is attempting to challenge the learner in an educative way by cultivating the learner's productive educative struggle with the material; however, the teacher cannot be certain that his or her planned question or challenge about a given subject matter will not over- or underchallenge the learner. In other words, the teacher cannot be sure (in advance of the interaction with the learner) exactly how the learner will experience the interruption. Thus, the "Learner-Teacher Point of Engagement" (point 3) locates the moment when the learner responds to the teacher's challenge (T ← L) (the response could be verbal or nonverbal; e.g., a look of confusion). This marks the moment when the teacher becomes aware if and to what extent the learner has been interrupted in a productive-educative way and, in turn, to what extent the learner's mind has opened to the new. In this moment, the teacher experiences a twofold form of negativity of experience: the teacher is interrupted by the learner's interrupted experience because the teacher did not know exactly how the learner would respond to the challenge (hence the dashed circle of both teacher and learner to indicated interrupted experience).

The difference between the two points of engagement is significant. The "Teacher-Learner Point of Engagement" is defined by the *teacher*, who is initiating the interruption in the learner's experience (in the sense that it is the teacher's question or challenge that she has designed for the learner). In contrast, the "Learner-Teacher Point of Engagement" is defined by the *learner* (in the sense that it is the learner's response to the teacher's challenge that determines the next step within the interaction). In reflecting on these two moments within the interaction (depicted in point 4 by an R for reflection), the teacher can recognize the *difference* between *what she is trying to teach* and *what the learner wants or needs to learn*. In other words, point 4 represents the moment when the teacher reflects on her own interruption in the experience of teaching and how it is interconnected to the interruption in the learner's experience of learning. The teacher's reflection aims to understand how the learner was interrupted by the initial challenge and, on that basis, determine to what extent the learner needs to be *reengaged* with a new, modified challenge (point 5). This new, modified challenge aims to support the learner to continue exploring possibilities within the learner's own learning process. It is in these moments that the teacher asks herself, "How do I proceed in a way that ensures that reflective educative forms of learning take place?"

The movement from point 1 through the "Teacher-Learner Point of Engagement" (point 2) to the "Learner-Teacher Point of Engagement" (point 3) identifies the learner's transition from established, taken-for-granted knowledge and ability to the interruption in the learner's experience. The interruption in the learner's experience (point 3) marks a *prereflective beginning of learning*. The learner may experience this interruption as confusion or uncertainty about what she knows and has already learned. By reengaging the learner with a modified challenge (point 5), the teacher is attempting to support the learner's transition from the *prereflective beginning of learning* to a *reflective-transformative beginning of learning* – thus, from an indeterminate situation to a problematic situation (as defined in Chapters 3 and 4). This transition may not be immediate. Therefore, the teacher and learner could continue to progress through the right side of the diagram proceeding from point 5 (the new challenge presented to the learner) through the moments of interaction represented in points 3 and 4. The learner's transition from point 5 to point 6 represents the successful transition from a *prereflective beginning of learning* to a *reflective-transformative beginning of learning*. Thus, point 6 represents the moment when the learner has identified her own difficulty (or the like) and reflectively attempts to understand it and to formulate possible solutions and new questions associated with it (depicted in 6 by R for reflection).

The model also leaves open the idea that reflective teacher-learner interaction could entail a movement *directly* from points 2 to 6. This would mean that the teacher's initial challenge to the learner (point 2) immediately initiates the learner's *reflective-transformative beginning of learning* (point 6). In other words, the teacher's challenge initiates the learner's reflective thought, such that the learner is able to identify her own difficulty. Whether the learner moves from the teacher's challenge (point 2) to a *prereflective beginning of learning* (point 3) or to a *reflective-transformative beginning of learning* (point 6) depends on both the type of challenge the teacher poses and the knowledge and ability the learner has already established through prior interruptions in experience.

Each of these moments within the teacher-learner interaction informs the teacher's ability to make judgments of pedagogical tact. Judgments of tact are complex, and this is shown in three particular ways in Figure 1. Such judgments presuppose that the teacher has made reflective judgments (point 1, with R indicating the teacher's reflection) informed by educational theory and practice about what environment and what materials are needed for reflective learning experiences to unfold. Furthermore, judgments of tact presuppose that the teacher has made judgments as to how to actively attempt to productively interrupt the learner's experience in a way that recognizes the perfectibility of the learner by encouraging, rather than discouraging, reflective learning processes (point 2). The teacher's pedagogical tact truly reveals itself in the way that she effectively responds *in the moment* (point 5) to the learner's needs and abilities when these become apparent (points 3 and 4). The teacher's response must be sufficiently reflective of how to transform the learner's interrupted experience into a reflective experiential learning process and not leave the learner lost, abandoned, or stuck.

This model of reflective teacher-learner engagement represents an experiential and experimental process of interaction in which the teacher comes to know the learner and the learner comes to know the teacher. For the teacher, the interaction aims at creating an educative atmosphere in which the learner develops trust for the teacher as one who will support – and not hinder – her in coming to understand herself and her relation to the world. To enact reflective teacher-learner engagement in the classroom entails that the teacher learns to create a space for dialogue within the learning environment. Creating a space for dialogue involves the art of knowing how to challenge students in a way that brings them out of their comfort zone and, at the same time, supports their attempts to think differently, test their ideas, and listen to one another in ways in which they are not accustomed. Teaching in this way involves risk, because there is always a chance that things will not turn out as planned; there is a chance one will be interrupted and experience disillusionment. However, I believe teachers must challenge themselves to create these dialogic spaces, for when students begin to see themselves differently, they begin to learn not only about the subject matter at hand, but also about themselves as human beings. In these spaces – when they are fruitful – a certain kind of trust can be established that forms the basis for educational relations, a trust that is granted to the teacher by the learner. This trust is only granted when the learner recognizes the teacher as someone who is willing and able to cultivate the learner's reflective learning processes.

Chapter 8

Perfectibility and Recognition of the Other

To teach seriously is to lay hands on what is most vital in a human being. It is to seek access to the quick and the innermost of a child's or an adult's integrity.
— George Steiner, *Lessons of the Masters*[1]

1   LEARNING AS HUMAN — HUMAN AS LEARNER

Teachers need to be given room to judge classroom situations on the basis of recognizing the learner as a learning being. This requires making the student the "point of orientation" (in Herbart's words) for all judgments of what to do in educational situations. Similarly, as Dewey stated, the learning individuals in our classrooms need to be recognized as human beings and not simply as pupils. Teachers must recognize that, in order to learn, students must be allowed to make errors in judgment, become frustrated, or find themselves in anguish as they break with routines or once-trusted ideas. The practice of teaching with pedagogical tact fulfills these conditions.

In many classrooms around the world, teachers are faced with reforms that stifle their ability to productively respond to the ever-changing nature of educational situations. They are pressured with testing, accountability measures, and increased calls for efficiency in achieving learning objectives and curriculum outcomes. This technical-reductionist version of the classroom situation in its most extreme form attempts to erase failure from the educational equation.[2] *These attempts also seek to erase the individual learner.* The learner breaks open the educational situation with his or her unexpected voice, which makes teaching personal and interpersonal. Of course, in the

---

[1] Reprinted by permission of the publisher from *Lessons of the Masters* by George Steiner, p. 18, Cambridge, M.A.: Harvard University Press, Copyright © 2003 by George Steiner.
[2] On this point and for a critique of Reynold's "Highly Reliable Schools," see Nigel Blake, Paul Smeyers, Richard Smith, and Paul Standish, *Education in the Age of Nihilism*, pp. 2–5 (London: Routledge, 2000).

classroom, just as in everyday life, it is not possible to account for all unexpected situations; it is not possible to erase the negativity in teachers' and learners' experiences of encountering one another as learning beings in the world. The danger is that school administrators, policy makers, and the public will continue to choose to ignore these negative experiences and operate as if they are educationally insignificant. In doing so, they make it impossible for teachers to cultivate pedagogical tact and transformative learning in schools because, under these circumstances, as Herbart stated so long ago, schools will not provide teachers the opportunity to "connect to individuals."

Herbart presented an underlying dilemma that philosophers and educators would have to face in creating situations for educative teacher-learner interaction in practice. He notes that, for open and meaningful educational environments to exist in schools, there needs to first be an "educational spirit" (*pädagogischer Geist*) in society, that is, a public state of mind that believes in and supports the rich potential of such environments.[3] Yet, for such an educational spirit to come into being in society, society must first witness the fruits of these environments.[4] This is a dilemma that we can locate in the dialectic between democracy and education that lies at the heart of Dewey's work. This aporetic situation still faces philosophers and educators, who strive to understand the conditions under which transformative education can take place.

If policy makers and those outside the lived situations of education continue to attempt to make the classroom environment controlled and controllable, they may eventually succeed in their efforts to remove the personal and interpersonal side of teaching and reduce teachers to automatons awaiting the next command. The genuine problem that faces humanity as a whole in halting and reversing these efforts is that good teaching and true pedagogical tact is difficult to observe from the outside. This is because it is connected to specific situations, it is something *felt* and *directly experienced* by the learner within the educational teacher-learner relation. Pedagogical tact, when it hits the right note, meets the existential need of the learner such that the learner feels recognized in her being as a *learning being* and forgets the pain of the foregoing difficulty. In this way, the immediate impression of pedagogical tact is, in a certain sense, forgotten by the learner. This connects to the fact that, as

---

[3] Johann Friedrich Herbart, "Über Erziehung unter öffentlicher Mitwirkung (1810)," in *Joh. Friedr. Herbart's Sämtliche Werke in Chronologischer Reihenfolge*, edited by Karl Kehrbach, Vol. 3, pp. 73–82, 81 (Langensalza: Hermann Beyer und Söhne, 1888).

[4] Ibid., p. 81.

adults, we generally remember our bad teachers by *what they did* – the ones who yelled, threw things, were not attentive, or said we were not good at a particular subject, whereas we typically remember our good teachers not for something specific that they did, but more often for *who they were* as people. By tactfully encountering students, true caring and professional teachers make teaching appear easy. Just as ballet dancers are seen as masters of their art when they make the difficult look graceful and effortless, truly pedagogically tactful teachers make teaching appear so effortless that some might believe anyone could do it.

Policy makers, administrators, and the public on the whole, who look in and observe education happening in classrooms from an external perspective, will observe that when everything is working, it looks smooth and easy. This fact perpetuates the present problem that strategies for the measurement of teaching start from the *results*, that is, they start from those situations in which good teaching has already been learned. When these strategies fail to work upon implementation, policy makers, school boards, and administrators continue to believe that they have simply not yet perfected their strategies and techniques, and, in the meantime, in certain cases, lower standards so far that no "failure" is recorded. In reality, such reformists are taking a fundamentally wrong approach that no amount of superficial adjustment can rectify.

Cross-cultural dialogue about education is a starting point for creating the educational spirit in society. Such dialogue must surround questions of how to create situations in which every human being is recognized as a *learning being* and given promising opportunities to learn. A precondition for such a discussion is that we, as philosophers, educators, and human beings, establish the *Bildsamkeit* of every individual as the starting point for our inquiry into education. The darkest periods of oppression in human history were connected to the lack of recognition of human beings as learning beings based on group affiliations such as race, gender, or religion. This injustice hits us at the core of who we are. To recognize another person as a learning being means not simply recognizing that he or she is *capable of learning*, but also that he or she can be *learned from*.

2 TEACHING AS RECOGNITION OF THE OTHER

A grave misreading of the preceding chapters would be to assume that the argument presented justifies poor teaching, as if it were being argued that, as long as the learner is experiencing discontinuity and is frustrated or confused (without qualification of what this experience is based in), then the learner will learn and the teacher has done her job. It is important that educators discuss how to define bad teaching and clearly discuss the limits of the teacher's task. I have sought to begin this dialogue by distinguishing between productive and destructive interruptions in learner's experiences. Only the former is an act of recognition of the learner as *perfectible* (*bildsam*), that is, able to learn in the way I have sought to define throughout this book. This distinction must be part of an ongoing dialogue about the teacher's task.

Teachers can begin to ask themselves how they would establish this distinction by reflecting on the negativity of experience within their own learning history with their former teachers and educators in and out of school. This reflection can begin by asking oneself, "Did I learn *in light of* or *in spite of* that teacher's actions?" Good teaching requires understanding how to create spaces for learning in which learners can find their voice. *What shape must this space take on in order for the learner's own sound to come out?* The answer to this question is not clear; it will be based in what the teacher identifies as the needs of the learners in her classroom, and her imaginative view of the possibilities for these learners. One starting point to answering this question can be found in Dewey's idea of the classroom as a space for learners to cultivate complexity of thought, engage with varied materials of learning and with other learners, develop a plurality of ideas and forms of practice, and exchange differing perspectives.

In Chapter 1, I identified two conclusions regarding what it means to recognize the perfectibility of the learner. To these we must add a third: the recognition of the other as a learning being implies that *the learner is unique and can always choose differently than the teacher*. Thus, the teacher must recognize that the otherness of the learner represents a certain blind spot – one that reminds teachers that, despite their best intentions, there is always a chance they can get it wrong. In all teacher-learner interaction, there must remain this space for difference and surprise, for something that the teacher had not thought of and could not foresee but is nonetheless essential and valuable for the continued *educative* interaction.

To teach is to accept the responsibility of recognizing another's humanity. This makes teaching a profession that requires a learned disposition – a disposition that cannot be attained by acquiring a handful of techniques and strategies; *it is the disposition of pedagogical tact*. Teachers can and must learn to prepare learners for the experience of interruption. That means that teachers must prepare themselves for the places where learners might get lost within a planned lesson. Teachers can plan for the possibility that learners will get lost, even if they do not know the exact way a particular learner will get lost. This does not imply manipulation of the learner's experience, but rather entails creating a learning environment and context in which getting lost can help learners find their own limitations and become self-reflective and self-questioning persons. Furthermore, recognizing that a learner can get lost is a recognition of the perfectibility of the learner; it is a recognition of the fact that, in order to learn, one must find one's own way. This path is untrodden for the learning individual – it is a path riddled with the new and unfamiliar.

Part of the question of *what education is* has to remain open; it has to recognize that the dialogue about education itself will have blind spots, things that we presently do not understand, that we may not ever fully understand, despite inquiry into the past. We have to leave the question open for the next generation to continue to uncover and explore. At the same time, this recognition of our own fallibility as a society is not a call to drop out of the dialogue, resigned to believing that we cannot ever fully figure out what education consists of. Instead, it is a call to recognize that education is not merely an additive, reductive process of getting to right answers, but rather that education is a transformative process. On this understanding, education entails a recognition of human perfectibility – that is, a recognition of every human being's ability to become interrupted, to break with themselves, potentially make new choices that recognize the other, and learn on that basis.

When teachers interrupt learners' experiences and allow them to feel the excitement of inquiry into the interruption, learners begin to trust the process of learning. The excitement experienced by learners is part of their becoming aware that, as individuals, their perspectives can change, they can come to see things differently, and that new encounters with otherness can lead them to call things into question. In this process, *the questions that were once posed to them by another* may become *their own questions*, a starting point for a renewal of life. Presently, schools are headed toward forcing students to take ownership of error, frustration, or confusion in schooling through the process of testing. But this process teaches them little to nothing about taking ownership of frustrations and error in *life*. Their errors are on paper, and that is where they remain. Standardized tests have come to represent finalities, closed concepts, and finished ideas; such tests tell learners that everything has already been learned – they simply need to catch up.

Teachers need to teach learners in a way that allows learners to take ownership of their own learning process within and outside the context of schooling. To do this, we must begin with understanding the role of inter-ruptions in experience that I have discussed throughout this book. When learners begin to trust in the process of learning, they begin to understand that they can continue to change the choices they make in their own life in ways that recognize the needs of others around them.

When we view learning as transformative, then we can begin to see that we can actively seek out the new and unfamiliar – the otherness within oneself and within society – and embrace it as a possibility for transforming individual and social experiences. In other words, we can come to regard ourselves as perfectible beings living in a perfectible society. In this endeavor, seeking out the new is at once painful and exciting.

We could go on with our lives indifferent to the other because of an indifference to the other within ourselves, to the otherness that gets drawn out in the negative experiences of everyday life. However, if we become aware of the otherness within ourselves, we can learn to be open to the other in ourselves *and* the other in the world around us. We have to ask ourselves if we would rather have the new disturb our comfort or risk not experiencing the new at all. Which path we take as human beings becomes a question of whether we value the discomfort of the negativity of experience and the educational possibilities that arise therein.

3   CONCLUSION: PRESERVING THE IN-BETWEEN OF EXPERIENCE FOR EDUCATION

What could it mean to preserve the in-between of experience for education? By reading Herbart and Dewey, as well as contemporary theorists' thoughts on the educative meaning of experiences such as inner struggle, felt difficulty, resistance, doubt, disillusionment, and fear, I have sought to demonstrate why we *should* preserve the in-between of experience for education, as well as how we could do so. In teacher-learner interaction, preserving the in-between means that learners are given a sense of how to find the in-between for themselves, how to create encounters with the new and unfamiliar that lead them to self-critical thought. The significance of the in-between of learning is grasped when we begin to understand that, in learning processes, the space that opens up when one is interrupted – confronted by something new and unfamiliar – is an experimental space for one to learn about oneself (one's limits and capacities) and about the world. In this space, learners can gain a sense of their own perfectibility.

As I have stated, learning processes entail that we are interrupted in our experience of the world. This means that learning processes are not simply positive and affirmative, but also discontinuous and negative, such that the *negativity of experience* is constitutive of processes of learning and those of teaching. In closing, I identify three dimensions of the negativity of experience that can further our grasp of how to continue to locate, investigate, and inquire into what it means to preserve the in-between in educational theory and practice. These three dimensions are a corporeal-existential dimension, a theoretical-experimental dimension, and a moral-practical dimension.

The corporeal-existential dimension is experienced when one is interrupted in such a way that one becomes aware of the fact that one's body mediates one's interactions with the world. In this way, our experience of the world is not merely constructed and planned, but also suffered, felt, noticed, undergone, and traversed *through and with* the body.

The theoretical-experimental dimension of the negativity of our experiences is grounded in precognitive and thus prereflective moments of interruption of the sort that we cannot knowingly and willingly create. Rather, these forms of interruption always in some way take us by surprise and connect to what we consider mistakes, errors of judgment, confusion. This fact points to what I call a "double-blindness" entailed by the negativity of experience. One part of this is that each individual is blind to what will interrupt her; each moment of interruption is unique in that it is based in a dialectic interaction between the individual's own learning history and the historical circumstances in which she finds herself. In this sense, we remain blind to our own future. Another part of this is that the interruption is a precognitive moment, and, as such, we cannot ever know exactly and with certainty what happened to us when we were interrupted – we must always search from "ahead" by looking back on our experience. In this sense, we remain blind to our own past. On my account, this double-blindness points to the fact that our blindness to what is *to come* relates to our blindness to what has gone before – just as we cannot fully know whether we have accurately found the full reason for an interruption in experience, we also cannot ever fully know how previous interruptions in our experiences relate to what is *to come* to interrupt us anew. However, to face this blindness, we can inquire experimentally into ourselves and the world around us, by asking questions about our experience of interruption, engaging in dialogue with others about their experiences, and thus challenge ourselves to find new ways of seeing the world and being in the world.

Finally, the negativity of experience also has a pragmatic-moral dimension. This relates to the fact that crisis situations, those that occur when we find ourselves struggling to decide what to do, cannot be resolved simply by recourse to established principles or naïve trust in a random trial of some new way of acting. Rather, the crisis situation must be reflectively struggled through, met with self-critique, and dealt with by paying attention to all of its particularities.

If negative experiences are to become part of educative experiences, we need to understand all three dimensions of the negativity of experience, so that, along with our corporeal-existential experience of the world, we develop a theoretical-experimental attitude toward the world, as well as an ability to pragmatically experiment *with* others in the world to develop forms of reciprocal respect.

The notions of discontinuity and *negativity of experience*, as I have developed them throughout this book, underscore the general phenomenon of the experience of limitation. Our experience of discontinuity presupposes such negativity of experience, that is, it presupposes that an unknown or blind spot always exists in what we do and how we think in the world. As I have sought to demonstrate here, this experience contributes to our understanding of ourselves, the world, and others. However, as I hope to have made clear, bringing together these varied notions of how we experience limitation does not diminish (or negate) the distinctions between these phenomena.

I believe that educational theory, research, and practice must continue to find ways to preserve the in-between. This means that we must consider all three dimensions of the negativity of experience, observe how they play out in concrete learning environments with particular learners, and anticipate how they might transform within the ever-changing nature of an individual's learning process. Furthermore, we must consider how to incorporate these dimensions of the negativity of experience into learning processes so that they play a nondestructive, educative role within the teacher-learner relationship.

Epilogue

Should Teachers Think? – Re(dis)covering the Meaning of Philosophy for the Education of Teachers

Philosophy of education is a discipline that has supported teachers' ability to think about the practice of teaching and about how children learn. The theories of education that are discussed in philosophy courses with preservice and in-service teachers aim to expose teachers to the underlying questions and problems of education and help them understand the difficulty of teaching. Yet, in several countries, including the United States, the United Kingdom, and Canada, teacher education programs are eliminating the philosophical component. The trend in decreasing theoretical inquiry for teachers corresponds to an increase in standardized testing as a measure, not just of learning, but also of good teaching. Is this correspondence merely a coincidence, or do these trends have something in common? A closer look at the current discourse on educational reform may tell us that they have more in common than we might at first think.

The rhetoric of reform in the United States, the United Kingdom, and Canada has been focused on teacher "accountability." But what exactly are teachers to be accountable for? To make teachers responsible for student learning seems reasonable and necessary. Indeed, the job of the teacher is to support and enhance learning. However, the central problem is in the attempt to fix teacher accountability to students' standardized test scores. Why is this a problem? Because a learner's test score does not tell us what decisions a teacher made to get the learner to that score. Was the teacher simply teaching to the test and demanding rote learning, or was the teacher really taking into account each individual learner and supporting his or her learning process?

The key problem is that such methods of teacher evaluation leave out entirely what goes on in classrooms on a day-to-day basis: they leave out how the teacher is actually teaching. Policy makers must be kept aware that teachers are willing and able to earn trust. Trust is earned in teaching, as in any profession, by making good judgments. So, the fundamental question that continually needs to be asked in the discourse on education reform is: What counts as good judgment in teaching?

Common ideas of teaching and lesson planning make those on the outside of the classroom, including parents, continue to think that teaching situations can be fully predetermined to guarantee learning. However, much of what goes on in the classroom is based on decisions made by teachers "in the moment," when a teacher sees that something is *not working* and *decides to make a change* (as described in my account of pedagogical tact). As I have discussed throughout this book, good teachers are able to decide when a student's learning process has become stuck and then determine what is needed to continue that student's learning process.

But this brings up the issue of freedom and autonomy for teachers to make judgments about learning, which leads us to another problem. Good judgment in teaching, just as in other professions, is often learned by making mistakes, that is, by first making *bad* judgments. Can we allow teachers to make mistakes when our children are involved? If teachers are given autonomy to make decisions in the classroom, then it follows that they should be held accountable for their decisions. Parents and society at large have the right to ask for, and demand, teacher and school accountability.

However, evaluations of teachers based on student test scores do not evaluate the process of teaching, only its ends. Thus, the evaluation cannot tell us whether the teacher was in fact a good teacher. Would we say a doctor was good because his patient went from obesity and high blood pressure to being thin and trim? Presumably, we first would want to ask how these results were achieved: Was it by surgery, or by the promotion of healthy eating and exercise? Whereas statisticians and economists calculating test scores to demonstrate school "progress" to other nations may not care about the answer to these questions, parents, teachers, and the students themselves should.

Standardized test scores cannot really tell us whether a student is learning. They often do not illuminate the process of the learner's thinking. A good example of this came from an actual preservice teacher, who saw in her practicum that the test assessing probability and likelihood in her Grade 5 classroom was less than adequate for measuring what students knew. On the test, students were asked to remark on the likelihood of having a birthday this year, and many students marked "impossible." Surprised that so many students got the answer wrong (according to the test), she questioned her students about their answers. One student explained, for example, "well my birthday was in January and now it's November." Also, on other answers, this teacher-in-training soon found that her students were thinking and learning – and were in a certain sense *right* – even though their test scores showed wrong answers.

Finding out how students are thinking, not just whether they got an answer right or wrong, is important for teachers because it tells them where to go next in the lesson. When teachers learn what it is that is confusing a student or why the student is having difficulty understanding something, then they can figure out ways to help the student reflectively learn. Teachers can begin finding the interruptions in learner's experiences that have already occurred by asking questions directed at the discontinuity in learning, like the one asked by the teacher, François, in the French film, *The Class* (*Entre les murs*). He asks his students, "Are there other words [in the book] that you *don't* understand?"[1] The question seeks to identify the unknowns, the difficulties and confusions in the students' learning process. These moments of difficulty or confusion in a student's thinking process should not be dismissed; they are vital for the teacher to be able to properly assess the learning process. Test scores erase these vital moments of learning because they erase the necessary moments of confusion or difficulty that are part of every learning process and thereby *erase the individual learner from the educational equation.*

Teachers and other educators who have acquired pedagogical tact can be equated with what Canadian Poet Laureate and educator Lorri Neilsen calls "motivated educators," those who "think and act courageously according to their students' needs and their own professional imperative."[2] As a society, we are at risk of creating unreflective teachers – those who do not think – if we continue with the sort of policies that hold teachers accountable for the outcomes of students' learning without, or independent of, any evaluation of teachers' decision-making processes that led to these outcomes. If we continue to create policies that do not address the underlying process of teaching, then we are essentially telling teachers *not* to think. That is, we are telling them that what they think and how they judge an educational situation is not valued. If we are not expecting teachers to think on their own, how can we legitimately hold teachers accountable for whether learning is occurring in their classrooms?

If we continue down the current path, then teaching will return to being construed as transmitting predetermined outcomes to students, and

[1] *The Class*, DVD, directed by Laurent Cantet, written by François Bégaudeau, Robin Campillo, and Laurent Cantet, 2008, France (original title, *Entre les murs*), Sony Pictures Home Entertainment, 2008, 8:10.
[2] Lorri Neilsen, *A Stone in My Shoe. Teaching Literacy in Times of Change*, p. 13 (Winnipeg: Peguis, 1994).

standardized testing will remain the primary means of verifying that students have achieved these outcomes. Philosophy of education is needed to assist teachers in finding justifications and criteria for judgment of complex and challenging educational situations in schools. Philosophy of education teaches teachers to think when faced with a problem of practice, consider all the alternatives, come up with varied solutions, and form judgments about what to do based on the learner's needs and the demands of the profession. The more we make teaching a mechanical, unreflective activity, the less we will attract creative and intelligent personalities to the profession, as Dewey pointed out in his 1925 essay, "What Is the Matter with Teaching?"[3]

The need to think and judge in educational situations makes teaching a moral endeavor, not simply a set of skills and strategies for managing a classroom. If teachers know not only *what* they are doing in classrooms, but also understand *why* they are doing it, then they can contribute to the discussion on good teaching. If we want things to change in the current discourse on education, then we desperately need thoughtful teachers – those who care about learners and the future of the profession – to contribute to this discussion. Can we afford not to allow teachers to think, and not to teach them to think like good teachers by making judgments with the learner as a learning being in view?

For learners to experience the transformational learning processes, teacher education programs must teach teachers how to cultivate such transformations. Thus, learning to teach involves more than learning a subject well. It entails learning to understand and cultivate the interruptions that arise in learners' experiences with the unknown and unfamiliar, such that learners can transform these into something new. On this understanding, teaching is a certain type of experimental practice.

Educational researchers, theorists, policy makers, and practicing educators must dispense with the idea that teachers need simply to find "what works." Rather, on my view, teacher evaluation must include evaluating teachers in the basis of their understanding of the differences between *what was planned* and *what was unexpected* in any given lesson or teacher-learner interaction. Evaluations of teaching efficacy should incorporate how teachers deal with the unexpected in practice. What is important in such evaluations is not that teachers avoid the unexpected or attempt to bring the unexpected into an all-encompassing plan without surprises. Rather, evaluations of teaching efficacy

---

[3] John Dewey, "What Is the Matter with Teaching? (1925)," *John Dewey: The Later Works*, edited by Jo Ann Boydston, Vol. 2, pp. 116–23 (Urbana: Southern Illinois University Press, 2008). Special thanks to William Hare for pointing out this connection to Dewey.

must aim to evaluate to what extent teachers are able to transform these unexpected moments into educative moments that support learners' reflective experiences.

I believe philosophy of education still has a critical role to play in teacher education and professionalization.[4] Teacher education must find ways to open up, pull apart, and make explicit the space of interruptions in teaching that typically do not affect experienced teachers in the same way they can affect novice teachers. By making this process explicit, teacher education programs can come to recognize the specific difficulties involved in learning to listen and question, and learning to teach.

It is *philosophers of education* who ask how we pass on the tradition of human thought and activity to the next generation of learners in such a way that they also learn to criticize and revise it. My discussion in this book hopes to bring up related questions surrounding teacher education and professionalization for philosophers and educators to continue to ask, such as: How can philosophy support preservice teachers in learning how to create classroom environments that promote thoughtful interaction among students, openness to difference, and engaged listening to the other? How can philosophy in teacher education invite teachers to continue to ask questions and think critically about education throughout their career? How can philosophy of education continue to provide preservice and in-service teachers with the theoretical guidance needed to assess the ethical situations they face in their attempt to educate future generations? What role can philosophy play in helping teachers understand and address the interruptions and blind spots in their experience of teaching, and those in the experiences of learners?

The "blind spots" of practice and experience are not something we can ever fully avoid. Rather, these blind spots are to be cherished; they remind us that we cannot fully foresee the future. They are what keep us humble and reveal to us that we are only human and cannot know everything. It would be a dire situation if we could know everything and foresee the future such that there were no surprises and no interruptions – which, in turn, would mean no innovation, no need for exploration, no learning from difference. A society that claims to have all the answers, such that we could all stop looking, would be a society that has fallen into the clutches of dogmatism. In the words of Hannah Arendt, "Our hope always hangs on the new which every generation

---

[4] The central role of philosophy of education in teacher education is notably something that philosophers who come from what have been considered disparate traditions – namely, Herbart, Dewey, R. S. Peters and others – have agreed on.

brings; but precisely because we can base our hope only on this, we destroy everything if we so try to control the new that we, the old, can dictate how it will look."[5] Teacher education can and must help prospective teachers understand how to reflectively deal with the difficulty inherent in their practice, a difficulty intimately tied to the fact that teachers have to acquaint the next generation with the world as it is while preparing them for a future yet to be discovered.

---

[5] Hannah Arendt, "The Crisis in Education," in *Between Past and Future. Eight Exercises in Political Thought*, edited by Jerome Kohn, pp. 170–93, 189 (Harmondsworth: Penguin, 1997); see also the original German version, Hannah Arendt, "Die Krise in der Erziehung," in *Zwischen Vergangenheit und Zukunft*, edited by Ursula Lutz, pp. 255–76, 273 (München: Piper, 1994).

Bibliography

Works of Herbart

Herbart, Johann Friedrich. "Aphorismen zur Pädagogik." In *Johann Friedrich Herbart's Sämmtliche Werke*, edited by G. Hartenstein. Vol. 11, Part 2, Schriften zur Pädagogik, 419–506. Leipzig: Leopold Voss, 1851.

"Pestalozzi's Idee eines ABC der Anschauung (1802 and 1804)." In *Joh. Friedr. Herbart's Sämtliche Werke in Chronologischer Reihenfolge*, edited by Karl Kehrbach, Vol. 1, 151–258. Langensalza: Hermann Beyer und Söhne, 1887.

"Über die ästhetische Darstellung der Welt, als das Hauptgeschäft der Erziehung (1802–1804)." In *Joh. Friedr. Herbart's Sämtliche Werke in Chronologischer Reihenfolge*, edited by Karl Kehrbach. Vol. 1, 259–74. Langensalza: Hermann Beyer und Söhne, 1887.

"Zwei Vorlesungen über Pädagogik (1802)." In *Joh. Friedr. Herbart's Sämtliche Werke in Chronologischer Reihenfolge*, edited by Karl Kehrbach. Vol. 1, 279–90. Langensalza: Hermann Beyer und Söhne, 1887.

"Allgemeine Pädagogik aus dem Zweck der Erziehung abgeleitet" (1806). In *Joh. Friedr. Herbart's Sämtliche Werke in Chronologischer Reihenfolge*, edited by Karl Kehrbach. Vol. 2, 1–139. Langensalza: Hermann Beyer und Söhne, 1887.

"Allgemeine Praktische Philosophie" (1808). In *Joh. Friedr. Herbart's Sämtliche Werke in Chronologischer Reihenfolge*, edited by Karl Kehrbach. Vol. 2, 329–458. Langensalza: Hermann Beyer und Söhne, 1887.

"Über Erziehung unter öffentlicher Mitwirkung (1810)." In *Joh. Friedr. Herbart's Sämtliche Werke in Chronologischer Reihenfolge*, edited by Karl Kehrbach. Vol. 3, 73–82. Langensalza: Hermann Beyer und Söhne, 1888.

"Kurze Anleitung für Erzieher, die Odyssee mit Knaben zu Lesen." In *Joh. Friedr. Herbart's Sämtliche Werke in Chronologischer Reihenfolge*, edited by Karl Kehrbach Vol. 3, 3–58. Langensalza: Hermann Beyer and Söhne, 1888.

"Umriss pädagogischer Vorlesung (1835 and 1841)." In *Joh. Friedr. Herbart's Sämtliche Werke in Chronologischer Reihenfolge*, edited by Karl Kehrbach. Vol. 10, 65–206. Langensalza: Hermann Beyer und Söhne, 1902.

"Introductory Lecture to Students in Pedagogy (1802)." In *Herbart's ABC of Sense-Perception and Minor Pedagogical Works*, edited and translated by William J. Eckoff, 13–28. New York: D. Appleton, 1896.

"The ABC of sense-perception (1802 and 1804)." In *Herbart's ABC of Sense-Perception and Minor Pedagogical Works*, edited and translated by William J. Eckoff, 132–278. New York: D. Appleton, 1896.

Letters and Lectures on Education, translated by Henry M. Felkin and Emmie Felkin. London: Swan Sonnenschein and Co. Ltd., 1898.

"On the Aesthetic Revelation of the World (1804)." In *The Science of Education, its general principles deduced from its aim, and The Aesthetic Revelation of the World*, translated by Henry M. Felkin and Emmie Felkin, 57–77. Boston: D. C. Heath & Co., 1902.

"The Science of Education" (1806). In *The Science of Education, its General Principles Deduced from its Aim, and The Aesthetic Revelation of the World*, translated by Henry M. Felkin and Emmie Felkin. Boston: D. C. Heath & Co., 1902.

Outlines of Educational Doctrine, translated by Alexis F. Lange. New York: MacMillan Company, 1913.

Works of Dewey

Dewey, John. "Democracy and Education" (1916). *The Middle Works*, edited by Jo Ann Boydston. Vol. 9. Carbondale: Southern Illinois University Press, 2008.

"The Need for a Recovery of Philosophy (1917)." *The Middle Works*, edited by Jo Ann Boydston. Vol. 10, 3–48. Carbondale: Southern Illinois University Press, 2008.

"Reconstruction in Philosophy (1920)." *The Middle Works*, edited by Jo Ann Boydston. Vol. 12, 77–202. Carbondale: Southern Illinois University Press, 2008.

"What Is the Matter with Teaching? (1925)." *The Later Works, 1925–1953*, edited by Jo Ann Boydston. Vol. 2, 116–23. Carbondale: Southern Illinois University Press, 2008.

"How We Think" (1933). *The Later Works*, edited by Jo Ann Boydston, Vol. 8, 105–352. Carbondale: Southern Illinois University Press, 2008.

"Art as Experience" (1934). *The Later Works*, edited by Jo Ann Boydston. Vol. 10. Carbondale: Southern Illinois University Press, 2008.

"Logic: The Theory of Inquiry" (1938). *The Later Works*, edited by Jo Ann Boydston. Vol. 12. Carbondale: Southern Illinois University Press, 2008.

"Experience and Education" (1938). *The Later Works*, edited by Jo Ann Boydston, Vol. 13, 1–62. Carbondale: Southern Illinois University Press, 2008.

"Time and Individuality (1940)." *The Later Works*, edited by Jo Ann Boydston. Vol. 14, 98–114. Carbondale: Southern Illinois University Press, 2008.

"Inquiry and Indeterminateness of Situations (1942)." *The Later Works*, edited by Jo Ann Boydston. Vol. 15, 34–41. Carbondale: Southern Illinois University Press, 2008.

and John L. Childs. "The Underlying Philosophy of Education (1933)." *The Later Works*, edited by Jo Ann Boydston. Vol. 8, 77–103. Carbondale: Southern Illinois University Press, 2008.

Other Works Cited

Arendt, Hannah. "The Crisis in Education." In *Between Past and Future. Eight Exercises in Political Thought*, 170–93. Harmondsworth: Penguin, 1997.

"Die Krise in der Erziehung." In *Zwischen Vergangenheit und Zukunft*, edited by Ursula Lutz, 255–76. München: Piper, 1994.

The Life of the Mind. New York: Harcourt Brace Jovanovich, 1981.

Aristotle. *Nichomachean Ethics*, edited and translated by Roger Crisp. Cambridge: Cambridge University Press, 2000.

Bellmann, Johannes. "Re-Interpretation in Historiography: John Dewey and the Neo-Humanist Tradition." *Studies in Philosophy and Education*, 23, no. 5, 2004: 467–88.

Benner, Dietrich. *Johann Friedrich Herbart: Systematische Pädagogik*. Vol. 2, *Interpretationen*. Weinheim: Deutsche Studien Verlag, 1997.

Allgemeine Pädagogik: Eine systematisch-problemgeschichtliche Einführung in die Grundstruktur pädagogischen Denkens und Handelns. Weinheim: Juventa, 2001.

"Kritik und Negativität. Ein Versuch zur Pluralisierung von Kritik in Erziehung, Pädagogik und Erziehungswissenschaft." *Zeitschrift für Pädagogik*, 46, 2003: 96–110.

"Der Andere und das Andere als Problem und Aufgabe von Erziehung und Bildung." In *Bildungstheorie und Bildungsforschung*, 45–57. Paderborn: Ferdinand Schöningh, 2008.

"Negative Moralisierung und experimentelle Ethik als zeitgemäße Formen der Moralerziehung." In *Bildungstheorie und Bildungsforschung*, 146–67. Paderborn: Ferdinand Schöningh, 2008.

Benner, Dietrich, and Wolfdietrich Schmied-Kowarzik. *Herbarts Praktische Philosophie und Pädagogik: Möglichkeiten und Grenzen einer Erziehungsphänomenologie*. Ratingen: A. Henn, 1967.

Benner, Dietrich, and Friedhelm Brüggen. "Bildsamkeit und Bildung." In *Historisches Wörterbuch der Pädagogik*, edited by Dietrich Benner and Jürgen Oelkers, 174–225. Weinheim: Beltz, 2004.

Benner, Dietrich, and Andrea English. "Critique and Negativity: Toward the Pluralisation of Critique in Educational Practice, Theory and Research." *Journal of Philosophy of Education*, 38, no. 3, 2004: 409–28.

Berding, Joop W. A. "War John Dewey ein (neo)Herbartianer. Die Debatte zwischen den 'alten' und der 'neuen' Erziehung." In *Herbart und Dewey: Pädagogische Paradigmen im Vergleich*, edited by Klaus Prange, 7–18. Jena: IKS Garamond, 2006.

Bernstein, Richard J. *John Dewey*. New York: Washington Square Press, 1966.

Biesta, Gert J. J., and Nicholas C. Burbules. *Pragmatism and Educational Research*. Oxford: Rowman & Littlefield, 2003.

Biesta, Gert J. J. *Beyond Learning: Democratic Education for a Human Future*. Boulder, CO: Paradigm, 2006.

"Mead, Intersubjectivity, and Education: The Early Writings." *Studies in Philosophy and Education*, 17, no. 2, 1998: 73–99.

Blake, Nigel, Paul Smeyers, Richard Smith, and Paul Standish. *Education in an Age of Nihilism*. London: Routledge, 2000.

Bohnsack, Fritz. *Demokratie als erfülltes Leben. Die Aufgabe von Schule und Erziehung. Ausgewählte und kommentierte Aufsätze unter Berücksichtigung der Pädagogik John Deweys*. Bad Heilbrunn: Klinkhardt, 2003.

Erziehung zur Demokratie: John Deweys Pädagogik und ihre Bedeutung für die Reform unserer Schule. Ravensburg: Otto Maier Verlag, 1976.

Boisvert, Raymond D. "The Nemesis of Necessity: Tragedy's Challenge to Deweyan Pragmatism." In *Dewey Reconfigured: Essays on Deweyan Pragmatism*, edited by Casey Haskins and David I. Seiple, 151–68. Albany: State University of New York Press.

Bolle, Rainer. "Herbarts Beitrag zur Theorie sittlicher Persönlichkeitsbildung – Weiterführende Impulse aus der Individual Psychologie Alfred Adlers." In *Johann Friedrich Herbart 1806–2006: 200 Jahre Allgemeine Pädagogik. Wirkungsgeschichtliche Impulse*, edited by Rainer Bolle and Gabrielle Weigand, 39–72. Münster: Waxmann Verlag, 2007.

Bollnow, Otto Friedrich. *Existenzphilosophie und Pädagogik*. Stuttgart: Kohlhammer, 1965.

Die Pädagogische Atmosphäre: Untersuchungen über die gefühlsmäßigen zwischenmenschlichen Voraussetzungen der Erziehung. Essen: Die blaue Eule, 2001.

Boostrom, Robert. "Teaching by the Numbers." In *Teaching and its Predicaments*, edited by Nicholas C. Burbules and David T. Hansen, 45–64. Boulder, CO: Westview Press, 1997.

Brüggen, Friedhelm. "Lernen-Erfahrung-Bildung oder Über Kontinuität und Diskontinuität im Lernprozess." *Zeitschrift für Pädagogik*, 34, no. 3, 1988: 299–313.

Buck, Günther. *Lernen und Erfahrung*. Stuttgart: W. Kohlhammer, 1969.

Hermeneutik und Bildung. München: Wilhelm Fink Verlag, 1981.

Herbarts Grundlegung der Pädagogik. Heidelberg: Carl Winter, 1985.

Burbules, Nicholas C. "The Tragic Sense of Education," *The Teachers College Record*, 91, no. 4, 1990: 469–79.

Dialogue in Teaching. Theory and Practice. New York: Teachers College Press, 1993.

"Teaching and the Tragic Sense of Education." In *Teaching and its Predicaments*, edited by Nicholas C. Burbules and David T. Hansen, 163–74. Boulder, CO: Westview Press, 1997.

"Aporia: Webs, Passages, Getting Lost, and Learning to Go on." In *Philosophy of Education 1997*, edited by Susan Laird, 33–43. Urbana, IL: Philosophy of Education Society, 1998.

"Aporias, Webs, and Passages: Doubt as an Opportunity to Learn." *Curriculum Inquiry*, 30, no. 2, 2000: 171–87.

"What Is Authority?" In *Key Questions for Educators*, edited by William Hare and John Portelli. San Francisco: Caddo Gap Press, 2007.

Burbules, Nicholas C., and Suzanne Rice. "Dialogue across Difference: Continuing the Conversation." *Harvard Educational Review*, 61, no. 4, 1991: 393–416.

Burgos, Rosa Nidia Buenfil. "Negativity: A Disturbing Constitutive Matter in Education." *Journal of Philosophy of Education*, 38, no. 3, 2004: 429–40.

Chinnery, Ann, William Hare, Donald Kerr, and Walter Okshevsky. "Teaching Philosophy of Education: The Value of Questions." *Interchange*, 38, no. 2, 2007: 99–118.

Cuffaro, Harriet K. *Experimenting with the World: John Dewey and the Early Childhood Classroom*. New York: Teachers College Press, 1995.

Dunkel, Harold B. *Herbart and Education*. New York: Random House, 1969.

Herbart and Herbartianism: An Educational Ghost Story. Chicago: University of Chicago Press, 1970.

Elik, Nezihe, Judith Wiener, and Penny Corkum. "Pre-Service Teachers' Open Minded Thinking Dispositions, Readiness to Learn, and Attitudes About Learning and Behavioural Difficulties in Students." *European Journal of Teacher Education*, 33, no. 2, May 2012, 127–46.

English, Andrea. "Negativity and the New in John Dewey's Theory of Learning and Democracy: Toward a Renewed Look at Learning Cultures." *Zeitschrift für Erziehungswissenschaft*, 8, no. 1, 2005a: 28–37.

"Negativität der Erfahrung, Pragmatismus und die Grundstruktur des Lernens – Erziehungswissenschaftliche Reflexion zur Bedeutung des Pragmatismus von Peirce, James und Mead für Deweys Theorie der reflective experience." *Zeitschrift für Pädagogik*, 49 (Special Issue "Erziehung, Bildung, Negativität," edited by Dietrich Benner), 2005b: 49–61.

Bildung – Negativität – Moralität: Systematisch-vergleichende Analysen zu Herbarts und Deweys Konzepten der Erziehung. Ph.D. Dissertation, Berlin: Humboldt University Berlin Library Archives, 2005c.

"Die Experimentelle Struktur menschliches Lehrens und Lernens: Versuche über die Rolle negativer Erfahrung in den Lehr-Lerntheorien von Herbart und Dewey." In *Johann Friedrich Herbart: 200 Jahre Allgemeine Pädagogik. Wirkungsgeschichtliche Impulse*, edited by Rainer Bolle and Gabriele Weigand, 97–112. Berlin: Waxmann, 2007a.

"Nietzsche, Deception, and Education: A response to Katz's Nietzschean Puzzle." In *Philosophy of Education 2006*, edited by Daniel Vokey, 401–03. Urbana, IL: Philosophy of Education Society, 2007b.

"Interrupted Experiences: Reflection, Listening and Negativity in the Practice of Teaching." *Learning Inquiry*, 1 (Special Issue "Listening and Reflecting," edited by Leonard J. Waks), no. 2, 2007c: 133–42.

"Wo *doing* aufhört und *learning* anfängt: John Dewey über Lernen und die Negativität in Erfahrung und Denken." In *Dem Lernen auf der Spur*, edited by Konstantin Mitgutsch, Elizabeth Sattler, Kristin Westphal, and Ines M. Breinbauer, 145–58. Stuttgart: Klett-Cotta, 2008.

"Transformation and Education: The Voice of the Learner in Peters' Concept of Teaching." *Journal of Philosophy of Education*, 43, Issue Supplement s1 (Special Issue "Reading R. S. Peters Today: Analysis, Ethics and the Aims of Education, edited by Stefaan Cuypers and Christopher Martin), 2009a: 75–95.

"Listening as a Teacher: Educative Listening, Interruptions and Reflective Practice." *Paideusis: International Journal of Philosophy of Education* (Special Issue "Open-mindedness and the Virtues in Education" honoring William Hare, edited by Michelle E. Forrest) Vol. 18, no. 1, 2009b: 69–79.

"Should Teachers Think?: Autonomy, Accountability and Philosophy of Education." *Teacher: Newsmagazine of the BC Teachers' Federation*, 23, no. 5, March 2011: 5.

"Critical Listening and the Dialogic Aspect of Moral Education: J. F. Herbart's Concept of the Teacher as Moral Guide." *Educational Theory*, 61, no. 2 (Special Issue "Philosophies of Listening," edited by Sophie Haroutunian-Gordon and Megan Laverty), 2011: 171–89.

"Negativity, Experience and Transformation: Educational Possibilities at the Margins of Experience – Insights from the German Tradition of Philosophy of Education." In *Education and the Kyoto School of Philosophy: Pedagogy for Human Transformation*, edited by Paul Standish and Naoko Saito, 203–20. Dordrecht: Springer Publishers, 2012.

"Intelligence and the Unexpected: Considering Dewey's Tragic Sense." In *Philosophy of Education 2012*, edited by Claudia Ruitenberg. Urbana, 227–229. IL: Philosophy of Education Society, 2013.

English, Andrea, and Barbara Stengel. "Exploring Fear: Rousseau, Dewey and Freire on Fear and Learning." *Educational Theory*, 60, no. 5, 2010: 521–42.

Feinberg, Walter. "The Conflict Between Intelligence and Community in Dewey's Educational Philosophy." *Educational Theory*, 19, no. 3, 1969: 236–48.

Forrest, Michelle. "Sensitive Controversy in Teaching to be Critical." *Paideusis*, 18, no. 1, 2008: 80–93.

Freire, Paolo. *Teachers as Cultural Workers. Letters to Those Who Dare Teach.* Boulder, CO: Westview Press, 2005.

Gadamer, Hans-Georg. *Truth and Method* (1960), Second revised edition, translation revised by Joel Weinheimer and Donald G. Marshall. New York: Continuum, 2000.

Garrison, James. "A Deweyan Theory of Democratic Listening." *Educational Theory*, 46, no. 4, 1996: 429–51.

"John Dewey's Philosophy as Education." In *Reading Dewey. Interpretations for a Postmodern Generation*, edited by Larry Hickman, 63–81. Indianapolis: Indiana University Press, 1998.

"The 'Permanent Deposit' of Hegelian Thought in Dewey's Theory of Inquiry." *Educational Theory*, 56, no. 1, 2006: 1–37.

"Teacher as Prophetic Trickster." *Educational Theory*, 59, no. 1, 2009: 67–83.

Gartmeier, Martin, Johannes Bauer, Hans Gruber, and Helmut Heid. "Negative Knowledge: Understanding Professional Learning and Expertise." *Vocations and Learning: Studies in Vocational and Professional Education*, 1, July 2008: 87–103.

Good, James A. *A Search for Unity in Diversity: The 'Permanent Hegelian Deposit' in the Philosophy of John Dewey.* New York: Lexington Books, 2005.

Gordon, Mordechai. "Listening as Embracing the Other: Martin Buber's Philosophy of Dialogue." *Educational Theory*, 61, no. 2 (Special Issue on Listening, edited by Sophie Haroutunian-Gordon and Megan Laverty), April 2011: 207–19.

Greene, Maxine. *Releasing the Imagination: Essays on Education, the Arts, and Social Change.* New York: Jossey-Bass Publishers, 1995.

The Dialectic of Freedom. New York: Teachers College Press, 1988.

Hansen, David T. "Being a Good Influence." In *Teaching and Its Predicaments*, edited by Nicholas C. Burbules and David T. Hansen, 163–74. Boulder, CO: Westview Press, 1997.

Exploring the Moral Heart of Teaching: Toward a Teacher's Creed. New York: Teachers College Press, 2001.

Hare, William. "Has Listening Had a Fair Hearing." *Agora*, 3, no. 1–2, 1975: 5–13.

Open-mindedness and Education. Montreal: McGill-Queen's University Press, 1983.

"Reflections on the Teacher's Tasks: Contributions from Philosophy of Education in the 20 th Century." *Educational Research and Perspectives*, 27, no. 2, 2000: 1–23.

Harkins, Mary Jane, Michelle Forrest, and Terrah Keener. "Room for Fear: Using Our Own Personal Stories in Teacher Education." *Journal of Teaching and Learning* 6, no. 1, 2009: 15–23.

Haroutunian-Gordon, Sophie. "Listening – in a Democratic Society." In *Philosophy of Education 2003*, edited by Kal Alston, 1–18. Urbana IL: Philosophy of Education Society, 2004.

"Listening and Questioning." *Learning Inquiry*, 1, no. 2 (Special Issue "Reflection and Listening"), 2007: 143–52.

Learning to Teach Through Discussion: The Art of Turning the Soul. New Haven, CT: Yale University Press, 2009.

Hellekamps, Stephanie. *Erziehender Unterricht und Didaktik*. Weinheim: Deutscher Studien Verlag, 1991.

Hickman, Larry A. "Dewey's Theory of Inquiry." In *Reading Dewey. Interpretations for a Postmodern Generation*, edited by Larry Hickman, 167–86. Indianapolis: Indiana University Press, 1998.

Hogan, Pádraig. "The Integrity of Learning and the Search for Truth." *Educational Theory*, 55, no. 2, 2005: 198.

Hook, Sydney. *Pragmatism and the Tragic Sense of Life*. New York: Basic Books Inc., 1974.

John Dewey: An Intellectual Portrait (1939). Westport, CT: Greenwood Press, 1971.

Huber, Ludwig. "Stichwort Fachliches Lernen. Das Fachprinzip in der Kritik." *Zeitschrift für Erziehungswissenschaft*, 3, 2001: 307–31.

Humboldt, Wilhelm von. "Theorie der Bildung des Menschen." In *Wilhelm von Humboldt, Werke in Fünf Bände*, edited by Andreas Flitner and Klaus Giel. Vol. 1, Schriften zur Anthropologie und Geschichte, 234–40. Darmstadt: Wissenschaftliche Buchgesellschaft, 1969.

"Über den Geist der Menschheit." In *Wilhelm von Humboldt, Werke in Fünf Bände*, edited by Andreas Flitner and Klaus Giel. Vol. 1, Schriften zur Anthropologie und Geschichte, 506–18. Darmstadt: Wissenschaftliche Buchgesellschaft, 1969.

"Theory of Bildung." In *Teaching as a Reflective Practice: The German Didaktik Tradition*, translated by Gillian Horton-Krüger, edited by Iain Westbury, Stephan Hopmann, and Kurt Riquarts, 57–61. Mahwah, NJ: Lawrence Erlbaum Associates, 2001.

James, William. "Lecture II: What Pragmatism Means (1907)." In *The Works of William James: Electronic Edition*, edited by Frederick H. Burkhardt, Fredson Bowers, and Ignas K. Skrupskelis. Vol. 1: Pragmatism, 27–44. Charlottesville, VA: InteLex Corporation, 2008.

"Lecture VI: Pragmatism's Conception of Truth (1907)." In *The Works of William James: Electronic Edition*, edited by Frederick H. Burkhardt, Fredson Bowers, and Ignas K. Skrupskelis. Vol. 1: Pragmatism, 95–114. Charlottesville, VA: InteLex Corporation, 2008.

"Talks to Teachers (1899)." In *The Works of William James: Electronic Edition*, edited by Frederick H. Burkhardt, Fredson Bowers, and Ignas K. Skrupskelis. Vol. 12: Talks to Teachers on Psychology, 13–115. Charlottesville, VA: InteLex Corporation, 2008.

Kant, Immanuel. *Fundamental Principles of the Metaphysics of Morals* (1785), translated by T. K. Abbott. New York: Prometheus Books, 1988.

Katz, Michael S. "Teaching with Integrity" In *Philosophy of Education 2008*, edited by Ronald Glass, 7–11. Urbana, IL: Philosophy of Education Society, 2009.

Kerdeman, Deborah. "Pulled Up Short: Challenging Self-Understanding as a Focus for Teaching and Learning." *Journal of Philosophy of Education*, 2003: 293–308.

"Pulled Up Short: Challenges for Education." In *Philosophy of Education 2003*, edited by Kal Alston, 208–16. Urbana, IL: Philosophy of Education Society, 2004.

Klafki, Wolfgang. "Didaktik Analysis of the Core of Preparation of Instruction (1958)." In *Teaching as a Reflective Practice: The German Didaktik Tradition*, edited by Ian Westbury, Stephan Hopmann, and Kurt Riquarts, 139–60. Mahwah, NJ: Lawrence Erlbaum Associates, 2000.

Neue Studien zur Bildungstheorie und Didaktik. Zeitgemässe Allgemeinbildung und kritisch-konstruktive Didaktik, 6th ed. Beltz: Weinheim, 2007.

Klemp, Nathaniel, Ray McDermott, Jason Raley, Matthew Thibeault, Kimberly Powell, and Daniel J. Levitin. "Plans, Takes and Mis-Takes." *Critical Social Studies*, 10, 2008: 4–21.

Koch, Lutz. *Bildung und Negativität. Grundzüge einer negativen Bildungstheorie.* Weinheim: Deutscher Studien Verlag, 1995.

"Eine pädagogische Apologie des Negativen." *Zeitschrift für Pädagogik*, 49 (Special Issue "Erziehung – Bildung – Negativität," edited by Dietrich Benner), 2005: 88–104.

Kolenda, Sandy. *Unterricht als bildendes Gespräch: Richard Rorty und die Entstehung des Neuen im sprachlichen Prozess.* Opladen: Barbara Budrich, 2010.

Laverty, Megan. "Dialogue as Philosophical Inquiry in the Teaching of Sympathy and Tolerance." *Learning Inquiry*, 1, no. 2 (Special Issue "Reflection and Listening," edited by Leonard Waks), 2007: 125–32.

Løvlie, Lars, and Paul Standish. "Introduction: Bildung and the Idea of Liberal Education." *Journal of Philosophy of Education*, 36. no. 3, August 2002: 317–40.

Margolis, Joseph. *Reinventing Pragmatism: American Philosophy at the End of the Twentieth Century.* Ithaca, NY: Cornell University Press, 2002.

Martin, Christopher. "Education Without Moral Worth? Kantian Moral Theory and the Obligation to Educate Others." *Journal of Philosophy of Education*, 4, no. 3, 2011: 475–92.

McClintock, Robbie. *Enough: A Pedagogical Speculation.* New York: The Reflective Commons, 2012.

"On (Not) Defining Education: Questions about Historical Life and What Educates Therein." *Theoretical Perspectives on Comprehensive Education: The Way Forward.* Hervé Varenne and Edmund W. Gordon, eds, pp. 27–60. Lewiston, NY: The Edwin Mellen Press, 2009.

McCourt, Frank. *Teacher Man.* New York: Scribner, 2005.

Mead, George Herbert. "A Pragmatic Theory of Truth." In *Selected Writings George Herbert Mead*, edited by Andrew J. Reck, 320–45. Chicago: University of Chicago Press, 1964.

Meadows, Elizabeth. "Transformative Learning through Open Listening: A Professional Development Experience with Urban High School Students." *Learning Inquiry*, 1, no. 2 (Special issue "Reflection and Listening," edited by Leonard Waks), 2007: 115–23.

Meyer, Meinert A. "John Deweys Vorstellungen bezüglich der Inhalte des Unterrichts – Eine Untersuchung zur historischen Curriculumtheorie." In *Modernisierung von Rahmenrichtlinien*, edited by Josef Keuffer, 49–80. Weinheim: Deutscher Studien Verlag, 1997.

"Stichwortartikel: Alte oder Neue Lernkultur." *Zeitschrift für Erziehungswissenschaft*, 1, 2005: 5–27.

Meyer-Drawe, Käte. "Phänomenologische Bemerkungen zum Problem des Lernens." *Vierteljahresheft für wissenschaftliche Pädagogik*, 58, no. 4, 1982: 510–24.

"Lernen als Umlernen – Zur Negativität des Lernprozesses." In *Lernen und seine Horizonte. Phänomenologische Konzeptionen Menschlichen Lernens – Didaktische Konsequenzen*, edited by Käte Meyer-Drawe and Winfried Lippitz, 19–45. Frankfurt: Scriptor, 1984.

"Die Belehrbarkeit des Lehrenden durch den Lernenden: Fragen an den Primat des pädagogischen Bezugs." In *Kind und Welt*, edited by Käte Meyer-Drawe and Winfried Lippitz, 63–73. Frankfurt am Main: Athenaeum, 1987.

"Von Anderen lernen. Phänomenologische Betrachtungen in der Pädagogik." In *Deutsche Gegenwartspädagogik*, edited by Michele Borrelli and Jörg Ruhloff, Vol. 2, 85–98. Hohengehren: Schneider, 1996.

"Die Herausforderung durch die Dinge: Das Andere im Lernprozess." *Zeitschrift für Pädagogik*, 46, 1999: 329–36.

"Anfänge des Lernens." *Zeitschrift für Pädagogik*, 49, 2005: 24–37.

Diskurse des Lernens. München: Wilhelm Fink, 2008.

Mintz, Avi I. "The Happy and Suffering Student? Rousseau's Emile and the Path Not Taken in Progressive Educational Thought." *Educational Theory*, 62, no. 3, 2012: 249–65.

Mitgutsch, Konstantin. "Lernen durch Erfahren: Über Bruchlinien im Vollzug des Lernens." In *Dem Lernen auf der Spur*, edited by Konstantin Mitgutsch, Elizabeth Sattler, Kristin Westphal, and Ines M. Breinbauer, 263–77. Stuttgart: Klett-Cotta, 2008.

Lernen durch Enttäuschung, Eine pädagogische Skizze. Vienna: Braumüller, 2009.

Müssener, Gerhard. *Johann Friedrich Herbarts "Pädagogik der Mitte": Sieben Analysen zu Inhalt und Form*. Darmstadt: Wissenschaftliche Buchgesellschaft, 1986.

Muth, Jakob. *Pädagogischer Takt. Monographie einer aktuellen Form erzieherischen und didaktischen Handelns*. Heidelberg: Quelle und Meyer, 1967.

Neilsen, Lorri. *A Stone in My Shoe. Teaching Literacy in Times of Change*. Winnipeg: Peguis, 1994.

Nietzsche, Friedrich. "Über die Zukunft unserer Bildungsanstalten." In *Friedrich Nietzsche: Sämtliche Werke, Kritische Studienausgabe*, edited by Giorgio Colli and Mazzino Montinari, Vol. 1, 643–752. München: Deutscher Taschenbuch Verlag, 1988.

Okshevsky, Walter. "Kant's Catechism for Moral Education: From Particularity Through Universality to Morality." In *Philosophy of Education 2000*, edited by Lynda Stone, 94–102. Urbana, IL: Philosophy of Education Society, 2001.

Oser, Fritz. "Negative Moralität und Entwicklung. Ein undurchsichtiges Verhältnis." *Ethik und Sozialwissenschaft*, 9, no. 4, 1998: 597–608.

"Negatives Wissen und Moral." *Zeitschrift für Pädagogik*, 49 (Special Issue "Erziehung-Bildung-Negativität," edited by Dietrich Benner), 2005: 171–81.

Oser, Fritz, Tina Hascher, and Maria Spychiger. "Lernen aus Fehlern. Zur Psychologie des 'negativen' Wissens." In *Fehlerwelten-Vom Fehlermachen und Lernen aus Fehlern*, edited by Wolfgang Althof, 11–41. Opladen: Leske and Budrich, 1999.

Paley, Grace. *The Collected Stories*. New York: Farrar, Straus and Giroux, 1994.

Passmore, John. "On Teaching to be Critical." In *The Concept of Education*, edited by Richard S. Peters, 192–211. London: Routledge and Kegan Paul Ltd., 1967.

Peirce, Charles Sanders. "Lecture 2: The Universal Categories." In *The Collected Papers of Charles Sanders Peirce: Electronic Edition*, edited by Charles Hartshorne and Paul Weiss, Vol. 5: Pragmatism and Pragmaticism, § 1, 41–§ 3, 65. Charlottesville, VA: InteLex Corporation, 1994.

"Paper 4: The Fixation of Belief." In *The Collected Papers of Charles Sanders Peirce: Electronic Edition*, edited by Charles Hartshorne and Paul Weiss, Vol. 5: Pragmatism and Pragmaticism, § 1, 358–§ 5, 387. Charlottesville, VA: InteLex Corporation, 1994.

"Paper 5: How to Make Our Ideas Clear." In *Collected Papers*, edited by Charles Hartshorne and Paul Weiss, Vol. 5: Pragmatism and Pragmaticism, §1, 388–§4, 410. Charlottesville, VA: InteLex Corporation, 1994.

"Paper 6: What Pragmatism Is." In *The Collected Papers of Charles Sanders Peirce: Electronic Edition*, edited by Charles Hartshorne and Paul Weiss, Vol. 5: Pragmatism and Pragmaticism, §1,411–§4,437. Charlottesville, VA: InteLex Corporation, 1994.

"Paper 7: Issues of Pragmaticism," In *The Collected Papers of Charles Sanders Peirce: Electronic Edition*, edited by Charles Hartshorne and Paul Weiss, Vol. 5: Pragmatism and Pragmaticism, §1, 438–§2, 463. Charlottesville, VA: InteLex Corporation, 1994.

Plato. "Apology," In *Plato Complete Works*, translated by G. M. A. Grube, edited by John M. Cooper and D. S. Hutchinson, 17–36. Cambridge, MA: Hatckett Publishing Company, 1997.

"Meno." In *Plato Complete Works*, translated by G. M. A. Grube, edited by John M. Cooper and D. S. Hutchinson, 870–97. Cambridge, MA: Hatckett Publishing Company, 1997.

"Republic." In *Plato Complete Works*, translated by G. M. A. Grube and C. D. C. Reeve, edited by John M. Cooper and D. S. Hutchinson, 971–1223. Cambridge, MA: Hatckett Publishing Company, 1997.

Prange, Klaus. "Die Funktion des pädagogischen Takts im Lichte des Technologie Problems der Erziehung." In *Urteilskraft und Pädagogik*, edited by Birgitta Fuchs and Christian Schönherr, 125–32. Würzburg: Königshausen und Neumann, 2007.

"Lernen im Kontext des Erziehens. Überlegungen zu einem pädagogischen Begriff des Lernens." In *Dem Lernen auf der Spur*, edited by Konstantin Mitgutsch, Elizabeth Sattler, Kristin Westphal, and Ines M. Breinbauer, 241–48. Stuttgart: Klett-Cotta, 2008.

Putnam, Hilary. *Pragmatism: An Open Question*. New York: Wiley-Blackwell, 1995.

Ramaekers, Stefan. "Multicultural Education: Embeddedness, Voice and Change." *Ethics and Education*, 5, no. 1, 2010: 55–66.

Ramseger, Jörg. *Was heisst "Durch Unterricht erziehen?": Erziehender Unterricht und Schulreform*. Weinheim: Beltz, 1991.

Raths, Louis E., Merrill Harmin, and Sidney B. Simon. *Values and Teaching: Working with Values in the Classroom*. Columbus, OH: Charles E. Merrill Publishing Co., 1966.

Reichenbach, Roland. "On Irritation and Transformation: A-Teleological Bildung and Its Significance for the Democratic Form of Living." *Journal of Philosophy of Education*, 36, no. 3, 2002: 409–19.

Rousseau, Jean-Jacques. *Discourse on the Origin of Inequality*, translated by Franklin Philip, edited by Patrick Coleman. Oxford: Oxford University Press, 1999.

Emile or On Education, translated and edited by Allan Bloom. New York: Basic Books, 1979.

Ruhloff, Jörg. "Bildung – Nur ein Paradigma im Pädagogischen Denken?" In *Skepsis und Widerstreit: Neue Beiträge zur skeptisch-transzendentalkritischen Pädagogik*, edited by Wolfgang Fischer and Jörg Ruhloff, 173–84. Sankt Augustin: Academia Verlag, 1993.

Ruitenberg, Claudia. "Giving Place to Unforeseeable Learning: The Inhospitality of Outcomes-Based Education." In *Philosophy of Education 2009*, edited by Deborah Kerdeman, 266–74. Urbana, IL: Philosophy of Education Society, 2010.

Rumpf, Horst. "Lernen als Vollzug und als Erledigung – Sich Einlassen auf Befremdliches Oder: Über Lernvollzüge ohne Erledigungsdruck." In *Dem Lernen auf der Spur*, edited by Konstantin Mitgutsch, Elizabeth Sattler, Kristin Westphal, and Ines M. Breinbauer, 21–32. Stuttgart: Klett-Cotta, 2008.

Säfstrom, Carl Anders. "Intelligence for More Than One: Reading Dewey as a Radical Democrat." In *Philosophy of Education* 2012, edited by Claudia Ruitenberg, 418–426. Urbana, IL.: Philosophy of Education Society, 2013.

Said, Edward. *Out of Place: A Memoir*. New York: Vintage Books, 1999.

Saito, Naoko. *The Gleam of Light: Moral Perfectionism and Education in Dewey and Emerson*. New York: Fordham University Press, 2005.

Scheffler, Israel. "In Praise of the Cognitive Emotions." In *In Praise of the Cognitive Emotions: And Other Essays in the Philosophy of Education*, 2–13. New York: Routledge, 2010.

Four Pragmatists: A Critical Introduction to Peirce, James, Mead, and Dewey. London: Routledge and Kegan Paul, 1974.

Schluss, Henning. "Negativität im Unterricht." *Zeitschrift für Pädagogik*, 49 (Special Issue Erziehung-Bildung-Negativität, edited by Dietrich Benner), 2005: 182–96.

Schön, Donald. *Educating the Reflective Practitioner*. San Francisco: Jossey-Bass, 1987.

The Reflective Practitioner: How Professionals Think in Action. Aldershot: Ashgate, 1983/2005.

Schultz, Katherine. *Listening. A Framework for Teaching a Across Difference*. New York: Teachers College Press, 2003.

Schütz, Egon. *Freiheit und Bestimmung. Sinntheoretische Reflexionen zum Bildungsproblem*. Ratingen: Henn, 1975.

Simpson, Douglas J., Michael J. B. Jackson, and Judy C. Aycock. *John Dewey and the Art of Teaching: Toward Reflective and Imaginative Practice*. London: Sage Publications, Inc, 2005.

Socrates for Six Year Olds. DVD, 1990, UK, produced by SAPERE, 2010.

Spychiger, Maria, Fritz Oser, Tina Hascher, and Fabienne Mahler. "Entwicklung einer Fehlerkultur in der Schule." In *Fehlerwelten–vom Fehlermachen und Lernen aus Fehlern*, edited by Wolfgang Althof, 43–70. Opladen: Leske and Budrich, 1999.

Spychiger, Maria, and Fritz Oser. *Lernen ist Schmerzhaft. Zur Theorie der Fehlerkultur und zur Praxis des Negativen Wissens*. Weinheim: Beltz, 2005.

Standish, Paul. "Moral Education, Liberal Education and the Voice of the Individual." In *Education in the Era of Globalization*, edited by Klas Roth and Ilan Gur-Ze'ev, 33–50. Dordrecht: Springer, 2007.

Steiner, George. *Lessons of the Masters*. Cambridge, MA: Harvard University Press, 2003.

Stengel, Barbara. "Facing Fear, Releasing Resistance, Enabling Education." *Philosophical Studies in Education*, 39, 2008: 66–75.

"The Complex Case of Fear and Safe Space." *Studies in Philosophy and Education*, 29, no. 6, 2010: 1–18.

The Class. DVD, directed by Laurent Cantet, written by François Bégaudeau, Robin Campillo, and Laurent Cantet, 2008, France (original title, *Entre les murs*), Sony Pictures Home Entertainment, 2008.

Thomson, Iain. *Heidegger on Ontotheology: Technology and the Politics of Education*. New York: Cambridge University Press, 2005.

Todd, Sharon. *Learning from the Other: Levinas, Psychoanalysis, and Ethical Possibilities in Education* Albany: State University of New York Press, 2003.

Tubbs, Nigel. *Philosophy of the Teacher: Journal of Philosophy of Education*, 39, no. 2 (Special Issue), 2005.

van Manen, Max. *The Tact of Teaching. The Meaning of Pedagogical Thoughtfulness.* London: Althouse Press, 1991.

Waddington, David I. "Uncovering Hegelian Connections: A New Look at Dewey's Early Educational Ideas." *Education and Culture*, 26, no. 1, 2010: 67–81.

Waks, Leonard J. "Reflective Practice in the Design Studio and Teacher Education." *Journal of Curriculum Studies*, 31, no. 3, 1999: 303–16.

"Listening and Questioning. The Apophatic/cataphatic Distinction Revisited," *Learning Inquiry*, 1, no. 2 (Special Issue "Reflection and Listening"), 2007: 153–61.

"Two Types of Interpersonal Listening." *Teachers College Record*, 112, no. 11, 2010: 2743–62.

"John Dewey on Listening and Friendship in School and Society." *Educational Theory* 61, no. 2, 2011: 191–205.

Waldenfels, Bernhard. *Das Zwischenreich des Dialogues.* Den Haag: Martinus Nihoff, 1971.

"Sich-sprechen Hören. Zur Aufzeichnung der phänomenologischen Stimme." In *Deutsch-Französische Gedankengänge*, 90–104. Frankfurt am Main: Suhrkamp, 1995.

"Antwort auf das Fremde. Grundzüge einer responsiven Phänomenologie." In *Der Anspruch des Anderen, Perspektiven phänomenologischer Ethik*, edited by Bernhard Waldenfels and Iris Daermann, 35–50. München: Fink, 1998.

Bruchlinien der Erfahrung. Frankfurt am Main: Suhrkamp, 2002.

"Die Macht der Ereignisse." In *Aesthetik Erfahrung, Interventionen*, edited by Jörg Huber, 155–70. Wien: Springer, 2004.

Westbrook, Robert B. *John Dewey and American Democracy.* Ithaca, NY: Cornell University Press, 1991.

Wright, Richard. *Black Boy. A Record of Childhood and Youth (1937).* New York: Perennial Library, 1989.

Index